Koala fingerprints are so similar
to human fingerprints that
Australian police are trained
to know the difference.

There are more than 400,000 different flowering plants in the world, including the lotus.

The cassowary, a 6-foot (1.8-m)-tall flightless bird, is often referred to as a "living dinosaur" because its inner toe is incredibly long and sharp, like a prehistoric raptor, and can kill with a single powerful kick.

Gladiator battles had referees to watch over and possibly stop fights before they got too dangerous.

TOTALLY RANDOM FACTS vol.2

3,219 Surprising, Strange, and Striking Things About the World

Melina Gerosa Bellows

BRIGHT MATTER BOOKS

NEW YORK

Contents

Awesome Animals:
Wings, Claws, Tails, and Teeth

Dot to Dot: 70 Totally Random Facts About SPOTTED CATS 2

Perfect Protection: 42 Totally Random Facts About ARMORED MAMMALS 6

Feathered Friends: 121 Totally Random Facts About BACKYARD BIRDS 8

Hide-and-Seek: 34 Random Facts About COLOR-CHANGING ANIMALS 14

Nature's Assassins: 49 Totally Random Facts About LETHAL ANIMALS 16

Oh, Baby! 99 Totally Random Facts About BABY ANIMALS 20

Cool Canines: 49 Totally Random Facts About DOGS 26

Mini Mammals: 72 Totally Random Facts About RABBITS, GUINEA PIGS, and GERBILS 30

Life in the Pack: 84 Totally Random Facts About WOLVES 34

Fly by Night: 51 Totally Random Facts About MOTHS 38

Marvelous Marsupials: 136 Totally Random Facts About KOALAS, KANGAROOS, and MORE 42

Slither and Strike: 75 Totally Random Facts About SNAKES 50

Bugging Out: 57 Totally Random Facts About INSECTS 54

Hello, Kitty! 58 Totally Random Facts About CATS 56

Chomp and Stomp! 53 Totally Random Facts About DINOSAURS 60

Here to Help: 32 Totally Random Facts About SERVICE DOGS and EMOTIONAL SUPPORT ANIMALS 62

Hey, Big Talker! 48 Totally Random Facts About PARROTS 64

Glow in the Dark: 32 Totally Random Facts About BIOLUMINESCENT ANIMALS 66

SPOT THE 13 RANDOM DIFFERENCES 68

There are more varieties of beetles than all the plants on Earth combined.

Planet Earth:

Rocks and Gems, Wild Weather, and Natural Wonders

Though diamonds are one of the rarest gems, a top-quality emerald can be worth more than a diamond.

Storm Surge: 67 Totally Random Facts About EXTREME WEATHER   72

Cool It! 73 Totally Random Facts About CLIMATE CHANGE   76

What a Gem: 84 Totally Random Facts About BIRTHSTONE GEMS   80

Fan the Flames: 93 Totally Random Facts About FIRE   84

The Power of Stem: 51 Totally Random Facts About TREES and FLOWERS   88

Into the Deep: 50 Totally Random Facts About the GRAND CANYON   92

Happening History:

A Peek at the Past

A Major Empire: 68 Totally Random Facts About ANCIENT ROME   96

Ye Olde Middle Ages: 66 Totally Random Facts About MEDIEVAL KNIGHTS and CASTLES   100

Change Makers: 53 Totally Random Facts About PEOPLE WHO CHANGED THE WORLD   104

Commander in Chief: 71 Totally Random Facts About U.S. PRESIDENTS   108

Splendid Sports:

Catching Waves, Making Moves, and Pushing the Goalpost

Gooooal! 49 Totally Random Facts About SOCCER   114

For the Win! 49 Totally Random Facts About ATHLETICS   116

Catching a Wave: 46 Totally Random Facts About SURFING   118

SPOT THE 13 RANDOM DIFFERENCES   120

Joan of Arc was a French female warrior who lived in the 15th century. When the English army was invading France, she fought back because she heard voices in her head that she saw as signs from God.

The world record for the largest cargo airplane today goes to the Antonov An-225 cargo jet, which is capable of carrying 280 tons (250 metric tons) —that's about 56 elephants!

Rain Forest of the Sea: 58 Totally Random Facts About the GREAT BARRIER REEF 146

A Fin-tastic Fish: 46 Totally Random Facts About SEAHORSES 150

Grab Masters: 51 Totally Random Facts About OCTOPUSES 152

To the Gills: 49 Totally Random Facts About MARINE FISH 156

The Amazing Human Body:

From Teeth to Toes and Everything in Between

Material Substance: 49 Totally Random Facts About ANATOMY 160

Eat It Up: 78 Totally Random Facts About TEETH and the HUMAN DIGESTIVE SYSTEM 164

Super Science and Terrific Tech:

Handy Tools, Impressive Inventions, and Things That Go

Human-Made Marvels: 93 Totally Random Facts About TOOLS, INVENTIONS, and MACHINES 124

Let's Go! 107 Totally Random Facts About TRANSPORTATION 130

Into the Ocean:

Coral Reefs, Cool Creatures, and More about the Deep Blue Sea

Rolling in the Deep: 107 Totally Random Facts About the OCEAN 138

Gentle Giants: 50 Totally Random Facts About WHALE SHARKS 144

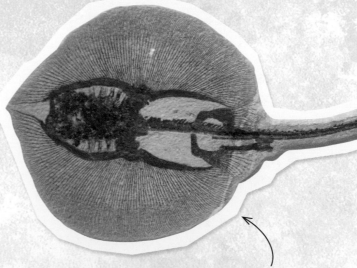

A fossil of a stingray. Stingrays have no bones, but instead have skeletons made of cartilage, which is the same stuff that makes up a human's ears and nose.

Using Your Head: 46 Totally Random Facts About the BRAIN   168

Vision Quest: 59 Totally Random Facts About EYES   172

—

Stellar Space:
Shining Stars, Exoplanets, and Magnificent Mars

Stellar Performance: 55 Totally Random Facts About STARS and CONSTELLATIONS   178

Out of This World: 36 Totally Random Facts About EXOPLANETS   182

Rockin' Red Planet: 72 Totally Random Facts About MARS   184

—

Random Roundup:
Rolling Rides, Enticing Eats, and Other Totally Cool Topics

Amazing Stays: 68 Totally Random Facts About UNIQUE HOTELS   190

Delicious and Nutritious: 44 Totally Random Facts About FRUITS and VEGGIES   194

That's Creepy! 45 Totally Random Facts to MAKE YOUR SKIN TINGLE   198

Play Stations: 51 Totally Random Facts About THEME PARKS   200

Full Spectrum: 46 Totally Random Facts About COLORS   204

Sweet Treats: 28 Totally Random Facts About CANDY   206

SPOT THE 13 RANDOM DIFFERENCES   208

Index   210

Photo Credits   214

Credits   215

The first part of an exoplanet's name is taken from the telescope that discovered it.

The average pomegranate can have as many as 1,400 seeds.

1,163 Totally Random Facts About

Awesome Animals

Wings, Claws, Tails, and Teeth

Dot to Dot

70 Totally Random Facts About SPOTTED CATS

Back view of a swimming jaguar

Jaguar

Cheetahs have "tear marks," black lines around their eyes that protect their eyes from the sun.

Jaguars have spots inside of their spots, in a bull's-eye shape.

Jaguars are the third largest big cat in the world, after tigers and lions.

Snow leopards live at the highest altitude of any cat species—up to 20,000 feet (6,096 m).

Snow leopards have wider nasal passages than other big cats. This means they can breathe more air in less time, allowing them to live at higher altitudes where the air is thinner.

Egyptian mau cats have been around for a long time: They were worshipped by ancient Egyptians.

Jaguars are excellent swimmers and will swim to get from place to place.

Rusty-spotted cats are one of the smallest wildcat species, weighing only about 3 pounds (1.4 kg). They are also nocturnal.

The tail of a jaguar can grow as long as 31 inches (80 cm).

Margay

The scientific name for a cheetah is *Acinonyx jubatus.*

Black-footed cats are the smallest wildcats in Africa. They grow up to 5 pounds (2.3 kg).

Female black-footed cats are called queens.

Ocelots are carnivores that hunt both on the ground and in trees.

Servals have extra-long necks to help them see over the tall grasses of the African savanna, one of the areas where they live.

In Africa, cheetahs have lost about 76 percent of their native range due to conflicts with and hunting and habitat destruction by people.

Cheetahs aren't found only in the wild in Africa; some live in Iran and they are being reintroduced to India.

Female black-footed cats will walk as far as 20 miles (32 km) to find food.

The word *jaguar* translates to "one who kills with one leap."

Rusty-spotted cats are found in India, Sri Lanka, and a small area in Nepal.

The margay cat is built to live in trees. It can even hang on a branch with just one foot.

Because of their ability to rotate their back legs, margay cats can run down trees.

Mother snow leopards line their dens with their own fur to make a warm and comfortable space for their cubs.

In addition to its fur, a cheetah's skin is spotted.

Domestic pixiebob cats are often born with extra fingers and toes.

Cheetahs growl when in danger.

The margay is the only cat that can rotate its back legs 180 degrees.

The word *ocelot* means "field tiger." It comes from the Aztec word *tlacoocelotl.*

Cheetahs can't roar, but they can chirp.

Jaguars are native to the southwestern United States, Mexico, and Central and South America.

The claws on a cheetah's feet help give the cat traction when it's running.

Asian leopard cat

Asian leopard cats have the widest range of any cat species. They are found in about 10 Asian countries.

Lions, tigers, leopards, and jaguars have cartilage along a bone in their skulls that prevents them from purring.

Rusty-spotted kittens eat chickens, frogs, birds, and small mammals such as rodents.

Jaguars make a noise called a "saw" because it sounds like someone is sawing wood.

Snow leopards wrap their tails around themselves to keep warm in their cold environments.

Jaguars are able to eat a variety of animals, including deer and tortoises.

SNOW LEOPARDS HAVE THE THICKEST COAT OF ANY BIG CAT SPECIES.

Snow leopard

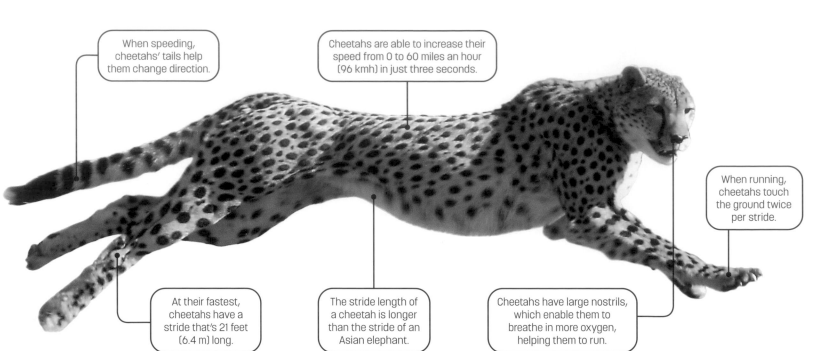

When speeding, cheetahs' tails help them change direction.

Cheetahs are able to increase their speed from 0 to 60 miles an hour (96 kmh) in just three seconds.

When running, cheetahs touch the ground twice per stride.

At their fastest, cheetahs have a stride that's 21 feet (6.4 m) long.

The stride length of a cheetah is longer than the stride of an Asian elephant.

Cheetahs have large nostrils, which enable them to breathe in more oxygen, helping them to run.

Female cheetahs usually live longer than male cheetahs.

Female jaguars have between one and four cubs in a single litter.

Snow leopards have very large paws, which act just like snowshoes, allowing them to walk on top of snow.

There are about 174,000 jaguars in the world today. This includes those in captivity.

JAGUARS ARE ABLE TO BITE WITH THE FORCE OF FOUR TIMES THEIR WEIGHT.

Half of all jaguars live in Brazil.

Deforestation is one of the great threats to jaguars, as it causes a loss of their natural habitat.

Domestic Savannah cats are a cross between an African serval and a domestic cat. They are able to leap 8 feet (2.4 m) in the air.

Snow leopards are called ghosts of the mountains.

Servals have the largest ears of all cat species.

Savannah cats live between 12 and 20 years.

Cheetahs kill by biting the throat of their prey, which cuts off their air supply.

Jaguars are most active at dawn and dusk.

Fishing cats have webbed toes to help them swim. Their front claws are used to help them catch fish in the wetlands of South and Southeast Asia where they live.

Serval

Jaguar attacking a caiman

Snow leopard

Best Buds!

KRIS AND REMUS ARE THE BEST OF FRIENDS. This is unusual because Kris is a cheetah and Remus is a dog! **In the wild, cheetahs are social animals, raised by their mothers along with their siblings.** Kris's mother abandoned him, so workers at the Cincinnati Zoo raised him themselves. But they were concerned that he might be lonely, **so they decided to find him a buddy at a local animal shelter.** When they met Remus, they learned that he and Kris had been born only a month apart, so they decided to adopt Remus. When Kris and Remus were first introduced, **Kris wasn't quite sure what to make of Remus—he'd never seen a dog before.** But now they are the best of friends. Kris and Remus aren't the only cheetah and dog buddy duo. Ruuxa the cheetah and Raina the dog from the San Diego Zoo are pals, too!

Snow leopards have more red blood cells in their bloodstreams than other cats to absorb the most oxygen possible in their mountainous habitats with less oxygen.

Oncillas are small wildcats that look like ocelots and margays, but smaller. They are also called little tiger cats.

Rusty-spotted cats have between one and three kittens in a litter.

Snow leopards are able to live in temperatures as cold as −40° F (−40° C).

The first Savannah cat was born in 1986. It had traits of both house cats and African servals.

Cheetah cubs have long hair, making them resemble a honey badger. The long hair tricks predators such as hyenas and lions into thinking the cubs aren't actually cubs, and helps prevent them from being hunted.

The scientific name for rusty-spotted cats is *Prionailurus rubiginosus*.

Female black-footed cats catch their prey 60 percent of the time. That's a very high rate in the wild!

Female cheetahs have an average of four cubs in each litter.

Including their tails, the largest snow leopards are 7 feet (2 m) long.

Cheetah mother and cubs

There are fewer than 7,500 wild cheetahs in the wild today. They are the most endangered big cat species in Africa.

Fewer than 8,000 snow leopards exist in the wild.

Climate change has decreased the snow leopard's habitat, as well as the populations of their prey, making it more difficult for the big cat to survive.

Perfect Protection

Porcupine

42 Totally Random Facts About ARMORED MAMMALS

There are 21 species of armadillos. • **Some porcupine species can live up to 30 years. That's a long time for a rodent!** • Hedgehogs are carnivores. • Baby porcupines are called porcupettes. • **The largest armadillo species is called the giant armadillo. Giant armadillos can be as many as 5 feet (1.5 m) long.** • The smallest armadillo species is the pink fairy armadillo, which is about 6 inches (15 cm) long. • **Echidnas have long beaks that can sense electrical signals from the body of the insects they eat.** • Hedgehogs live to be about seven years old. • **There are two distinct families of porcupines: Old World hedgehogs from Africa and Eurasia, and New World porcupines of North and South America.** • Armadillos spend 16 hours a day sleeping. • **There are four species of echidnas. All are found only in Australia and the island of New Guinea.** • Hedgehogs weigh as much as 2.4 pounds (1 kg) and grow as long as 14 inches (36 cm). • **Porcupines are nocturnal.** • An armadillo has overlapping plates all over its body. This is what makes up its armor. The plates cover the animal's back, head, legs, and tail. • **Along with the platypus, echidnas are the only living egg-laying mammals, or monotremes, on Earth.** • Hedgehogs don't leave the nest until they are

Echidna

One porcupine can have up to **30,000 QUILLS.**

three weeks old. • **Porcupines are rodents and grow bigger than hedgehogs, which are related to shrews and moles.** • In Spanish, *armadillo* means "little armored one." • **A baby echidna will stay in its mother's pouch until its spines start coming in. This takes about 50 days.** • Hedgehogs live in grasslands, woodlands, and meadows. • **Porcupine translates to "thorny pig" in Middle French, a version of French spoken in the 14th to 16th centuries.** • Every armadillo species is native to Central and South America, except for the nine-banded armadillo. Its range spans all the way from Argentina to the southern United States. • **Echidnas have a layer of fur below their quills, which helps keep them warm.** • As a way of protecting themselves from predators, hedgehogs coat themselves in plant poisons, which they are immune to, making their spines poisonous. They may also use poisons from frogs and toads.

Hedgehog

Three-banded armadillo

- **Porcupines are good swimmers.**
- The Rothschild's porcupine is the smallest porcupine species—it weighs only about 2 pounds (1 kg). •
- **The African crested porcupine weighs up to 44 pounds (20 kg), making it the largest porcupine species.** • Some hedgehogs hibernate.
- **Different armadillo species have different numbers of bands, or plates that overlap each other.** • A mother echidna's eggs are about the size of a grape. •

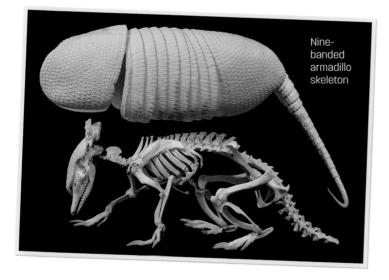

Nine-banded armadillo skeleton

A hedgehog's spines are short and soft at birth. • The quills of a porcupine are actually sturdy hairs with a covering of keratin, which makes them hard and sharp. • **Baby armadillos are called pups.** • Echidnas don't have teeth. Instead, they use their 6-inch (15-cm) tongue to slurp up insects and worms. • **Hedgehogs have from 5,000 to 7,000 spines on their backs.** • Porcupines are able to run backward. • **Porcupines chew animal bones to get the salt they need to survive.** • Baby echidnas are called puggles. • **Porcupine quills contain natural antibiotics that help prevent the growth of bacteria. Scientists think this might help prevent infection if they accidentally poke themselves.** • Each hedgehog spine, or quill, lasts one year before falling out. • **Some species of porcupines have air-filled quills, which act like life preservers and help them float.**

Feathered Friends

121 Totally Random Facts About BACKYARD BIRDS

The Oriole Bird, mascot of the Baltimore Orioles

The area of a black chickadee's brain in charge of memory grows 30 percent in the fall and shrinks once it's spring. This helps the bird remember where it hides seeds during the winter.

Not all robins migrate, but those that do really go the distance: up to 3,000 miles (4,828 km).

Blue jays will mimic the calls of different hawks to trick them or to warn other blue jays of a hawk's presence.

During World War I (1914–1918), soldiers trained pigeons to carry messages wrapped around their legs to allied troops.

Cardinals are native to the Americas.

Pine grosbeaks have pouches in their lower jaw to carry food.

The ruby-throated hummingbird has such short legs that it can't hop or walk.

Canada jays use their sticky spit to adhere berries to branches so they can eat the berries later.

Baltimore's baseball and football teams are both named after birds: the Baltimore Orioles MLB team and the Baltimore Ravens NFL team.

The drumming sound made by woodpeckers is their version of a birdsong.

Releasing a carrier pigeon from a tank

Chestnut-backed chickadees are found from California all the way to Alaska.

A robin can become drunk if it eats only honeysuckle berries.

A single brown thrasher knows more than 1,000 different tunes.

Birds have hollow bones to help them get enough air. Birds take in large amounts of oxygen to help them fly, which means their lungs expand a lot. Having hollow bones allows the air sacs in a bird's lungs to extend into its bones, giving it enough oxygen to soar.

The skeleton of a turkey

Robin chick

It's a myth that if a person returns a baby bird to its nest, the mother will reject the baby because it smells like a human.

Red-breasted nuthatches steal materials from other birds' nests so they can make their own.

In the wild, dark-eyed juncos sometimes mate with white-throated sparrows, making hybrid babies.

Hummingbirds are the world's smallest birds.

House sparrows are social birds that nest in colonies.

A male red-winged blackbird can have 15 mates at once.

Common redpolls dig 1-foot (30-cm)-long tunnels into snow to keep warm.

THE CARDINAL IS THE STATE BIRD FOR SEVEN U.S. STATES.

The American goldfinch call sounds like it's saying *po-ta-to-chip*.

During the winter, American goldfinches have brown feathers. In spring, the males' feathers turn a bright yellow.

Eastern bluebirds make their nests in tree holes made by woodpeckers. They move in when the woodpeckers no longer use the nests.

A flock of cardinals is known as a college, conclave, deck, radiance, or a Vatican.

Some baby eastern bluebirds stay in the nest to help their parents raise the next set of chicks.

Although ravens and crows may look similar in color and shape, ravens are bigger.

One penny weighs more than some species of hummingbirds.

In addition to carving out tree nests, woodpeckers use their sharp beaks to dig into tree bark to look for insects.

Male and female pileated woodpeckers take turns sitting on their eggs.

A group of blue jays is called a party.

EASTERN BLUEBIRDS PERFORM ACROBATICS IN THE AIR TO IMPRESS A MATE.

During mating season, a male cardinal will spend hours fighting its reflection thinking that it's another male.

An Italian sparrow is a hybrid species between a house sparrow and a Spanish sparrow.

Pigeons are one of the few animals that can recognize that their reflection isn't another pigeon.

Northwestern crows play games while flying.

American crows will stand on anthills and let ants climb all over them so the ants can eat the parasites living on the crow.

Pigeons can fly up to 6,000 feet (1,829 m) in the air.

White-throated swifts build their nests in the sides of cliffs.

Hooded orioles make their nests up to 45 feet (14 m) high in a tree.

Birds practice their songs in private before trying to use them to attract mates.

A female cuckoo will lay 12 to 22 eggs during a mating season. Each egg is laid in different birds' nests, leaving other species of birds to raise their chicks.

Crows live in family groups, and sometimes help raise babies that are not their own.

European starlings were introduced into Central Park, New York City, in 1890. About 50 years later, they were all over North America.

One flock of red-billed queleas can have more than 1,000 birds.

Onomatopoeic is the word used to describe a bird's name being derived from the calls it makes. An example is the hoopoe bird, which makes a *hoop-oe* sound.

Robins lay blue eggs to protect their babies from overheating and the sun's harmful UV radiation.

Northern mockingbirds can mimic the sounds of dogs and car horns perfectly.

If a crow encounters a hostile human, it will alert other crows to be wary of that specific person.

For 50 million years, birds didn't have beaks; they had snouts.

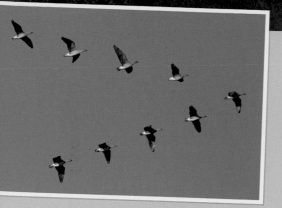

Most birds that migrate travel in a V formation.

When walking on a treadmill, pigeons don't bob their heads like they usually do when normally walking.

Budgies will yawn after seeing another budgie yawn. It can be contagious for them, just like it is for people.

Several species of cardinals are granivorous—animals that eat seeds or grain. Cardinals mostly eat seeds. They have rounded, small beaks that allow them to more easily pick seeds up.

The bones of many bird species weigh less than their feathers.

Pigeons mate for life.

When not in use, a woodpecker's tongue curls around the back of its head between the skull and skin.

A baby cuckoo hatched in another bird's nest will kick out other eggs so it gets all the food for itself.

The common raven is one of the most widespread bird species in the world.

Crows will gather and hold funerals for dead members of their group.

In winter, male house sparrows are in charge of the group. In spring, female house sparrows take over.

Both male and female pigeons produce a milk-like substance called "crop milk" from their stomachs and regurgitate it into a chick's mouth.

A mourning dove can drink water half as salty as seawater without getting sick.

A purple martin catches and eats food while flying.

A woodpecker's surprisingly long tongue

Cowbirds are considered parasites to yellow warblers. They will leave an egg in the nest of a yellow warbler. The cowbird chick might take nutrients away from yellow warbler chicks or even push out the other chicks.

A female northern mockingbird once laid a record 27 eggs in one season. These birds usually lay a maximum of about 18 eggs in one season.

THE COMMON CUCKOO IS THE CUCKOO SPECIES THAT MAKES THE *CUCKOO-CUCKOO* SOUND.

The white-tipped sicklebill has a curved beak to reach down deep into flowers for their nectar.

Birds can't sweat.

Baby hoatzin birds can climb trees by using claws on their wings.

Early golf balls were stuffed with bird feathers.

Some birds can use their bills to check the temperature of their nests.

In some bird species, only the males sing. Both male and female cardinals sing.

A woodpecker's tongue is two times as long as its beak.

Before migrating, hummingbirds will typically store 25 to 40 percent of their body weight in reserve fat.

Woodpeckers have a nose covered in small, furry feathers that keep dust and splinters out of their nostrils.

During mating season, male Baltimore orioles have territories equal to 2 to 3 acres (0.8 to 1.2 ha) of land.

Baltimore orioles build nests that hang from small tree branches.

To protect its eggs, a yellow warbler will cover a cover a cowbird egg left in its nest with another layer of nesting materials before laying her eggs. This will prevent the egg from incubating and hatching.

Yellow warbler nests have been found as many as six layers deep in places where there are more cowbirds.

Birds have three eyelids.

A mourning dove can store up to 17,200 seeds in a special sack in their bodies called a "crop."

CROWS USE TOOLS SUCH AS STICKS TO GET FOOD.

Brown-headed cowbirds steal nests from more than 220 other bird species.

A bluebird can spot an insect from 60 feet (18 m) away.

Purple martins drink by skimming water off the surface of a pond into their mouths.

Hummingbirds eat every 10 to 15 minutes.

Due to rare mutations, some cardinals have yellow feathers instead of red ones.

Turtledoves purr.

A hummingbird gets nectar from 1,000 to 2,000 flowers a day.

Most birds that have red and yellow feathers can only make those colors from eating certain foods.

Barn swallows snatch insects from the surface of water while in flight.

The crested treeswift glues its nests together with its spit.

Magpies don't like blue or shiny objects and seem to eat less if these objects are nearby.

Male hummingbirds stab each other with their beaks to compete over a mate.

The rainbow bee-eater rubs bees and wasps against trees to remove their stingers before eating them.

Robins learn to fly when they're only two weeks old.

A brown thrasher will sweep its beak back and forth like a broom to clear away leaves on the ground to find beetles hidden underneath.

A mourning dove eats 12 to 20 percent of its body weight every day.

Pigeons have been used as messenger birds since the fifth century in Syria and Persia.

Along with drinking nectar, hummingbirds need to eat insects for protein and other nutrients to survive.

A group of robins is called a round.

Pigeons bob their heads as they walk to get a better sense of the depth and distance of objects because their eyes face to the sides.

The sword-billed hummingbird's beak is longer than its body (excluding the tail).

You have a one-in-a-million chance of spotting a yellow cardinal.

British barn swallows are also known as house and chimney swallows since they're often seen near towns and other human establishments.

When alerting the rest of the flock of danger, the more *dee* sounds in a chickadee's call, the more serious the danger is.

Because Brewer's sparrows live in environments with little water, they can go weeks without needing to drink.

The ovenbird of North America covers its nests in leaves, making a dome-like shape that looks like an old-fashioned oven. This is also how it got its name!

Crows and ravens are believed to be as smart as chimpanzees.

Male Lucifer hummingbirds have purple feathers on their throats to help attract mates.

Golden-crowned kinglets of North America can survive nighttime temperatures reaching below −40 °F (−40 °C).

The scientific name for Cassin's kingbird, *Tyrannus vociferans*, translates to "vociferous tyrant," so named because of their aggressive nature and tendency to attack hawks much bigger than themselves.

A magpie's tail is as long as its body, allowing it to make swift turns in the air to avoid predators.

A bee hummingbird weighs about the same as a quarter of a teaspoon of sugar.

The ring-billed gull is the most widespread gull in North America.

Cardinals group together into flocks during the winter when resources are scarcer. They pool these resources to increase their chances of survival.

A group of pelicans is called a squadron.

A group of owls is called a parliament.

A GROUP OF FLAMINGOS IS CALLED A FLAMBOYANCE.

The Baron caterpillar's larvae blend in with the green leaves to which they are attached. • **The mimic octopus is able to change colors to look like other sea creatures, such as jellyfish and stingrays.** • The dead leaf mantis does in fact look just like a dead leaf! This striking camouflage helps protect it from predators. • **Stonefish have a rough, rocklike coat that mimics the color and texture of coral reefs, allowing them to easily blend into their surroundings.** • The gray owl has white and gray feathers, which help it blend with its snowy habitat in northern Asia, northern Europe, and northern North America. • **When the golden tortoise beetle is annoyed, it changes its color from yellow to red.** • The red-eyed flounder blends in with the seafloor by hiding among pebbles. Its clever camouflage helps this flat fish trap the small marine life it eats. • **Katydids' bodies look just like the leaves of** the plants they live on, keeping these insects hidden from predators, including snakes, frogs, and birds. • The tongue of an alligator snapping turtle looks just like a worm. They wiggle it to trick fish into coming close, then snap up their newest meal. • **The pygmy seahorse has white and pink skin with large red bumps that resemble the coral found among the reefs in which it lives.** • Stick insects have long, thin torsos that make them look so much like actual sticks that they disappear into the vegetation. • *Color matching* **is the term for camouflaging by having an exterior that matches your background or environment.** • *Mimic* is the term for when an animal looks as if it is something else either for camouflage or to trick other animals into thinking it's something else. • **The viceroy and monarch butterflies are examples of Mullerian mimicry. This is where two species mimic each other to the benefit of each animal.** • In the winter, snowshoe hares have white coats to blend with their snowy environment. In the summer, their coats turn brown to blend in with the plant life that surrounds them. • **The pattern of a rattlesnake's scales**

Snowshoe hare

Hide-and-Seek

34 Totally Random Facts About COLOR-CHANGING ANIMALS

Crab spider

looks just like desert sand, which allows the snake to blend right into its surroundings. • Wobbegongs are long, flat sharks with a boldly marked pattern on their bodies. They use this tricky camouflage to hide among rocks and to catch unsuspecting prey. • **Common potoos are nocturnal birds that have evolved to look just like the bark of a tree. They can stay motionless for long periods of time, blending into the bark.** • Snow leopards have evolved to grow fur in patterns that mimic rocks in their mountainous habitat. Their camouflage makes them so hard to spot that they have been nicknamed "ghosts of the mountains." • **The tail of a spider-tailed horned viper mimics a spider. It's used to lure birds, tricking them into thinking they are about to snag a meal. When a bird is close, the viper attacks.** • The Pederson's cleaner shrimp is translucent with blue spots, which allows this tiny creature to hide among the sea anemones in its tropical habitat. • **The nonvenomous scarlet king snake mimics the venomous coral snake to trick predators into thinking it's dangerous.** • Chameleons

Stick insect

will change color to cool down or to warm their bodies. The darker they are, the more heat they absorb, whereas the lighter they are, the less heat they take in. • **Chameleons also change colors to communicate with other chameleons.** • Flounders can only mimic the surroundings they are able to see, because their eyes send the color they see to the cells in charge of changing their skin's color. • **If a flounder's eyes are damaged, it can't change color.** • Scientists are still trying to figure out exactly why zebras have stripes, but they don't think the stripes are for camouflage. • **It takes crab spiders between 10 and 25 days to change from white to yellow. They change color to blend into the flower they are sitting on. Then, they wait for prey to go by and catch their food.** • Squid, cuttlefish, and octopuses are able to change the color of their skin through spots on their bodies that contain different pigments and can expand and contract to show more or less color. • **The Octopus cyanea is able to change the color and texture of its skin instantly.** • *Disruptive coloration* is the term for an animal's exterior having vibrant patterns to make it difficult for predators to see their bodies. Leopards are a good example of this. • **Humans first started using camouflage clothing in military uniforms during World War I.** • Pacific tree frogs change color to resemble the leaves on which they live. They also change color when the season and temperature change.

The mossy-leaf tailed gecko has skin that **IMITATES THE TEXTURE AND COLOR OF MOSS.** It is only found in the African country of Madagascar.

Nature's Assassins

Deathstalker scorpion

50 Totally Random Facts About *LETHAL ANIMALS*

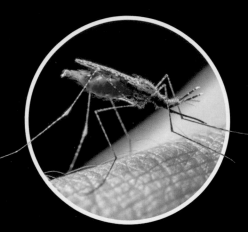

Mosquitoes kill more than a million people a year, more than any other animal. These insects can release deadly diseases and parasites into people's bloodstreams while drinking their blood.

The black-footed cat, an African wildcat, is an excellent hunter. It hunts under the cover of darkness and kills 10 to 14 prey animals each night.

Feathers of the hooded pitohui bird contain a toxin that scientists believe comes from the beetles they eat. This is one of the only toxic birds known on Earth.

Rough-skinned newts release a strong smell to warn potential predators that they are poisonous. Their toxin is contained in their skin.

The venom of a black widow spider is 15 times deadlier than a rattlesnake.

The cone snail, a marine snail found in the Pacific, Indian, and Atlantic Oceans, has venom powerful enough to kill the equivalent of 700 people.

The deathstalker scorpion is one of the most venomous scorpion species. Despite being only 3.9 inches (10 cm) long, it can strike its tail and deliver a deadly sting at 51 inches (130 cm) per second.

Because crocodiles cannot chew, they latch onto their prey and do a "death roll," where they spin and flip their prey, tearing it apart.

Many big cats attack the throat of their prey, but the jaguar has jaws so strong that it crushes the skull of its prey to kill it.

The Irukandji jellyfish is only about an inch (2.5 cm) long, but it has a nasty sting that is extremely dangerous. It can cause nausea, a high heart rate and high blood pressure, and fluids to build up in the lungs. Sometimes the jellyfish's sting can even lead to death.

The tiny blue-ringed octopus displays its blue rings only when it feels threatened and ready to release its extremely toxic venom. Its venom weakens or paralyzes the muscles of its victims and can kill.

Moose will use their huge antlers as weapons to protect their babies.

The cassowary, a 6-foot (1.8-m)-tall flightless bird, is often referred to as a "living dinosaur" because its inner toe is incredibly long and sharp, like a prehistoric raptor, and can kill with a single powerful kick.

The venom of the Sydney funnel-web spider of Australia is strong enough to kill a human in 15 minutes.

STINGERS

The world's largest lizard, the Komodo dragon of Indonesia, is a vicious predator that will kill and eat almost anything. Its bite contains spit filled with deadly bacteria that can kill most animals within a day.

The male duck-billed platypus is one of very few venomous mammals. It uses hooks on its hind legs to deliver a painful sting.

The stonefish has evolved to look like a rock. Using this camouflage, it waits for prey to get close before using the 13 spines on its back that inject the deadliest venom of any species of fish.

The Cape buffalo of Africa has massive horns that are used as weapons to kill predators.

The sloth bear of India will use its huge claws to slash predators if necessary. Its large claws are also used to tear apart termite nests, as the insects are part of the bear's diet.

During mating season, when male African elephants are competing with other males for a female's attention, they will attack nearly anything with little provocation.

Puffer fish are served as a delicacy food in some places, but they contain a deadly poison that is released if not cooked properly.

Between 1347 and 1351, fleas living on rats spread the bubonic plague, also known as the black death, killing around 25 million people.

A group of snakes known as spitting cobras have the ability to spit venom from their fangs. The venom can cause blindness if it gets into the eyes of their victims.

A crocodile's jaw is strong enough to snap bones in two with a single, powerful bite.

Puffer fish prepared for eating

The tsetse fly of Africa kills 10,000 people annually. Like mosquitoes, this fly releases a deadly parasite into the bloodstream while drinking a person's blood. If left untreated, it can kill a person in a few years.

BULL SHARKS ARE CONSIDERED TO BE ONE OF THE MOST DANGEROUS SPECIES OF SHARK BECAUSE OF THEIR AGGRESSIVE NATURE. THEY HUNT DURING BOTH THE DAY AND NIGHT AND EVEN EAT DOLPHINS.

Weaver ants have the ability to spray acid to defend themselves.

Triatomine bugs, also known as kissing bugs and assassin bugs, can transmit a deadly disease called Chagas' disease if they poop while drinking the blood from a face of a sleeping person.

Africanized bees, also known as killer bees, were created by breeding two different bee species, making them extremely aggressive.

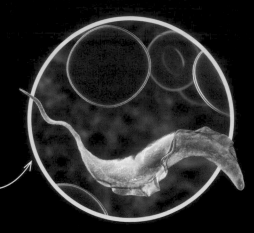

The parasite transmitted by triatomine bugs that causes Chagas' disease

THE BOX JELLYFISH, ONE OF THE MOST VENOMOUS ANIMALS ON EARTH, HAS VENOM SO DEADLY THAT SOME PEOPLE STUNG BY IT DIE BEFORE EVEN REACHING SHORE.

Africanized bees attack and sting their victims in massive swarms, with victims receiving more than 10 times as many stings than from the average bee swarm.

Because rhinos have poor vision, they're easily startled and will charge and ram into anything that scares them.

Spotted hyenas move in large packs, have bone-crushing jaws, and work together to bite, then tear down prey.

Though wolverines are only up to 34 inches (86 cm) long, they have been known to sometimes kill and eat full-grown caribou, mountain goats, and even moose.

The Tunisian fat-tailed scorpion is responsible for 90 percent of fatalities caused by scorpions in North Africa.

The bite of a Brazilian wandering spider can cause intense vertigo, nausea, irregular heartbeat, hypothermia, and more, within 30 minutes.

Freshwater snails carry a parasitic worm that carries a disease called schistosomiasis. This parasite can be transmitted to humans.

The cone snail injects its venom into its prey through a harpoon-like dart.

Despite being herbivores, hippos are considered the world's deadliest large mammals because they can easily kill with their massive, bone-crushing jaws and razor-sharp teeth.

The goliath tigerfish of the Congo has a mouthful of razor-sharp needlelike teeth and has been known to attack small crocodiles.

Asian giant hornets are the largest species of wasp in the world. They have been known to invade beehives, tearing bees apart with their mandibles.

A grizzly bear can catch and kill a 2,000-pound (907-kg) adult North American buffalo using its sharp teeth and claws.

In 2021, a group of about 70 orcas worked together to hunt and kill a blue whale, the biggest animal to have ever lived. The attack lasted more than three hours.

The *Lonomia* caterpillar of South America is a highly venomous insect that can severely damage the human brain.

Rats and mice are common carriers of various diseases that can be transmitted through their spit when they bite.

A full-grown grizzly bear has the strength equal to 2.5 to 5 humans when it's not in an aggressive state.

Using its powerful jaws, a tiger can kill and carry an animal twice its weight up a tree.

Lions have long, sharp canine teeth that they sink into the necks of their prey. The lion's bite can break the neck of their victim or suffocate it.

Humans have caused thousands of animal species to become endangered due to activities like burning fossil fuels, cutting down trees, and polluting the air and water.

A fish trapped in a discarded plastic net

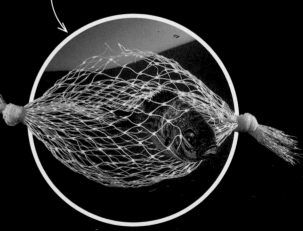

THE SLOW LORIS IS THE ONLY VENOMOUS PRIMATE. IT SECRETES VENOM FROM ITS ELBOWS AND MIXES IT WITH SPIT TO DELIVER A TOXIC BITE.

Oh, Baby!

99 Totally Random Facts About BABY ANIMALS

Baby giant panda

Compared to the size of their adult counterparts, baby giant pandas are among the smallest mammals when born, but by six months of age they have grown to 10 times their birth weight.

Baby elephant shrews have all their hair at birth.

Mother lions hide their cubs from the rest of the pride and from predators until they are six weeks old.

A group of lion cubs of the same age raised together by several mothers is called a crèche.

Often, female deer keep their twins hidden in different places.

Only 2 to 5 percent of cows have twins.

In their first two weeks of life, turkey chicks sleep under the wings of their mother.

Tigers can have as many as seven cubs in a single litter.

Quolls

Spiders can lay up to 3,000 eggs at once. And for many species, the babies are on their own from the start.

The *Toxeus magnus* jumping spider feeds her spiderlings a yellow milk-like fluid full of protein, fat, and sugar.

A baby quoll (a marsupial from Australia) is called a pup, and is only the size of a bean when born.

Baby swans are called cygnets. Though adult swans are white, cygnets are brown-gray with black bills.

Young owls are called owlets.

Most species of lizards are self-sufficient at birth and can walk, run, and eat without help from their parents.

Baby seahorses are around a half inch (8 to 16 mm) long when they're born. (An M&M is about 10 millimeters.)

Owl

Baby giant pandas grow a full coat of fur by about two months of age.

Baby rhinoceroses are born without horns. It takes a few months for their horns to begin growing in.

About 20 minutes after birth, zebras can walk. By the one-hour mark, they can run!

Baby rattlesnakes aren't able to rattle until they shed their skin at least two times.

The venom of baby rattlesnakes is still dangerous to humans.

Meerkats raise their young as a group. The mother leaves to find food and other members of the group will help protect her babies.

When opossums are born, they are the size of a honeybee.

Horn sharks lay eggs that are spiral-shaped.

Until they are a year old, baby anteaters move around by riding on their mothers' backs.

It takes only five months for bandicoots to become fully grown adults.

Female crabs carry millions of eggs beneath their bodies until they are ready to hatch.

Baby alligators have between 60 and 80 teeth when they are born. They eat snails, fish, worms, and even birds.

Baby hamsters' teeth begin to grow in at seven days old.

Whale calves are usually born tail first.

BABY FLAMINGOS ARE GRAY OR WHITE, NOT PINK, WHEN THEY HATCH.

After birth, cotton-top tamarin monkeys are raised by the group, not just by Mom.

Black bear cubs weigh about 1 pound (454 g) at birth and stay with Mom for about 16 months.

Meerkats

The African elephant carries her baby for about 22 months, longer than any other mammal on Earth.

Baby puffins are raised by both their mother and father.

Cotton-top tamarins have twins more often than they have single babies.

Baby alligators can't use their tongues.

All marsupial babies, such as koalas, wombats and wallabies, are called joeys, just like baby kangaroos.

The female pipefish releases her eggs in a male pipefish's pouch, and he cares for the eggs for about two weeks. Then they are ready to hatch.

Baby pygmy marmosets imitate their parents' sounds by babbling.

Young macaques play with snowballs.

Ostriches, the world's largest bird, are fully grown at six months of age.

Kangaroo

Ostrich

BABY DEER ARE CALLED FAWNS. *FAWN* COMES FROM THE OLD ENGLISH WORD FOR "GLAD."

Scientists have found that male pipefish have more babies if their mate is attractive.

Bonobo babies learn to make friends very early on. The bonds they make when they're young last into adulthood.

Orangutans take about eight years to mature into adults, the longest time of any of the great apes.

Baby elephant calves drink 2,200 gallons (8,328 L) of milk.

At just 10 inches (25 cm) tall, the royal antelope is the smallest antelope species in the world. Babies are just 2 pounds (1 kg) at birth.

Many reptiles, including crocodiles and turtles, are born with a special egg tooth that helps them crack out of the shell.

Two months after hatching, the egg tooth is reabsorbed into the reptile's mouth.

When playing, young chimps will sometimes make dolls out of sticks and pretend they are baby chimps.

Mother earwigs give birth to 60 babies at a time and favor the healthiest ones.

In southern Africa, where it's very dry, sandgrouse fathers bring water to their chicks by soaking themselves and flying back to the nest.

Puppies are born with 28 teeth and have 42 teeth by the time they reach adulthood.

Baby sloths are able to hold on to the fur of their mother within minutes of being born.

Sloths

Baby chickens, or chicks, communicate with their mothers by chirping through their shells.

Baby dolphins have spines on the sides of their tongues that act as zippers, keeping seawater out while the babies drink their mother's milk.

Baby skunks begin to spray their stinky scent with accuracy at about four months old.

Sows, or mother pigs, sing to their piglets.

Mother sea otters raise their pups on their own. Babies stay with Mom for about six months.

A squirrel that finds an abandoned baby squirrel will sometimes adopt it as its own.

A baby blue whale can gain 250 pounds (113 kg) in a day from drinking its mother's milk.

Baby turtles chirp and grunt at each other through their eggshells before they hatch. Researchers think that they communicate to coordinate hatching schedules.

Baby skunks cannot spray to defend themselves until they are about a month old.

Baby sea otters weigh about 5 pounds (2 kg) at birth, which is more than a polar bear cub.

At birth, baby chipmunks are the size of a jelly bean.

NEWBORN PIGLETS RUN TO THEIR MOTHER WHEN THEY HEAR HER VOICE.

Chipmunk

Kodiak bears

A Kodiak bear is about 1 pound (454 g) at birth but grows to be more than 1,000 pounds (454 kg)—that's 1,000 times its birth weight! If this were true of humans, adults would weigh more than 6,000 pounds (2,722 kg).

Sea otter mothers wrap their baby in seaweed to keep them in one place when they have to leave them.

Raccoon mothers feed their young for around three months. After that, the babies learn to forage for their own food.

Baby llamas are called crias.

The babies of some species of monkeys, such as the François' langur, are born with a different fur color than their parents.

SEAL PUPS CAN HOLD THEIR BREATH UNDERWATER FOR TWO MINUTES.

Puppies can be born as identical twins, which is rare in the animal world.

A baby pygmy hippo can drink milk from its mother even when underwater.

The eggs of the white-headed duck are the largest compared to body size of any duck, goose, or swan species.

Baby sharks are called pups.

A baby seahorse is called a fry.

Dusky leaf monkeys

Tiger

Tiger cubs have blue eyes when they are born.

Poult is the term for a baby turkey. Poults eat insects, seeds, and berries.

Like a mother chicken, a mother turkey is called a hen. She lays 10 to 12 eggs at a time.

A young female turkey is sometimes referred to as a jenny. A young male turkey is called a jake.

The babies of platypuses and echidnas are both called puggles.

Young geese are called goslings.

Young goats are called kids. When a mother goat is giving birth, it's called "kidding."

Baby mice are called pinkies. Mother mice carry their babies for 19 to 21 days before they are born.

Young skunks are called kits. So are young foxes and rabbits.

When a baby camel is born, its humps are not yet formed. As it gets older, the humps will grow as they fill with fat.

Lucky Ducklings

- Ducklings are able to swim one day after they are born with the help of an adult.

- **Ducklings are precocial, meaning they are almost fully developed when they are hatched.**

- Ducklings are born with soft, fluffy down feathers to help keep them warm.

- **Mother ducks coat their ducklings with a waterproof oil, allowing the babies to swim without getting wet.**

- Ducklings travel in packs, known as teams or flocks, to stay as safe as possible from predators.

- **Ducklings begin to fly at three months old.**

- Wood ducks make their nests in trees. Ducklings jump from the trees after they hatch and head to water.

- **It takes about 28 days for a duckling to hatch from its egg.**

- Like adult ducks, ducklings have few nerves in their feet, keeping their feet colder than the rest of their bodies. This helps them stay comfortable in lower temperatures.

- **Ducklings can spend 60 percent of the day eating, which helps them take in enough nutrients to grow feathers.**

- Only white ducks have yellow ducklings.

- **Within a month or two, most ducklings are able to fly.**

A dog sled team in Alaska

Cool Canines

49 Totally Random Facts About DOGS

Pekingese

Dogs have belly buttons.

Dogs belong to a family of mammals called Canidae.

There are more than 30 species in the Canidae family, including wolves, foxes, coyotes, dingoes, and jackals.

Dogs are the most diverse land mammal species.

In ancient China, Pekingese and Japanese Chin dogs were so revered that people prayed to them in temples, and they even had their own servants.

When wet, dogs can shake 70 percent of the water off their bodies in just four seconds.

Dogs were the very first animals to become domesticated, before even cats and farm animals such as chickens and cows.

There are hundreds of dog breeds, divided into eight classes: sporting, hound, working, terrier, toy, nonsporting, herding, and miscellaneous.

Golden retrievers, Labradors, and German shepherds are commonly used as guide dogs for people who are blind or have other disabilities.

Working intelligence and obedience intelligence refer to a dog's ability to learn from humans. Poodles and golden retrievers get high marks in this department.

Adult dogs have 42 teeth.

Beagles, English springer spaniels, and golden retrievers are trained to use their sense of smell as detection dogs—they can detect substances such as blood and dangerous materials.

Dogs are omnivores—they eat both meat and plants.

THE EARLIEST IMAGES OF DOGS appeared around 8,000 years ago on rock carvings in modern-day Saudi Arabia.

Just like wolves, dogs are highly social pack animals.

The Norwegian lundehund was originally bred to hunt puffins.

Dogs turn in circles before they lie down because their wild ancestors used to flatten grass to make a comfortable bed.

The average life span for a dog is 10 to 14 years.

On average, a dog can run around 19 miles an hour (31 kph).

Puppies are born with their eyes sealed shut. They don't open for three weeks.

During World War I, Belgian sheepdogs worked as message carriers.

Depending on the breed, dogs' ears have different shapes. Each shape has a unique name; for example, ears that point straight up are called prick ears.

Dachshunds were originally bred to hunt badgers.

The most expensive dog wedding in history cost $250,000. The event took place to raise money for animal welfare.

The longest dog on record was Zorba, an English mastiff who was more than 8 feet (2.4 m) long!

A 33,000 year-old canine skull fossil found in Siberia is the oldest confirmed fossil of a domestic dog.

Dogs evolved from a now-extinct species of gray wolf.

The largest canid is the Alaskan timber wolf. Larger males can grow upward of 155 pounds (70 kg).

Wild canids are found on all continents except Antarctica.

The smallest canid is the fennec fox, a desert-dwelling hunter with large ears. Adult fennecs are between 1.5 and 3.3 pounds (0.7 and 1.5 kg). This is about the size of a two-month-old kitten.

Two canid species are listed as critically endangered: the red wolf of the southeastern United States and the African wild dog.

Dogs are not native to Australia, although the dingo was introduced to the continent around 3,500 years ago, and the red fox around 1860.

According to a recent survey, the most popular name for a dog is Max. Other popular names include Molly, Sam, Zach, and Maggie.

I ♥ My Dog

Making eye contact with a dog can create a loving bond and **BRIGHTEN YOUR MOOD.** ♥

Puppies can be adopted as early as eight weeks of age. Until then, they should stay with their moms and littermates.

About 5 percent of dogs given to animal shelters are purebred dogs.

Dogs can raise, lower, tilt, and rotate each ear independently.

A dog's whiskers are so sensitive that they can detect tiny changes in airflow.

Dogs are capable of locating the source of a sound in a fraction of a second.

Taller dogs are more likely than shorter dogs to cooperate with humans.

The smallest breed of dog is the Chihuahua. It measures just 6 to 9 inches (15 to 23 cm) tall and weighs 3 to 6 pounds (1.4 to 2.7 kg).

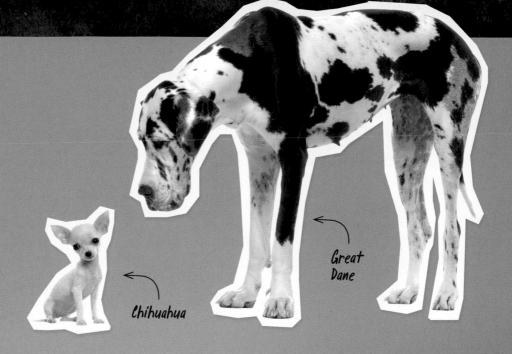

Chihuahua

Great Dane

The largest breed of dog is the Great Dane. The average Great Dane is around 40 inches (102 cm) tall and weighs 120 pounds (54 kg).

Japanese Chins have the habit of spinning in circles.

Humans and dogs have similarly structured brains when it comes to understanding language.

Dogs can hear frequencies that humans cannot.

Leaving clothes with your dog when you are absent can help keep them calm because they are able to pick up your scent.

Saint Bernards were once rescue dogs, helping monks save people caught in snowstorms in the snowy Alps between Switzerland and Italy.

There are three sizes of poodles: toy, miniature, and standard.

Just as humans are right-handed or left-handed, researchers have found that when dogs tilt their heads, they are either "right-tilters" or "left-tilters."

Genius Dogs!

ONE OF THE SMARTEST DOGS RECORDED WAS A BORDER COLLIE NAMED CHASER who could identify and retrieve more than 1,000 different toys by name. Chaser had a collection of 30 balls and could distinguish between them. She also understood adjectives, so not only could Chaser fetch a ball, but she could also understand directions to fetch a bigger or smaller ball. What made Chaser special is that once she learned a concept, she could use her brain and start to learn by inference—the process of reaching a conclusion from known facts—which is how human children learn. Her owner, who was a scientist, trained her. Chaser also has the distinguished reputation of having the largest tested memory of any nonhuman animal in the world.

Mini Mammals

72 Totally Random Facts About RABBITS, GUINEA PIGS, and GERBILS

Popcorning is a term for when guinea pigs jump up and down in one place. They do it when they're happy.

The teeth of guinea pigs and rabbits never stop growing.

A gerbil's teeth do stop growing, with the exception of their large front teeth known as incisors.

Rabbits are born blind and without fur.

Gerbils' coats can be one of 40 different colors.

Rabbits with pointy ears have the ability to rotate their ears up to 270 degrees.

Guinea pigs are most active at dusk and at dawn.

One of the reasons male and female gerbils leave their scents in different areas is to mark territory.

Rabbits spend their first few days in a soft, warm nest lined with fur.

Gerbils are native to Asia, Africa, and parts of eastern Europe.

It's possible to toilet train a gerbil.

Rabbits communicate worry by clenching their faces and changing the position of their bodies.

Gerbils sleep in short bursts that combine to an average of about 12 hours a day.

Guinea pigs talk to one another by squeaking, chirping, and purring.

Gerbils are naturally an orange color, which is called golden agouti.

Guinea pigs have two kinds of poop: dry pellets, which are regular poops, and cecotropes, which guinea pigs eat to digest leftover nutrients.

Gerbils are able to leap as high as 1 foot (30 cm).

Gerbils are also called desert rats.

Truffles the guinea pig holds the world record for longest guinea pig jump at 18.89 inches (48 cm).

GUINEA PIGS WERE KEPT AS FARM ANIMALS AND AS PETS AS FAR BACK AS 5000 BC.

Rabbits get lonely if they're alone. They need the companionship of other rabbits to be happy.

Gerbils are able to communicate with each other using ultrasonic tones that are too high for humans to hear.

It is illegal to own a gerbil in Hawaii because gerbils could become an invasive species.

Although pet gerbils are herbivores, wild gerbils are omnivores, eating insects, meat, and plants.

Insects are a good source of protein for wild gerbils and can be found even in their dry habitats.

Male gerbils also leave their scent to show dominance, while females use scent to attract their young.

Female rabbits carry their babies for only 30 days before giving birth. They have between 4 and 12 kits per litter.

A gerbil's tail is about the same length as its body.

Guinea pigs have a very warm body temperature of between 102° F and 104° F (39° C and 40° C).

A RABBIT CAN SEE NEARLY 360 DEGREES.

A rabbit's diet should be made up of 90 percent hay. Chewing hay prevents their teeth from overgrowing.

The largest gerbil species, known as the great gerbil, can be as large as 16 inches (40 cm) long.

When guinea pigs travel together, they move in a single-file line.

Jackrabbits are a species of superfast rabbits. They can move as fast as 45 miles an hour (72 kmh).

Gerbils enjoy boxing and wrestling with each other.

Rabbits express happiness by jumping, twirling, and moving their feet. Together these movements are called a binky.

Guinea pigs can live up to 10 years.

Gerbils clean themselves by covering their bodies in sand, which exfoliates dirt from their fur.

Horses and rabbits actually have a similar diet and similar eyes, teeth, and ears.

Gerbils evolved to live in dry, arid climates with little water, so they rarely pee.

Most of the pet gerbils in the United States today are descendants of 11 pairs of gerbils brought to the U.S. in 1954.

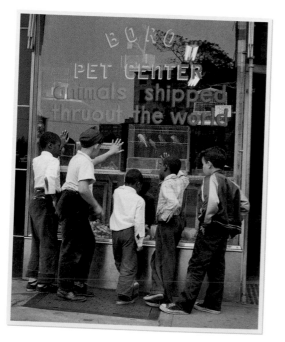

Cavia porcellus is the scientific name for a guinea pig.

Where wild gerbils are an invasive species, they can overeat native plants and be harmful to the environment.

Rabbits release body heat through their ears to help them stay cool.

Carrots are not actually a part of a rabbit's natural diet.

Wild gerbils dig networks of burrows in their dry habitats, which include the Gobi desert, located in Central Asia.

Guinea pigs can walk as soon as they are born.

The earliest written record of gerbils in the Western Hemisphere was in 1866. The species that has become a common pet is native to the Asian country of Mongolia.

Pointy-eared rabbits can hear two sounds at once.

To protect themselves, gerbils can shed their tails to get away from a predator.

Guinea pigs are not related to pigs. They get their name from the short, round shape of their piglike bodies.

Gerbils emit a high-pitched noise and kick their back legs to warn other gerbils of danger.

When flipped on their back, rabbits can go into a state of "tonic immobility," in which their bodies shut down to appear dead to predators.

Gerbils are about the same size as hamsters.

There are two types of guinea pigs: long-haired and short-haired. Most pet guinea pigs are short-haired.

There are more than 110 species of gerbils.

Guinea pig

WILD GERBILS LIVE IN GROUPS OF UP TO 20 INDIVIDUALS THAT ALL SHARE A DEN.

Like people, guinea pigs can't make their own vitamin C. They need to get it from the foods they eat or supplements.

Guinea pigs are rodents.

Over the course of one year, a female rabbit can have as many as 800 babies, grandkids, and great-grandkids.

Guinea pigs have four toes on their front feet and three on their back feet.

Every gerbil has a unique scent, which other gerbils use to identify them.

Flash holds the world record as fastest guinea pig for running 32.8 feet (10 m) in 8.81 seconds.

Like rabbits, guinea pigs are social animals and need the company of other guinea pigs.

The 5-foot (1.5-m)-tall *Josephoartigasia monesi* was a larger distant relative of guinea pigs.

Queen Elizabeth I of England had a guinea pig as a pet.

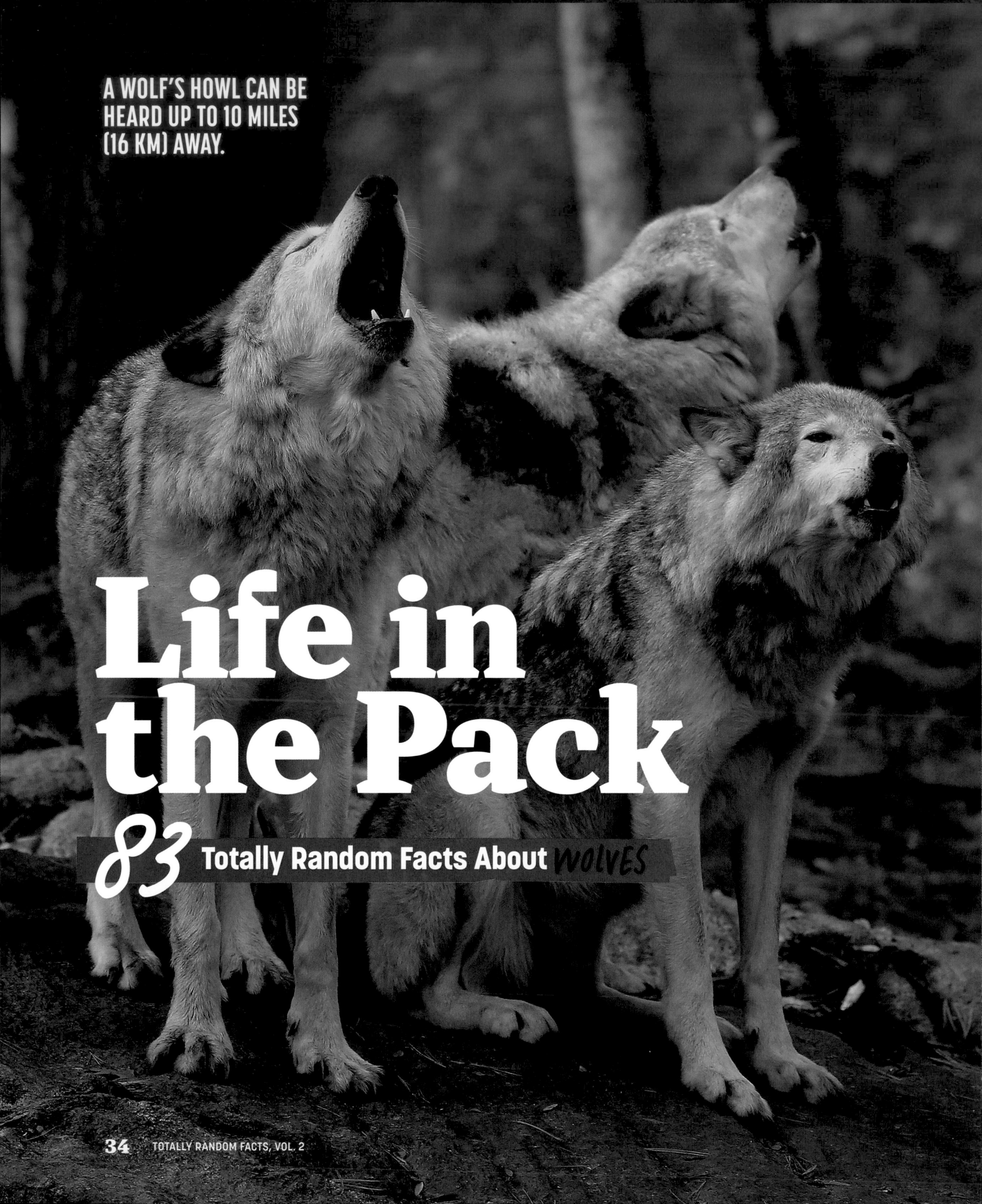

A WOLF'S HOWL CAN BE HEARD UP TO 10 MILES (16 KM) AWAY.

Life in the Pack

83 Totally Random Facts About WOLVES

Wolves are the largest species of canids, a family that includes dogs and foxes. • **Modern-day domestic dogs are the result of thousands of years of humans domesticating and breeding wild wolves.** • There are two main species of wolves in the world: red wolf and gray wolf. • **Gray wolves have two layers of fur. The top layer keeps moisture off their coats and the bottom layer helps keeps them warm. These layers help them survive frigid temperatures.** • Snow that gets stuck on a gray wolf's fur doesn't melt. • **The average adult male gray wolf can weigh between 75 and 120 pounds (34 and 54 kg).** • The average adult female gray wolf can weigh between 60 and 95 pounds (27 and 43 kg). • **A wolf's jaws can exert up to 1,500 pounds (680 kg) of pressure per square inch, which is six times as powerful as the jaws of a rottweiler dog.** • A wolf can sprint up to 45 miles an hour (72 kmh) in short bursts. • **Wolves that live in colder climates tend to be bigger.** • A wolf's mouth has about 42 teeth, just like a dog's. • **Between 84 and 87 percent of deer manage to escape when being hunted by wolves.** • North America is home to five subspecies of the gray wolf. • **A wolf can eat up to 20 percent of its own body weight in one meal.** • Scientists think the eastern timber wolf might be a distinct species of wolf, separate from the gray and red wolf species. • **The Arabian wolf is a subspecies of gray wolf that lives in the desert climate in small pockets of the Middle East. It was once much more widespread.** • Wolf packs are generally made up of parents and their offspring. • **Wolf parents are the leaders of the pack.** • When prey is brought to a wolf pack, usually the hungriest wolf eats first. • **Like birds, wolves will chew, swallow, and then throw up food for their pups. This makes it easier for the pups to eat because their jaws are not strong enough to chew tough meat.** • Gray wolves howl to regroup the pack or to ward off rival packs. • **Gray wolf packs have between**

4 and 9 members on average, but some packs have been known to have up to 30 individuals. • If a pack gets too big, some wolves will break off and start their own pack. • **Wild wolves tend to live between 8 and 13 years. Wolves in captivity can live to be 15 years old.** • Gray wolves are not just gray: They can be black, tan, brown, white, or a combination of black, tan, and brown. • **Female gray wolves carry their babies for only 63 days before giving birth.** • The Mexican wolf, a subspecies of the gray wolf, is also known as *el lobo*, which means "the wolf" in Spanish. • **On average, a female gray wolf gives birth to between four and six pups at once.** • When a wolf howls alone, it's either to attract a mate or to alert the rest of the pack to its location if they have been separated. • **A wolf may show submission to a dominant wolf by rolling onto its back and showing its belly or by whimpering and tucking its tail between its legs.** • Wolves will show submission to prevent a fight from breaking out among pack members. • **A wolf can smell 100 times better than a human.** • "Scent marking" is a practice in which wolves go to the bathroom in certain places to mark their territory. Dogs do this, too. • **Wolf packs that hunt bison tend to have more members than packs that mostly hunt deer.** • Wolves bark to scare off animals that threaten their pups or invade their territory.

WOLVES HUNT IN PACKS TO KILL ANIMALS MUCH BIGGER THAN THEMSELVES, INCLUDING BISON.

Newborn pups are blind and deaf. • **All wolves have blue eyes at birth. Wolves' eyes change color at around eight weeks old.** • A newborn gray wolf pup only weighs 1 pound (0.5 kg). • **Wolves are naturally afraid of humans.** • Wolves are vital for ecosystems because they regulate the populations of other animals. • **There are only about 7,000 gray wolves left in the Lower 48 of the United States.** • In a wolf pack, the "breeding pair" are the parents of the other wolves in the pack. • **When a wolf is pregnant, she will dig a den where she can protect**

IT'S A MYTH THAT WOLVES HOWL AT THE MOON.

and raise her pups once they're born. • A wolf's den can be between 6 and 14 feet deep (1.8 to 4 m). • **Wolves can recognize which howl and bark belongs to which wolf.** • Wolves are most active during dawn and dusk. • **Wolves tend to hunt old, young, and sick prey because they're easier to catch.** • When wolves are old enough, they'll leave their pack and set out in search of a mate to start their

own pack. • **Wolves are mature enough to leave the pack between one and three years of age.** • Wolves take down larger prey by separating from one another to surround it. • **Arctic wolves, a subspecies of the gray wolf, will follow herds of caribou as the caribou migrate, waiting for the perfect time to strike their prey.** • Coastal wolves are a subspecies of the gray wolf found in the Pacific Northwest of North America. They can swim several miles between islands in search of food. • **Himalayan wolves, believed**

Wolf parents hold their tails up high to show their dominance.

An angry wolf will stick its ears straight up and bare its teeth.

You can tell a lot from a wolf's body language. Here are some ways wolves use nonverbal communication.

Less dominant wolves hold their tails down and lower their bodies while pawing at the ground near the dominant wolves.

Young wolves will tuck their tails, crouch, and lick the muzzles of their parents to show submission.

A scared wolf will flatten its ears against its head.

A wolf who wants to play will bow and dance.

From Wolf to Woof!

DID YOU KNOW THAT YOUR PUP HAS A WILD STREAK? In fact, all dogs—no matter what breed—are genetically related to wolves. **Scientists believe that dogs became their own species between 15,000 and 40,000 years ago.** With this evolution came a number of differences. Although wolves and dogs share the same number of teeth, wolf teeth are larger and stronger. The digestive system of a wolf is able to break down raw meat. **Dogs might have a hard time digesting raw meat or get sick from the bacteria it contains.** Wolves have more slanted eyes and pointed ears, as opposed to the floppy ears that some dogs have. Wolves also have much larger paws than dogs. Wolves are far more independent than dogs, too. Most dogs can't survive in the wild without the help of humans. **Generally, wolves are shy and hesitate to approach people, so wolf attacks are rare.** Dogs, as anyone who has been on the receiving end of a slobbery kiss can attest, tend to be much friendlier.

to be the same species as Tibetan wolves, have adapted to live at high altitudes. They are usually found above an elevation of 13,000 feet (3,963 m). • Despite living in packs, Ethiopian wolves are solitary hunters because their diet is mostly made up of rats.

• **The average height of a wolf is 2.2 to 2.7 feet (0.67 to 0.82 m) tall at the shoulder.** • Red wolves are the most endangered wolves in the world. • **As of 2021, there were between 8 and 15 red wolves left in the wild. They are all found in eastern North Carolina.** • Red wolves once lived from Pennsylvania to Texas. • **The average red wolf weighs 45 to 80 pounds (20 to 36 kg).** • In the very rare instance of encountering an aggressive wolf, the best thing to do is just back away slowly and make yourself look big by standing tall. • **Wolves will growl at a potential predator or at another wolf invading their territory, but they don't snarl and growl at animals they're hunting.** • If wolf parents are away, other adult wolves care for the pups until the parents return. • **Adult wolves produce one litter of pups every year.** • Wolf pups mostly chase each other, wrestle, and play hide-and-seek as they grow up, like many dogs do. • **Humans began domesticating wolves around 10,000 to 15,000 years ago, before any other animals had been domesticated.** • Because the frost prevents Arctic wolves from digging dens for shelter, they live in rocky caves. • **Arctic wolves are the only wolf subgroup that isn't threatened by poaching or habitat destruction, because they live so far away from humans.** • Red wolves are on

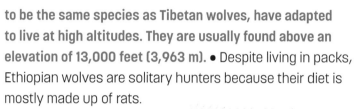

average 26 inches (66 cm) tall and 4 feet (1.2 m) long from nose to tail. • **Wolf pups begin hunting at about six months old.** • At only 45 pounds (20 kg), the Arabian gray wolf is the smallest subspecies of wolf in the world. • **Wolves can eat almost everything off a carcass, even the bones.** • In 2012, the African golden jackal was discovered to actually be a species of wolf. It's since been renamed the African golden wolf. • **The African golden wolf is the first new species of canine discovered in more than 150 years.** • The biggest species of canine ever was the dire wolf, which lived during the Ice Age and grew to be 5 feet (1.5 m) long. It weighed around 150 to 200 pounds (68 to 91 kg).

Atlas
moth

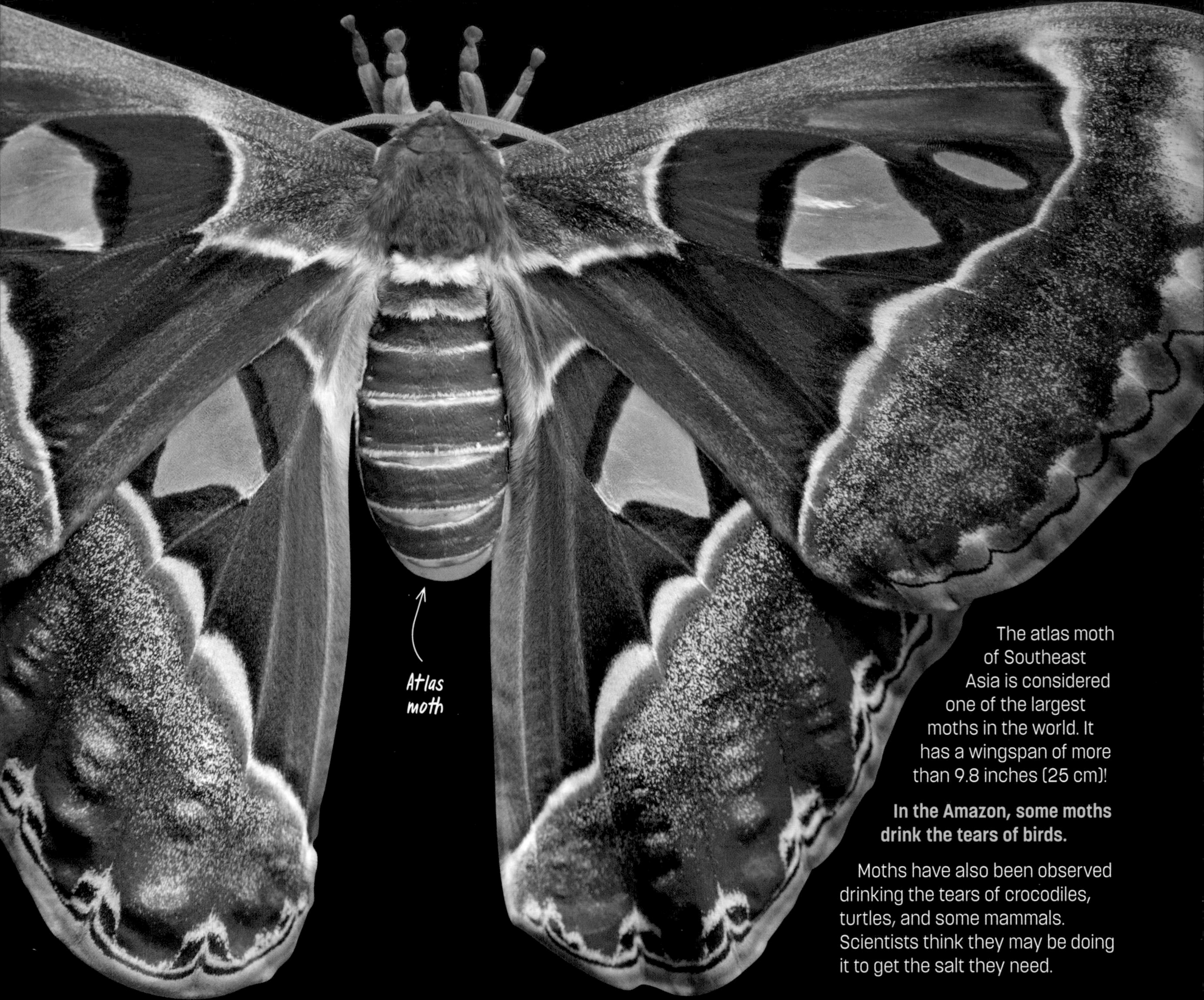

The atlas moth
of Southeast
Asia is considered
one of the largest
moths in the world. It
has a wingspan of more
than 9.8 inches (25 cm)!

**In the Amazon, some moths
drink the tears of birds.**

Moths have also been observed
drinking the tears of crocodiles,
turtles, and some mammals.
Scientists think they may be doing
it to get the salt they need.

Fly by Night
51 Totally Random Facts About MOTHS

Moths are a group of insects related to butterflies. Both belong to the order Lepidoptera.

There are 160,000 species of moths in the world, compared with 17,500 species of butterflies. This means there are about 10 moth species for every single species of butterfly.

Like butterflies, moths have scales covering their wings. They are the only two kinds of insects in the world with this trait.

Another characteristic that links moths to butterflies and separates them from other animals is the ability to furl and unfurl their proboscis—what we usually think of as their tongue.

The smallest moth in the world is Mexico's *Stigmella maya*. Its front wing measures just 0.04 inch (1 mm).

There are about 11,000 species of moths in the United States.

Moths are attracted to light because it confuses their navigational system.

There are more moth species in the United States than all the bird and mammal species of North America combined.

Moths live in every environment in the world except the polar regions.

Moth caterpillars eat nonstop.

Most moth caterpillars eat leaves and flowers. Others eat fruit, beeswax, and fur. Some are even carnivores, eating other smaller insects.

Adult moths drink nectar.

Most moths are nocturnal, but numerous species are active during the day.

If you want to tell the difference between a moth and a butterfly, inspect its antennae. Moths have antennae that are usually wispy and feathery, whereas butterflies have antennae that are round at the end, like clubs.

The white witch moth has a wingspan that reaches up to 11 inches (28 cm), or about the size of a dinner plate.

Some male moths can detect a female moth 7 miles (11 km) away.

The adult luna moth doesn't eat. It has no mouth and only lives for about a week.

Moths **DETECT SCENT** through their antennae.

Death's head hawk moth

The death's head hawk moth has a skull-shaped pattern on its body, and squeaks loudly when disturbed.

Moth caterpillars are food for almost everything else. Even when they grow into adults, they are still prey for many animals, especially bats.

About 95 percent of birds that make nests feed insects to their young, and caterpillars are a favorite for baby birds.

Tiger moths defend themselves by producing clicking noises that jam bats' sonar.

Unlike most moths that have dull coloring, the sunset moth of Madagascar is multicolored with shades of green, blue, orange, and pink.

As prey, moths and caterpillars provide a great deal of protein to animals that eat them.

In addition to protein, moth caterpillars provide important minerals, including potassium, calcium, zinc, and iron.

Moths use chemical senses to find one another in the dark.

Most moth species live for only one year.

Hornet moth

The hornet moth is harmless, but it looks exactly like a hornet to trick predators.

Some moths mimic other animals as a defense mechanism to avoid being eaten by predators.

Some moths use a "startle display" by flashing a brightly colored underwing to distract prey.

Just like butterflies, some moths migrate.

Moths are attracted to fermenting sweet smells such as rotting fruit.

The wood nymph moth mimics the shape and coloring of bird droppings to avoid being eaten.

Some moths eat animal dung for protein.

Hummingbird moths unfurl their long tongues to **SIP NECTAR FROM FLOWERS** such as honeysuckle.

Silk produced by moths has been used for making textiles such as woven fabrics.

Moths don't eat sweaters—but their larvae do.

Moths like white, fragrant flowers because they are easy to spot at night.

Moths will sip from mud puddles to get the minerals they need.

The vampire moth will suck the blood of any vertebrate (an animal with a backbone).

The polyphemus moth has bold eyespots to startle and confuse predators.

Moths evolved before butterflies.

In 2018, scientists discovered the oldest known evidence of existence of moths and butterflies, which showed that these insects lived about 50 million years earlier than originally thought. The wing scales were about 200 million years old.

In some African countries, moth and butterfly caterpillars are eaten as a source of protein.

Some moths have a coloring that camouflages them to look like tree bark.

The Blackburn's sphinx moth, Hawaii's largest native insect, is facing extinction in part because the plant that it eats is in decline due to clearing of its native habitat.

The caterpillars of the Blackburn's sphinx moth can be either gray or bright green, and all have white stripes along each segment of their bodies and white specks.

Flowers that bloom at night depend on moths for pollination.

Roasted moth caterpillars for sale in Zambia

ONCE OUT OF THE POUCH, KOALA JOEYS SPEND SIX
MONTHS HANGING ON TO THEIR MOTHER'S BACK.

Marvelous Marsupials

136 Totally Random Facts About KOALAS, KANGAROOS, and MORE

Marsupials are born prematurely and fully develop within their mother's pouch where they get nutrients from their mom's milk.

Most of the world's marsupial species—about 350 altogether—are found in Australia. They include koalas, kangaroos, wallabies, opossums, and possums, among others.

Marsupials evolved around 200 million years ago in North America.

Most marsupials are nocturnal. They use their senses of hearing and smell to find their way around at night.

Koala fingerprints are so similar to human fingerprints that Australian police are trained to know the difference.

The red kangaroo, which can weigh up to 200 pounds (91 kg), is the world's largest living marsupial.

Unlike any other animal, koalas have two opposable thumbs on each hand. Humans, apes, and a few other animals have one opposable thumb per hand.

A red kangaroo can move at speeds of 30 to 40 miles an hour (48 to 64 kmh).

Only two species of marsupials live in North America: the Virginia opossum and the Mexican mouse opossum.

There are more than 40 species of kangaroos.

Kangaroos can survive months without water because they get water from the grasses they eat.

Male kangaroos flex their biceps to attract mates.

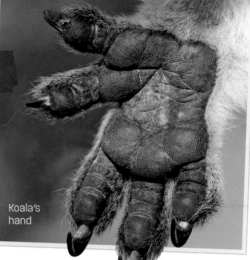

Koala's hand

Opossums live in the Americas, as well as in Australia, New Guinea, and parts of Indonesia.

Male kangaroos are called boomers.

Female kangaroos are called flyers.

Baby kangaroos are called joeys.

Wallaroos are a species of kangaroo, and so are wallabies. Wallaroos are smaller than kangaroos, but larger than wallabies.

A newborn red kangaroo only weighs 0.03 ounces (1 g) and stays in its mother's pouch for about 235 days.

The word *marsupial* comes from the word *marsupium*, meaning "pouch."

Male kangaroos box with each other when vying for a mate.

The opening of the wombat's pouch is toward the rear, not the top as with most other marsupials.. This prevents dirt from getting in while the wombat is digging.

The numbat and musky rat kangaroo are the only marsupials active only during the day, and not at night, dusk, or dawn.

The mountain pygmy possum is the only Australian marsupial that lives in a climate where it snows most of the year.

A NEWBORN KOALA IS AS SMALL AS A JELLY BEAN.

All marsupials have great senses of hearing and smell.

Opossums will play dead to avoid predators.

At any given time, a mother wallaroo could have a baby in her uterus, a newborn feeding in her pouch, and a young joey hopping around her.

A Virginia opossum can carry up to 13 babies on its back.

Most marsupials live alone when it's not mating season.

Most marsupials give birth to multiple babies at once.

As a defense strategy, wombats dig underground and leave their behinds exposed. Their bottoms are mostly made of cartilage, making them very durable.

A group of kangaroos is called a mob.

A group of wombats is called a wisdom.

A wombat can run at speeds of up to 25 miles an hour (40 kmh).

Mother kangaroos can produce full- and low-fat milk for their babies depending on the age of the joey. Younger joeys get lower-fat milk. Older joeys that are ready to explore outside the pouch get fattier milk.

Kangaroos are left-handed.

Kangaroos are great swimmers.

Kangaroos can't hop backward.

Like wombats, koalas have cartilage in their behinds. This helps them sit on rough branches for long periods of time.

Koalas mainly eat eucalyptus leaves, which are highly toxic to most other animals.

Koalas eat the leaves of only 50 of the 700 species of eucalyptus trees.

Tasmanian devil

The world's largest carnivorous marsupial is the Tasmanian devil.

Quokkas are small marsupials that are native to the southwest area of western Australia.

Quokkas store fat in their tails and use the fat for energy when there is not enough food.

Kangaroos lick their arms to stay cool.

A kangaroo can jump a distance of more than 30 feet (9 m) in a single hop.

Quokkas have two stomachs.

In 2021, wild Tasmanian devils were born on the mainland of Australia. It had been more than 3,000 years since these animals were born in the wild outside of the island of Tasmania.

Opossom with babies

Eucalyptus leaves don't have many nutrients and so they don't provide koalas with much energy. **This is part of the reason koalas sleep most of the day.**

There are two subspecies of koalas: southern and northern. southern koalas are larger than northern koalas.

Sugar glider

Sugar gliders are small marsupials that can fit in the palm of a hand. They are native to the forests of New Guinea and Australia.

Mother koalas feed their babies a special type of poop called "pap."

Baby koalas start eating pap when going from drinking milk to eating eucalyptus leaves.

Sugar gliders have prehensile tails, which are tails that help them grasp. They will use their tails to hold branches when moving around.

A BABY MARSUPIAL'S BODY DEVELOPS MORE IN THE POUCH AFTER BIRTH THAN IN THE WOMB.

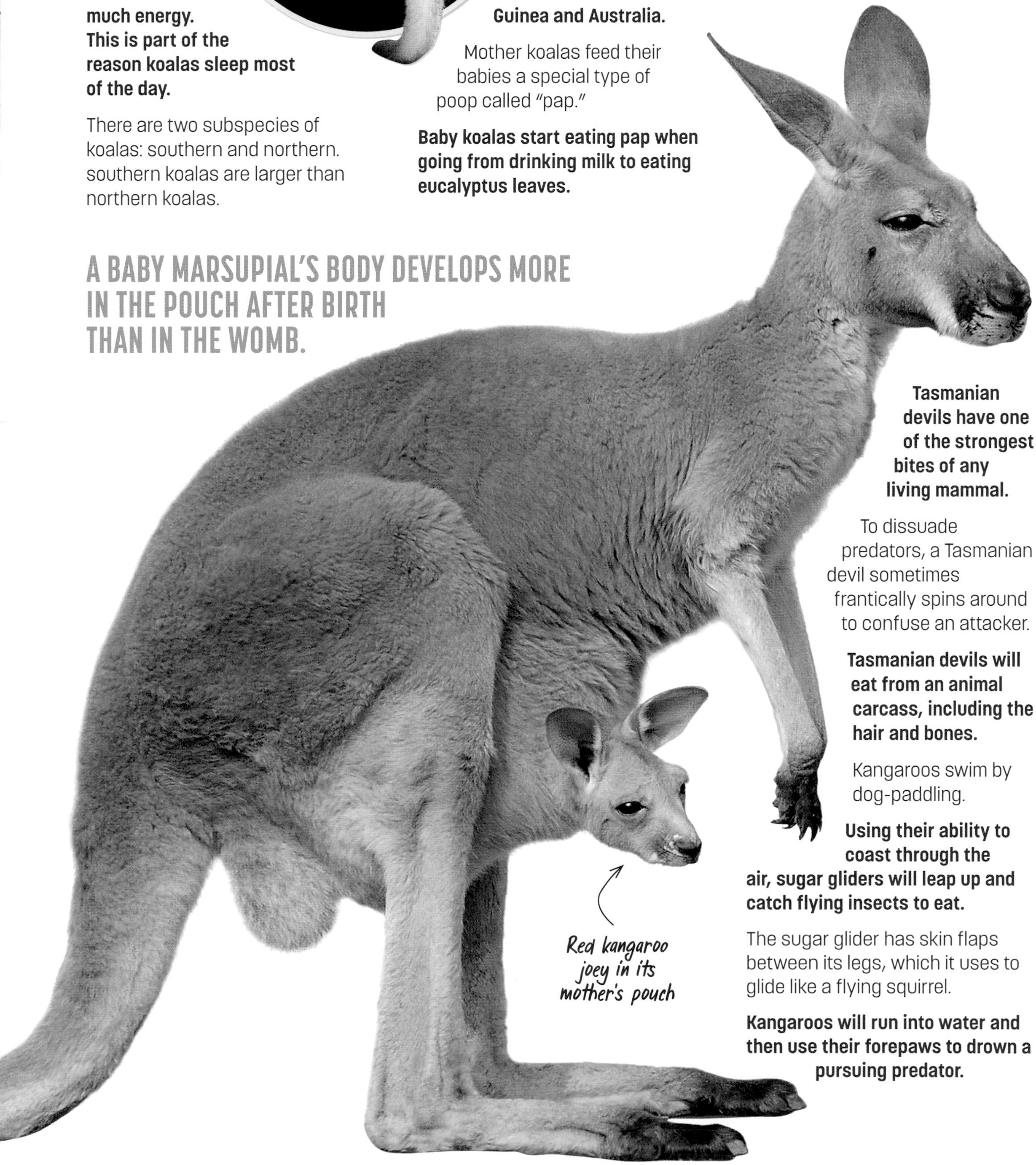

Tasmanian devils have one of the strongest bites of any living mammal.

To dissuade predators, a Tasmanian devil sometimes frantically spins around to confuse an attacker.

Tasmanian devils will eat from an animal carcass, including the hair and bones.

Kangaroos swim by dog-paddling.

Using their ability to coast through the air, sugar gliders will leap up and catch flying insects to eat.

The sugar glider has skin flaps between its legs, which it uses to glide like a flying squirrel.

Kangaroos will run into water and then use their forepaws to drown a pursuing predator.

Red kangaroo joey in its mother's pouch

TREE KANGAROOS CAN JUMP FROM A HEIGHT OF 60 FEET (18 M) TO THE GROUND WITHOUT GETTING A SCRATCH.

Mother kangaroos make clicking sounds to communicate with their babies.

The world's smallest marsupial, the long-tailed planigale, is less than 5 inches (13 cm) long.

Koalas have razor-sharp claws to help them grip trees.

Tree kangaroos are the largest tree-dwelling mammals in Australia.

Koalas spend most of their lives in eucalyptus trees.

Of the four hours they're awake each day, koalas spend three hours eating.

A kangaroo can dig up to 3 feet (1 m) underground in search of water.

A red kangaroo can jump 10 feet (3 m) in the air.

Brushtail possums have adapted to living in cities and suburbs. They are found in Australia and New Zealand.

Koalas have two extra vocal folds to help make their deep bellowing sound.

If a predator is chasing a mother kangaroo, the mother will sometimes force its baby out of the pouch and abandon it to escape.

Tree kangaroo

Koalas sometimes jump from tree to tree.

Brushtail possums will screech loudly in the middle of the night to warn others in their group of danger.

The *Procoptodon,* a giant prehistoric species of kangaroo, grew to be 9 feet (2.7 m) tall.

The *Procoptodon* couldn't hop; it just walked.

Bilby

Bilbies are rabbit-size marsupials that have ears similar to rabbits. They live alone in burrows up to 6 feet (2 m) underground.

A Tasmanian devil can eat up to 40 percent of its body weight in food in one day.

Male kangaroos chuckle while they attempt to attract a mate.

Tasmanian devils can sprint at speeds of 15.5 miles an hour (25 kmh) for an hour without resting.

A tree kangaroo can jump up to 30 feet (9 m) from branch to branch.

The long-tailed planigale doesn't eat the heads and wings of its insect prey.

Koalas screech when threatened.

If startled, koalas can sprint at speeds up to 18 miles an hour (30 kmh).

Male koalas make a loud bellowing sound during mating season.

Koalas have poor eyesight.

The yellow-footed rock wallaby can jump 13 feet (4 m) from rock to rock in the mountainous areas where it lives.

Some phalangers, which are a type of possum, can glide as far as 459 feet (140 m) away.

Green ringtail possums live in ball-shaped nests made of leaves and branches.

Herbert River ringtail possums use their tails to carry branches that they will use for making a nest.

Possums are more closely related to koalas than they are to opossums.

A parma wallaby's tail can be the same length as its entire body. It will sometimes use its tail as a fifth leg to help it move.

A prehistoric carnivorous marsupial, *Thylacosmilus* evolved long teeth similar to a saber-toothed cat.

Koalas can climb 150 feet (46 m) up into a tree.

Napoleon, the king of France during the early 1800s, had a pet wombat.

WOMBAT POOP IS CUBE-SHAPED.

Koalas sleep about 20 hours a day.

Koalas eat about 1 to 1.5 pounds (454 to 680 g) of eucalyptus leaves a day.

Sugar gliders make loud gurgling, grunting, and chirping noises when they eat.

Male koalas have scent glands on their chests that they use to mark their territory by rubbing against trees.

Unlike all other species of kangaroos, tree kangaroos have long forelimbs instead of long hindlimbs. This helps them climb, because they spend most of their time in trees.

Bilbies are native to Australia and once lived all over the continent. Due to human activity, they have been forced to live only in drier desert areas.

Kangaroos and wallabies are members of the genus *Macropus*, meaning "long foot."

Cuscuses are a group of seven species of fuzzy-looking possums that live in the Solomon Islands and northern Australia. They eat and sleep in a sitting position.

A kangaroo is featured on the Australian coat of arms.

Although cuscuses are normally docile, they'll bark and swipe their razor-sharp claws if threatened.

Kangaroo skeleton

Wombat

19th-century drawing of a Diprotodon skull →

Thylacinus

Water opossums are the only marsupials that live primarily semiaquatic lives.

The word *koala*, from an Aboriginal language, means "no drink," because it was believed koalas got all their water from eating leaves.

A newborn koala is born deaf and blind, and relies on touch and smell alone to find its way into its mother's pouch.

Using a special muscle, female koalas are able to open and close their pouches like a zipper.

Unlike most other mammals, marsupials don't have a corpus callosum, which is a bundle of nerves in the brain that connects the left and right hemispheres.

To dissuade predators, sugar gliders can produce a foul stench that smells like rotting fruit.

Water opossums have a water-repelling coat that also helps them float.

Wombats live in tunnels that can be more than 650 feet (198 m) long.

To alert others of approaching danger, kangaroos will repeatedly stomp on the ground or thump their tails.

Because a newborn baby kangaroo is too weak to suckle or swallow, a mother pumps milk down the baby's throat.

A koala's second and third fingers on their back legs are fused together. These fused fingers are used for grooming.

The *Thylacinus*, also known as the Tasmanian tiger, was a carnivorous marsupial that was native to Australia and New Guinea. It was hunted to extinction in the 1930s.

Quolls, small white-spotted opossum-like predators, generally don't live past their second mating season.

A PREHISTORIC COUSIN OF THE WOMBAT, THE *DIPROTODON* GREW TO BE THE SIZE OF A RHINO.

Quolls are the largest carnivorous marsupials in mainland Australia.

Cuscus fur colors have huge variation, including white, yellow, grayish green, and black.

A Virginia opossum has up to 50 teeth.

The oldest wombat lived to be 32 years old.

Koalas are mostly nocturnal.

A sugar glider has a territory equal to 2 acres (0.8 ha) of land, or a little more than a city block.

Quoll →

A male opossum is called a jack.

A female opossum is called a jill.

Koalas are able to recognize and avoid certain leaves that are too toxic for them.

Koalas mostly get their water from eating eucalyptus leaves, but will move from the trees and drink during a drought.

It takes about 100 hours for a koala to digest its food.

Water opossums have sensitive whiskers that help them find prey both at night and in the water.

WITH THEIR LONG FEET, RED KANGAROOS DELIVER KICKS POWERFUL ENOUGH TO SHATTER BONES. IT'S ONE OF THEIR DEFENSIVE MOVES.

Slither and

75 Totally Random Facts About SNAKES

There are around 3,000 species of snake in the world. They live on every continent except Antarctica.

Black mambas in Africa are named after the black coloration in their mouths.

The oldest known captive snake ever is a 62-year-old ball python.

Garter snakes in North America hibernate in large dens with up to 8,000 individuals cuddled together during the winter.

When squeezing its prey, a boa constrictor can sense its victim's heartbeat and loosens only once its heart has stopped beating.

The inland taipan of Australia has the most powerful and deadly venom of any species of snake.

Sidewinder snakes move in a motion called "sidewinding," where only two parts of the snake's entire body are on the ground at a time. This helps it both move faster as well as keep most of its body off the hot desert sand.

Some large species of pythons can swallow full-grown goats whole.

Snakes can't chew, so they have to swallow their prey whole.

"Pit holes" are sensory holes near a pit viper's eyes that allow it to see the heat an animal emits.

A snake's jaw is incredibly flexible, allowing it to swallow prey twice the size of its head.

Snakes have small bones in their lower jaws to detect the vibrations from things moving on the ground.

A rattlesnake skull

SNAKE VENOM EVOLVED FROM SPIT GLANDS.

Strike

An Indian snake charmer and his assistant

The saw-scaled viper, found in dry areas of Africa and Asia, is responsible for more human deaths than all other snake species.

The green anaconda is the heaviest species of snake in the world. It can weigh up to 550 pounds (250 kg).

Green anacondas live most of their lives in water. Their eyes and nostrils have evolved to be on the top of their heads so they can peek up above the water to ambush prey.

Snakes only attack humans if they feel cornered and can't escape.

A green anaconda can grow to be 30 feet (9 m) long and 12 inches (30.5 cm) wide.

Despite being very large, green anacondas can climb trees.

A snake smells by flicking its tongue out, collecting chemicals, and placing the tongue on the vomeronasal, a sensory organ at the roof of the mouth, which then sends signals to the brain.

Burmese rock pythons are about 12 to 18 inches long (31 to 46 cm) when they hatch. As adults they grow to be 15 feet (4.6 m) long and sometimes even longer.

A snake's forked tongue allows it to follow chemicals in the air from two different locations at the same time.

After eating a large meal such as a tapir or a crocodile, a green anaconda can go weeks or months without eating.

Snake charming is an Indian practice in which a person supposedly hypnotizes a snake, such as a king cobra, with a musical instrument called a pungi.

There are about 600 species of venomous snakes, but only around 200 of them can seriously hurt or kill a human.

Moving at a top speed of 18 miles an hour (29 kmh), a sidewinder known as the Peringuey's adder is the fastest snake in the world.

Unlike humans, snakes don't have fused jawbones, allowing them to stretch open their mouths much wider.

The nonvenomous milk snake has evolved to look similar to venomous snakes such as coral snakes as a defense mechanism: Because of its coloring, predators think that the snake is dangerous.

The sidewinder snake has small horns on top of each eye, which some scientists believe are meant to keep sand out of its eyes when buried in the sand.

Sidewinder

Rattlesnakes aren't born with their rattles. Instead, they have a tiny bump at the end of their tails called a "button," which will grow into a rattle as the baby sheds and grows.

Female Kenyan sand boas hatch their eggs inside their bodies and give birth to live young.

Once mating is complete, a female green anaconda will eat one or more of the male anacondas she mated with because she won't eat again until after she gives birth—seven months later.

A green anaconda gives birth to between 20 and 40 live young at a time. The record for most anaconda babies born at once is 82!

Snakes are good at slithering because their scales produce a thin layer of an oily substance that makes them slippery.

Rattlesnakes shake their rattles as a warning to predators to back off or else they'll bite.

The king cobra's venom is so deadly that it could kill an elephant.

King cobras are the only species of snake that make nests for their eggs.

Reticulated pythons can grow to be up to 33 feet (10 m) long, almost the length of a school bus.

SNAKES FIRST APPEARED AROUND 128 MILLION YEARS AGO DURING THE EARLY CRETACEOUS PERIOD.

The Pacific gopher snake scares away predators by pretending to be a rattlesnake–it hisses, strikes, and moves its tail.

Some people falsely believe that snakes can drink and digest milk. Snakes only drink water.

"Flying" snakes, like flying squirrels, glide from tree to tree by positioning their bodies to catch air beneath them as they jump from tree branches.

Some flying snakes can glide up to 330 feet (100 m) between branches.

A rattlesnake's rattle can shake back and forth at speeds of 60 shakes a second.

Puff adders in the United States are known to play dead when confronted by a predator.

Doctors have used the venom from snakes such as king cobras to treat venom bites and help with pain relief.

The red spitting cobra shoots its venom up to 6 feet (1.8 m) away from small holes in front of its fangs.

A red spitting cobra has incredible aim, almost always accurately hitting a target's eyes no matter their size.

A red spitting cobra's venom can cause permanent blindness if it enters a person's eyes.

Ball pythons are named after their tendency to roll into a tight ball when feeling threatened.

Male king cobras fight over mates by pushing their heads together. The first male pushed to the ground loses.

Some snakes eat only birds' eggs. These snakes have special bones in their throats that cut up the eggshells, allowing the snake to spit out the shells.

Amazon tree boa

King cobra

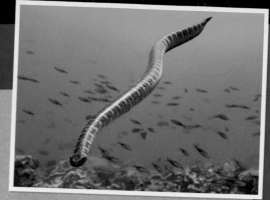

The iconic hood of king cobras is made by the cobra flattening its neck ribs as a way to make itself look bigger and more threatening to predators.

The babies of green tree pythons are born in a variety of colors, including yellow, red, and blue. Their scales turn bright green as they mature.

The scales of an Asian vine snake create a geometric pattern on its body. This snake will sometimes inflate its neck area when threatened, revealing bright colors between its scales.

The biggest species of snake to ever exist was the Titanoboa, which lived 59 million years ago in the region that is now the Amazon. It grew to be 45 feet (13.7 m) long.

The Titanoboa weighed around 1.25 tons (1.1 metric tons), about as much as a small car.

Green tree pythons spend almost their entire lives in trees and leave only during the night.

The tentacled snake of Southeast Asia has two small appendages sticking out from its nose that researchers believe help it either find prey or camouflage itself.

Copperheads can release a musk that smells like cucumber when touched.

Copperheads are one of the few species of venomous snakes that attack without warning when feeling threatened.

Young copperheads resemble caterpillars or worms. They will stay still and flick the tip of their tails to attract animals that confuse it for a worm. Then, they strike!

Full-grown copperheads eat only 10 to 12 meals a year.

A rattlesnake's rattle is made of keratin, the same material as a human's nails and hair.

New baby snakes shed their skin as a way to leave behind their scent. This technique helps protect them from predators.

Snakes of the Sea

- Olive sea snakes have been known to attack human divers during mating season because they mistake the diver's flippers for a competing male or either a female they wish to mate with.

- There are about 60 species of sea snakes, all of which are highly venomous members of the cobra family.

- Sea snakes have evolved paddle-like tails to help them swim.

- The sea snake family makes up 90 percent of all living marine reptile species.

- Most sea snakes live in the coastal regions of the Indian and western Pacific Oceans.

- Sea snakes can hold their breath up to eight hours.

- To go a long time without air while underwater, sea snakes' lungs have evolved to stretch the entire length of their bodies.

- Sea snakes give birth to live young in the water.

- Some species of sea snakes can't crawl on land because they don't have belly scales.

- Sea snakes can't drink saltwater. Instead, they drink freshwater from rain.

Titanoboa

Bugging Out

57 Totally Random Facts About INSECTS

Cockroaches can live for up to a week without their heads. • **All insects have six legs.** • All insects have three-part bodies (which include a head, thorax, and abdomen) encased in a hard exoskeleton, which is like a shell. • **All insects have a pair of antennae that they use to smell and sense hot and cold.** • There are more varieties of beetles than any other living creature. They make up about a third of all insect species. • **Insects live on every continent, but none live in the oceans.** • Only one insect species, a wingless midge called *Belgica antarctica*, lives on the continent of Antarctica. • **Insects do not breathe through their mouths. They breathe through little holes in their sides called spiracles.** • Unlike humans, insect respiratory systems aren't hooked up to their circulatory systems. Instead, they have a network of tubes to deliver oxygen and release carbon dioxide. • **Insects don't have veins and arteries; their blood flows freely, bathing their organs.** • The largest insect ever to fly was the ancient dragonfly called *Meganeuropsis*. It lived 275 million years ago and had a wingspan of up to 2.5 feet (0.8 m). •

DRAGONFLIES ARE OLDER THAN DINOSAURS.

Meganeuropsis **weighed about as much as a crow!** • The longest insects in the world are stick insects. In China, a species called *Phryganistria* stretches 24.6 inches (62.4 cm) long. That's more than 2 feet! • **Dragonfly larvae can live for two years underwater.** • Eighty percent of a dragonfly's brain is dedicated to sight. • **Insects have compound eyes, which can have many thousands of tiny lenses.** • An insect's lenses work like sensors to help them see fast movement and distinguish between light and dark. • **An entomologist once clocked a horsefly zooming at about 90 miles an hour (145 kmh).** • The longest lived insect is the termite queen. It can live for 50 years or more. • **Ants can lift 100 times their own body weight, and possibly much more.** • Houseflies find sugar with taste buds in their feet. • **When it comes to detecting sweet, flies' taste buds on their feet are 10 million times more sensitive than the taste buds on your tongue.** • It takes about 2,000 silkworm cocoons to make a single pound of silk. • **Golden tortoise beetle**

THAT'S SO RANDOM:

Leaf Me Alone!

THE GRAY'S LEAF INSECT MIGHT BE KNOWN AS THE KING OF CAMOUFLAGE. Gray's leaf insects are plant-eating herbivores that live in the tropical rain forests of Asia, Madagascar, Mauritius, and the Seychelles. **True to their name, these bugs look exactly like leaves** and can be very hard to spot. They are leaf-size at 2 to 5 inches (5 to 13 cm) long and extremely flat with irregularly shaped bodies, wings, and legs. **They even have veins on their leathery forewings that look exactly like the veins on leaves** of mango and guava trees where they like to find food. It's a good thing, too, because it keeps them safely hidden from birds, amphibians, and reptiles that want to eat them!

Ant carrying a piece of apple

larvae place their dried poop on their backs as a way to camouflage and protect themselves. • Bees can fly up to 60 miles (97 km) in a single day. • **Mexican jumping beans are seedpods that contain the larvae of a small moth.** • In Australia, scientists used dung beetles to clean up after cattle. • **Wasps can get drunk from rotting fruit.** • Some termite queens can lay 40,000 eggs per day. That's up to 365,250,000 eggs over a lifetime. • **Some honeybees quack.** • Honeybees have to make about 10 million trips to flowers to produce 1 pound (454 g) of honey. • **There are more varieties of beetles than all the plants on Earth combined.** • Many insects have a natural "antifreeze" inside them that keeps them from freezing in the winter. • **There is about the same number of ant and bird species in the world—9,000.** • The male silk moth can detect the chemicals of a female silk moth in the air from miles away. • **The oldest known fossil of an insect (a springtail) dates back 400 million years.** • The hearts of insects are shaped like tiny tubes. • **Mantids are the only insect capable of turning their head completely around so they can see behind them.**

Fantastic Fleas

- Fleas live by feasting on blood.
- **Female fleas can consume 15 times their own body weight in blood on a daily basis.**
- There are more than 2,500 species of fleas.
- **Fleas can jump about 30,000 times without resting.**
- Female fleas are incapable of laying eggs until after their first meal.
- **Fleas have claws.**
- Second only to the froghopper, fleas are the best jumpers of all animals in the world.
- **Fleas don't have ears.**
- Flea larvae eat the dung of their parents.

MANY CULTURES EAT INSECTS AS A SOURCE OF PROTEIN.

• Some museums use beetles to clean animal bones. • **Fire ants cling together to form a raft so they can float during a flood.** • Stinkbugs release a foul smell when they feel threatened. • **Ladybugs have been to space.** • Beetles clean their legs with their antennae. • **Insects don't have bones.** • Stick insects can grow a leg back after losing it. • **The trap-jaw ant can close its mandible at 145 miles an hour (233 kmh), faster than any other animal.**

Hello, Kitty!

58 Totally Random Facts About *CATS*

Cats can move each ear independently and rotate them 180 degrees.

Cats have 30 vertebrae, or bones, in their spines. Humans have 33.

A cat born with more than 18 toes is called a polydactyl. In Greek, *poly* means "many," and *daktylos* means "finger."

The largest cat breed is the gray tabby Maine coon.

The smallest cat breed is the Singapura.

One of the oldest cat breeds is the Egyptian Mau. This cat can change its facial expressions, and even its eye color from green to turquoise, according to mood.

Cats can drink seawater.

A cat's purr can lower your blood pressure and calm your nerves.

Cheetahs meow like house cats.

The loose flap of skin some cats have on their belly is called a primordial pouch. It lets the cat extend fully while running and also protects its organs when in a fight.

Domestic cats can hold their tails vertically while walking.

A cat has about 12 whiskers on either side of its nose.

Whiskers are the same width as the cat's body. This helps a cat judge if it can fit through a tight space.

Merlin, a black-and-white cat from Torquay, United Kingdom, held the record for the loudest purr. His purr was so loud that it sounded like a shower!

Cats have 32 muscles that control their outer ears (humans have only 6, and only 3 of those muscles are used for movement).

Unlike domestic cats, wildcats can't hold their tails vertically when walking. Instead, they hold their tails horizontally or between their legs.

Cats identify one another by scent.

When your cat gives you a long, slow blink, it may be telling you it loves you.

Cats' whiskers help them "see" in the dark by brushing up against things.

Up to 85 percent of white cats with blue eyes will also suffer from congenital deafness.

ALL KITTENS ARE BORN WITH BLUE EYES. EYE COLOR STARTS TO CHANGE WHEN A KITTEN IS ABOUT EIGHT WEEKS OLD.

A Maine coon at a cat exhibition in Bishkek, Kyrgyzstan

Barivel, an Italian Maine coon cat is the longest cat in the world at an impressive 3 feet 11.2 inches (120 cm) long. That's longer than the longest golf clubs!

Cats usually have between 20 and 23 bones in their tails.

Cats can hear about five times better than people can.

ADULT CATS HAVE 30 TEETH.

Most cats have no eyelashes.

Cats cannot see directly beneath their noses.

The oldest cat in the world lived to be 38 years old.

Cats have scent glands on many parts of their bodies, including their tails, cheeks, and paws.

A cat named Didga could do 24 tricks, including ride a skateboard.

The richest cat in the world inherited $13 million when his owner died.

Cats have an average of four kittens per litter.

In seven years, one female cat and her offspring can produce 420,000 cats.

Carnivora, the group of animals to which domestic cats belong, emerged about 50 million years ago.

Cats are digitigrade, meaning they walk on their toes.

A cat's jaw can't move sideways, so a cat can't chew large chunks of food.

Cats have about 130,000 hairs per square inch (20,155 hairs per sq cm).

Cats and some other animals might be able to detect earthquakes before they occur.

A cat draping its tail over another cat or a person is a sign of friendship.

When your cat's tail is held straight up and twitching, it means your cat is delighted to see you.

Cats are color-blind.

A cat's heart beats between 130 and 240 beats per minute.

MANY EGYPTIANS WORSHIPPED THE GODDESS BASTET. SHE HAD A WOMAN'S BODY AND A CAT'S HEAD.

Like humans, kittens have baby teeth. They fall out and are replaced with adult teeth starting around six months of age.

A cat's normal body temperature is 102° F (38.9° C); a human's is 98.6° F (37° C).

Cats breathe at a rate of 20 to 30 breaths per minute.

A female cat is pregnant for approximately 63 days.

Cats have been known to survive very high falls, even from 32 stories (346 ft) up!

Domestication of cats occurred in the Fertile Crescent, a region of the Middle East, about 10,000 years ago.

Cats kill their prey with their teeth, not their claws. They use their claws to hold the prey.

More than 5,300 years ago, Chinese farmers began to use cats to help keep rodent populations down.

Cat urine glows under black light.

Calico and tortoiseshell cats are almost always female.

Ginger cats are more likely to be male than female.

Cats can make about 21 different vocalizations.

An adult cat can jump five to six times its height.

When a cat arches its back, it usually means the cat feels threatened.

A cat's pupils turn into vertical slits in bright light. In the dark they turn round.

THAT'S SO RANDOM:

House Cats and Tigers Have a Lot in Common!

A STUDY LED BY A TEAM OF INTERNATIONAL SCIENTISTS DISCOVERED THAT HOUSE CATS AND TIGERS SHARE 95.6 PERCENT OF THEIR GENETIC MAKEUP, which means they have many similarities. Consider their bodies: Both are designed for hunting, which is clear from their anatomy and flexibility. But a closer look reveals another unique trait they have in common: **Both have five toes on their front paws and four on their back paws,** a characteristic that makes them agile, speedy, and silent, all useful traits for when stalking prey or dashing away from predators. **Both wild and domestic cats spend between 16 to 20 hours a day sleeping.** When they're awake, they both spend 30 to 50 percent of their time grooming. **They both also have great senses of smell and will open their mouths to take in even more smells.** In addition, both are carnivores, mark their territory with urine, and usually hunt early in the day.

Chomp and

53 Totally Random Facts About **DINOSAURS**

Some plant-eating dinosaurs ate as much as 1 ton (0.9 metric ton) of food per day; piled together, that would take up about the space of a bus. • **Some dinosaurs may have lived 200 years!** • The majority of carnivorous—or meat-eating—dinosaurs walked on two feet, enabling them to move faster to catch their prey. • **Many species of dinosaurs had feathers.** • The majority of plant-eating dinosaurs walked on four feet to support their heavy torsos. • **Paleontologists recently discovered a dinosaur limb with its skin preserved. They think this dinosaur might have been killed on the same day the asteroid that wiped out the dinosaurs hit Earth.** • The genetic ancestors of dinosaurs were called archosaurs, which means "ruling reptiles." • **Scientists aren't sure why dinosaurs got so big.** • The majority of dinosaur species and dinosaur fossils have been found in China, Argentina, and North America. • **Badlands are areas in different parts of the world where soil is dry and eroded and where many dinosaur fossils are found.** • Some dinosaurs were as small as a chicken. • **Dinosaurs could be as large as 85 feet (26 m) long.** • The majority of dinosaurs—about 60 percent—were plant-eaters. • **About 40 percent of dinosaurs were meat-eaters.** • *Suchomimus* looked similar to a crocodile, and its name means "crocodile mimic" in Greek. • **Scientists first discovered dinosaurs**

Suchomimus had more than **100 LARGE TEETH** lining its strong jaws.

had feathers when they uncovered the fossil of a dinosaur called *Archaeopteryx*, which had feathers clearly visible in the rock formation. • *Thrinaxodon*, a dog-size animal that lived alongside dinosaurs, was one of the first animals that had the characteristics of a mammal. • **Fossils are rocks! They are the preserved remains of bones that have been replaced with minerals.** • *Pegomastax* was a dinosaur that looked like it was part porcupine and part parrot. • *Suzhousaurus megatherioides* was furry, and it waddled. Its name means "giant sloth-like reptile from Suzhou," because it looked a bit like the ancient giant ground sloth. • Dinosaurs roamed the planet 64 times longer than humans have been on Earth. • **The skulls of some dinosaurs were the size of a car.** • All meat-eating dinosaurs belong to a group called theropods. • **Meat-eating dinosaurs had sharp claws on their toes. Plant-eating dinosaurs had**

A paleontologist holding a dinosaur egg

Stomp!

Archaeopteryx

toenails or hooves that were blunt. • At up to 92 feet (28 m) long, *Diplodocus* is the longest dinosaur known. Its neck alone was more than 21 feet (6.5 m). • **Argentinosaurus was as long as four fire trucks placed end to end.** • A portion of the Chicxulub crater—the impact site of the asteroid that scientists believe killed all nonflying dinosaurs—is located underwater in the Gulf of Mexico. • **The event that led to the extinction of dinosaurs wiped out about 80 percent of animals on Earth.** • Though they're still trying to figure it out, scientists think that all dinosaurs could have been warm-blooded. • **Some dinosaur eggs were the size of basketballs.** • Because birds are considered dinosaurs, the bee hummingbird is the smallest known dinosaur at 2 inches (5 cm) in length. • **Liopleurodon was a marine reptile that lived alongside dinosaurs. It grew up to 85 feet (26 m) long—about the size of a blue whale.**

• The majority of carnivorous dinosaurs had hollow bones. • **The brain of a human baby is larger than the adult brains of most dinosaur species.** • Some dinosaurs may have shed their skin, similar to the way lizards and snakes do today. Others may have shed in pieces, similar to birds and mammals. • **Dinosaurs existed for roughly 174 million years.** • *T. rex* ate as many as 22 tons (20 metric tons) of meat each year. • **The length of a *T. rex*'s arms was roughly the same length of an adult human's arms.** • The largest dinosaur footprints discovered were 4 feet (1 m) across. • **Scientists believe that *Deinonychus* had one of the strongest bites of all dinosaurs.** • The nose of *Corythosaurus* contained a large hollow space, allowing it to make loud sounds. •

Liopleurodon

The name *Struthiomimus* translates to "ostrich mimic," because these dinosaurs resembled ostriches. • The *T. rex* was able to run at a top speed of 18 miles an hour (28 kmh). • **The sound of the *T. rex*'s footfalls in the movie *Jurassic Park* was created using the sound of a sequoia tree falling to the ground.** • All dinosaurs reproduced by laying eggs. • **Paleontologists in Montana believe they found a nesting colony when they discovered fossils of duck-billed dinosaurs with eggs, hatchlings, young, and adults all together.** • Sauropods were the largest land animals ever to have lived on Earth. • **Plant-eating dinosaurs that had horns and beaked mouths are known as ceratopsians.** • *Triceratops* was the last of the ceratopsian dinosaurs to live on Earth. • **Most dinosaur fossils have been found in dry, desertlike areas because these environments lack soil, trees, and other plant matter that would otherwise hide fossils.** • Some asteroids are named after dinosaurs. Asteroid 9954 is named for *Brachiosaurus*. Asteroid 9951 is named Tyrannosaurus.

Colorado is known as the **STEGOSAURUS STATE** because the first *Stegosaurus* ever discovered was found in Morrison, Colorado.

Here to Help

32 Totally Random Facts About SERVICE DOGS and EMOTIONAL SUPPORT ANIMALS

There are approximately 222,900 service and emotional support animals in the United States.

Service animals are not considered pets—they are working animals.

In the 1920s, service dogs were only for people who were visually impaired. They were referred to as "Seeing Eye dogs."

Service dogs that assist the visually impaired are known as guide dogs.

Under the U.S. Americans with Disabilities Act, only dogs and some miniature horses can officially be considered service animals.

Miniature horses are also used as therapy animals in nursing homes, hospitals, and children's centers.

Service dogs are trained to help people with disabilities live more independent lives.

There more than 15,000 service dogs in the United States.

The first service animals were German shepherds.

Pigs, especially potbellied pigs, are known to be good support animals. They are highly intelligent and able to help with many tasks.

A service dog's U-shaped harness allows people to communicate with their dog by moving the harness in different directions.

It costs more than $25,000 to train a service dog.

Guide dogs are able to navigate crowded areas and help their person cross streets.

Service dogs that help with medical issues are known as medical alert or medical response dogs.

Service animals for people who have seizures are able to move a person to their side during a seizure, alert others to help, and even fetch medication.

Fewer than 50 percent of animals make it through the training necessary to become service animals.

Service animals assist those with mobility impairments by retrieving objects, navigating automatic doors, and pulling wheelchairs up hills and ramps.

Service dogs for those with allergies are able to detect an allergen and alert their owners to avoid it.

Service dogs handled by people with diabetes are able to alert their people of blood sugar changes—the dogs can smell the chemical changes!

Service animals for those who are hard of hearing can alert their handlers when a noise is made. The animal will use touch, then lead them to the source of the noise.

Some service dogs wear vests or other clothing to identify them, but it is not required.

Helping Horses!

LARRY MARK GUTHRIE OF PINE, COLORADO, IS NO ORDINARY PET OWNER. He cares for and trains miniature horses to become service animals **to assist those who have visual or mobility impairments.** Guthrie first became interested in raising his furry helpers when he was diagnosed with an illness that affected his nervous system, causing his body to shake uncontrollably. According to Guthrie, **the process of caring for the animals each day is calming and can be healing.** He enjoys the daily tasks of dressing his horses in halters, training them to follow commands, feeding them, and cleaning their stalls. Guthrie takes his mini horses Chunky Monkey, Fancy Dancer, Glitter Bug, and Patty Cake for outings whenever possible—even to the grocery store!

Capuchin monkeys have been trained as service animals. They are particularly helpful in grasping and retrieving items and can perform manual tasks such as opening a car door.

An emotional support animal's job is to calm their handler, whereas a service dog's job is to help their handler with their disability.

The Americans with Disabilities Act, passed in 1990, made it law for people with disabilities to be allowed accompaniment by a service dog.

Animals that drop out of service training make wonderful pets.

The most common dog breeds to be trained as service dogs are Labradors, golden retrievers, and German shepherds.

Courthouses in some states allow therapy or service dogs to help calm adults with disabilities or children called into court during a trial.

Ferrets can be emotional support animals. They are able to sense seizures before they occur.

PARROTS can be emotional support animals.

Any business that allows the public to enter their building is required to also allow service animals, too.

It can take anywhere from one and a half to two and a half years for service dogs to complete their training.

Boa constrictors can be emotional support animals! People with obsessive-compulsive disorder, bipolar disorder, panic disorder, or who experience seizures may benefit from having one.

Hey, Big Talker!

48 Totally Random Facts About PARROTS

Scientists have said that parrot intelligence is equal to that of a five-year-old human.

Parrots use pebbles to break mollusk shells, one example of birds using tools.

Unlike most birds, which have three toes in the front and one in the back, parrots have two toes in the front and two toes in the back.

Parrots eat just about anything, including meat.

There are about 350 species of parrots.

The beak of a parakeet continuously grows throughout the bird's life.

The maroon-fronted parrot lives on mountains 6,000 feet (1,829 m) high.

Males and females of most parrot species have a very similar pattern of feathers. This is not the case for many bird species. Males are often brighter or more colorful than females.

Parrots mostly taste food on the top of their mouths.

The kakapo is a flightless parrot native to New Zealand. It weighs as much as a house cat.

The world's smallest parrot, the buff-faced pygmy parrot, is the size of a human finger.

The world's oldest bird was an 83-year-old pink cockatoo named Cookie.

Parrot feathers produce bacteria-resistant pigments that help protect their feathers from damage.

Parrots can copy and say human words and phrases.

A blue parakeet named Puck could say more than 1,700 words.

Parrots copy sounds from other birds and animals to be accepted into a group.

Cockatoos have a set of feathers on their head that they display like a mohawk to attract mates.

Parrots are very social birds, and many live together in large groups.

Galahs, which are pink-breasted cockatoos, mate for life.

Parrots don't have vocal cords.

A macaw has enough bite force in its beak to bite off a human finger.

Parrots can use their muscular tongues to hold nuts in place while their beaks crack them open.

A macaw's feather pattern on its face is believed to be as unique as a **FINGERPRINT**.

Kea

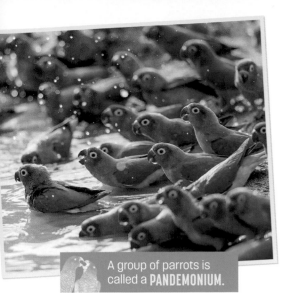
A group of parrots is called a **PANDEMONIUM.**

Sometimes parrots dance when they hear music.

Macaws can fly up to 15 miles (24 km) a day to find food.

Parrots can climb up trees with their feet.

Lorikeets are sometimes referred to as "brush-tongued" parrots because they have hairs on their tongues that let them more easily catch nectar and pollen from flowers to eat.

A lorikeet spends 70 percent of its time awake eating.

Some species of parrots eat dirt to get minerals such as sodium, or salt.

A macaw will groom the feathers of its mate.

One-third of all parrot species are endangered.

Most species of parrots don't migrate.

Male and female eclectus parrots have such different-colored feathers that for many years, scientists thought they were different species.

Parrots were common pets among pirates because of their colorful feathers and ability to copy words.

Keas, which are New Zealand mountain parrots with long bills, have been known to flock together to attack and even kill full-grown sheep.

Because of the shape of their beak, palm cockatoos physically can't close their mouths completely shut, which lets them hold nuts while cracking them at the same time.

When it's raining, palm cockatoos will sometimes hang upside down and spread out their wings and tail like they're taking a shower.

Wild parrots address other individuals with specific calls that function as names.

Lovebirds are parrots that mate for life and continuously show affection for each other.

Lovebirds were named after how they feed their mates by exchanging food in an act that can be interpreted as kissing.

Peach-faced lovebirds in Phoenix, Arizona, make nests by digging holes into cacti.

In the United States, more than 25 percent of bird owners have at least one parakeet.

Cockatiels sleep on average 14 hours a day.

The flightless kakapo is one of the most endangered birds on Earth, with approximately 200 individuals left.

The night parrot of Australia, despite leading a nocturnal lifestyle, has terrible night vision.

The national flag of Dominica has a sisserou parrot in the center. It's a species only found in that country.

Instead of talking, cockatiels whistle.

THAT'S SO RANDOM:

Parrots Showing Kindness!

SCIENTISTS HAVE LONG KNOWN THAT PARROTS ARE INTELLIGENT. But according to a recent study, these birds are also capable of performing acts of kindness. The Max Planck Institute of Ornithology in Germany conducted a study with African gray parrots. **The birds had already been trained to understand that tokens, in the form of small metal rings, could be exchanged for treats.** If the bird passed a ring through a small exchange window in its cage, it would be rewarded with a walnut. In the experiment, the first bird had a lot of tokens, but no way to retrieve the treats because the exchange window in its cage was covered up. The second bird, in the next cage, had no tokens, but did have an open window. **As the scientists watched, the first bird transferred all of its 10 tokens to the second bird, who could trade them in for treats.** The first bird didn't get any of the walnuts, so the reward could have only been to help out his feathered friend. In a follow-up experiment, the roles were reversed. The scientists witnessed the same generous behavior, suggesting that courtesy is contagious even in the animal world!

Bioluminescence is a chemical process through which a living organism produces light.

There are three main categories of bioluminescent creatures: marine, land, and microorganisms.

More than 1,500 fish species are bioluminescent.

Bioluminescent animals contain a compound called luciferin. When luciferin reacts with oxygen, it produces light.

Fireflies use bioluminescence to attract mates. Female fireflies flash from their abdomens. Males use signals to get females to respond to them.

Unlike light the sun produces, light from bioluminescence is produced through a chemical reaction that releases very little heat.

The color of light that an animal or organism produces—which can be red, yellow, green, blue, or violet—depends on the species and its habitat.

Most bioluminescent ocean creatures emit a blue or green light. Many bioluminescent land animals emit a yellow light.

A firefly's light can be yellow, green, or orange!

Quantula striata, **the only bioluminescent land snail, emits a yellow glow.**

Bioluminescent prey use their light to distract predators so they can quickly escape.

Bioluminescent prey also use light to warn predators that they may be toxic, a sign to leave them alone!

Some squid use a bioluminescent liquid instead of black ink to startle predators and jet away.

Seventy species of fungi, including mushrooms and toadstools, are bioluminescent.

When night falls, bioluminescent mushrooms named little ping-pong bats light up, illuminating the trees they grow on. They get their name from the fact that they look like tiny ping-pong paddles.

Glow in the Dark

Firefly

32 Totally Random Facts About *BIOLUMINESCENT ANIMALS*

Bioluminescent plankton

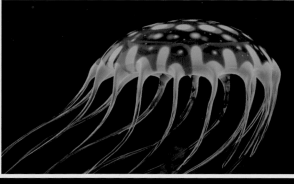

ABOUT 76 PERCENT of ocean animals are bioluminescent, including jellyfish, sharks, and sea stars.

The American pocket shark, which is only 5.5 inches (14 cm) long, releases bioluminescent fluid beneath its fins to draw in prey.

Some bays in Florida and other parts of the tropics glow blue and green when bioluminescent plankton, tiny organisms beneath the surface of the water, are disturbed.

Hawaiian bobtail squid, which are not bioluminescent, have a special relationship with bacteria that are. The squid feed the bacteria and in return use their bioluminescence as camouflage.

Sometimes, sperm whales live among bioluminescent plankton. The plankton glow to keep fish from eating it. This alerts the sperm whale that fish are nearby and it's time to eat.

Only some of the more than 2,000-plus species of fireflies produce a glow.

When enough bioluminescent bacteria are in once place, they use chemical signals to trigger bioluminescence so they all glow at the same time.

Only one glowing creature—the limpet, a snail native to New Zealand—is known to live in a freshwater habitat.

Sometimes fireflies synchronize their flashing so they are all doing it at the same time.

Firefly light is the most efficient light in the world. Almost all of the energy in the chemical reaction shines as light, with almost none of it going to waste.

Scientists have extracted and used the protein that causes the crystal jelly to glow to help identify the effects of genes in medical research.

Bright Lights!

- Biofluorescent animals cannot create their own light. Instead, they absorb light and can then emit that light from their bodies in a different color.

- **Under a black light, the fur of some flying squirrels glows a bright pink.**

- The first documented case of biofluorescence in a wild reptile was captured on camera in 2015, when a glowing hawksbill sea turtle swam by a team of marine biologists filming biofluorescent coral.

- **Firefly larvae sometimes glow to tell predators they taste really bad.**

- Scorpions emit a bluish green glow under ultraviolet light. Scientists aren't sure why.

- **In 2017, scientists discovered the first fluorescent frog species. The polka dot tree frog, found in the Amazon rain forest, emits a blue-green glow under ultraviolet light. Scientists think the glow might help the frogs see one another in the dark.**

SPOT THE 13 RANDOM DIFFERENCES:

Turn to page 215 for the answers!

Planet Earth

Rocks and Gems, Wild Weather, and Natural Wonders

There are 13 types of storms: tornadoes, squalls, gales, windstorms, dust devils, hailstorms, blizzards, snowstorms, thunderstorms, ice storms, firestorms, hurricanes, and flooding.

A blizzard is a severe snowstorm with gusty winds of more than 35 miles an hour (56 kmh) that lasts for more than three hours.

Winds from blizzards can cause already-fallen snow to fly around, making it very hard to see in what is known as a "whiteout condition."

Earthworms surface during rainstorms as the rain gives them the moisture they need to survive and be able to move. Some can move farther distances on the soil than they can underground, through the soil.

To be classified as a hurricane, winds must be faster than 74 miles an hour (119 kmh).

The fastest hurricane wind speed ever recorded occurred during Hurricane Camille in 1969. The wind blew at 190 miles an hour (306 kmh).

More tornadoes occur in the United States than in any other country.

Hurricanes form near the equator where ocean water is warm.

A storm surge is caused by winds from a hurricane pushing ocean water to shore, thus increasing water levels.

The center of a hurricane is called an eye.

A tsunami is a series of gigantic wave caused by an event such as a volcanic eruption or earthquake.

Tsunami waves can reach higher than 100 feet (30 m).

Some tornadoes occur in a funnel shape, whereas others occur in a spiral.

Flash floods occur very quickly—within three to six hours of heavy rainfall.

A gale is a strong current of wind.

Floods can also be caused by large amounts of thawing ice.

Storm Surge

67 Totally Random Facts About EXTREME WEATHER

BREAKING NEWS — **HURRICANE SLAMS COAST**

LIVE NEWS · Ra

Tornadoes are most likely to occur between the hours of three and nine p.m. By then, the sun has heated the air and ground enough for a thunderstorm to occur.

Tornadoes can travel a path of more than 200 miles (322 km).

Flash floods can produce water as high as 20 feet (6 m) in only minutes.

Tornadoes are translucent until they pick up dirt and other debris, which makes them darker.

A tornado that occurs on water is called a waterspout. They sometimes suck up fish and birds!

A squall is a sudden and violent gust of wind.

A waterspout sometimes moves from water to land, where it becomes a tornado.

THAT'S SO RANDOM:

It's Twisted!

EVER WONDER HOW A TORNADO WORKS? Although these dramatic weather events seem mysterious, scientists have figured out some of the conditions and causes that contribute to these chaotic columns of swirling air. Most tornadoes occur during spring and summer thunderstorms. **These rapidly spinning cylinders of air form when cold and warm air meet inside thunderstorms, which makes the atmosphere unstable.** Because cold air weighs more than warm air, it rapidly pushes warm air upward from below, causing a spinning air current. Tornadoes are some of the strongest occurrences of extreme weather—**they can be more powerful than hurricanes. Wind speeds of a tornado can top 310 miles an hour (500 kmh),** lifting and hurling large, heavy objects such as cars and houses, and uprooting trees. Eyewitnesses report that tornadoes are as loud as a high-speed freight train going by. Thank goodness, **most tornadoes don't last long** and many don't cause damage.

TSUNAMI IS A JAPANESE WORD THAT TRANSLATES TO "HARBOR WAVE."

Flooding in New Orleans after Hurricane Katrina

A *haboob* is the Arabic name for an intense dust storm caused by a thunderstorm.

About 80 percent of all tsunamis take place in a region called the Ring of Fire in the Pacific Ocean.

In certain weather conditions, a tornado can travel backward.

Tornadoes are also called twisters.

In 1899, the entire length of the Mississippi River completely froze over.

Hurricanes begin as a group of thunderstorms that combine over the ocean.

Eyes of hurricanes are between 20 and 30 miles (32 and 48 km) wide.

The edge of a hurricane's eye is surrounded by clouds.

Tornadoes can form when a hurricane makes landfall.

Hurricanes are named in alphabetical order.

El Niño is a weather occurrence that takes place in the Pacific Ocean.

When El Niño occurs, the temperature of the ocean's surface increases. This causes an increase in rainfall across North, Central, and South America.

About 90 percent of natural disasters that occur in the United States include a flooding.

The Guinness World Record for the place with the largest temperature range is Siberia's Pole of Cold, at the Russian Antarctic station, where it can be as hot as 100.4 °F (38 °C) and as cold as −90 °F (−68 °C).

A firestorms happens when the heat from a wildfire causes its own wind.

Hurricane names are selected from a list created by the World Meteorological Organization.

Because El Niño causes changes in water temperature in the ocean, creatures such as seals, sea lions, and fish that need particular temperatures to thrive often relocate.

Extreme weather can also force people to relocate because of a lack of farm crops and drinkable water, or rising sea levels.

Tsunamis can move as fast as 500 miles an hour (805 kmh).

For two months in 1684, the River Thames in the United Kingdom completely froze.

After 900 Burmese pythons escaped captivity during a hurricane in Florida, there was a 99 percent decrease in the population of racoons and opossums. Certain rabbit and fox species disappeared completely.

It doesn't snow often in Antarctica, but when it does, the snow can be so heavy that you can't see your hand held up to your face.

El Niño in Spanish translates to "the child."

SCIENTISTS THINK DUST STORMS CAN CARRY INFECTIOUS DISEASES FROM ONE PLACE TO ANOTHER.

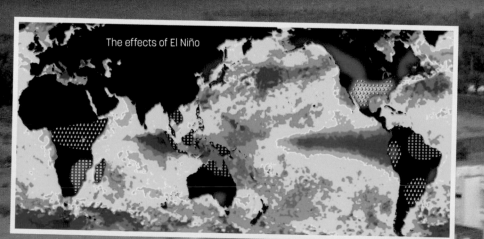
The effects of El Niño

El Niño occurs in a cycle that ranges in two- to seven-year intervals. The largest known El Niño on record took place in 1997.

A rainband is an area of clouds and rainfall that stretches in a long band.

A rainband can be as wide as 10 miles (16 km).

Hurricane John was the longest tropical cyclone in history. Spinning in the eastern Pacific, it lasted 31 days, from August 11 until September 11, 1994.

Peak hurricane season in the Atlantic Ocean happens during the months of August and September.

About 85 percent of fatal lightning strike victims are men.

The world's longest drought occurred in Arica, Chile, from October 1903 to January 1918— during this time, not a drop of rain fell.

Scientists are able to predict when tsunamis will occur partly by studying the start time of a triggering earthquake.

The world's largest desert, Antarctica, gets only 2 inches (50 mm) of precipitation per year.

The world record for heaviest hailstorm occurred in Gopalganj, Bangladesh, on April 14, 1986. The largest hailstones weighed in at 2.25 pounds (1 kg).

If lightning hits sand, it can fuse the grains together to create fulgurites, small glass-like tubes that follow the shape the lightning strike took as it dispersed through the sand.

Lake Maracaibo, Venezuela, gets more lightning strikes than anywhere else on Earth. There, lightning storms happen up to 160 nights per year.

Extreme weather affects the migration patterns of animals, especially grazers like wildebeests, gazelles, zebras, and other African animals.

Wildebeest

When the Ground Shakes

- Earthquakes occur when tectonic plates, large chunks of rock that make up Earth's crust, move.

- **More severe earthquakes occur when one tectonic plate is forced beneath another.**

- The underground location where a fault (fracture in Earth's crust) starts to rupture is called the hypocenter.i

- **The first recorded earthquake in the state of California occurred in 1769.**

- The largest recorded earthquake in U.S. history occurred in Alaska on March 27, 1964. It was a magnitude 9.2.

- **The largest known earthquake in the world occurred in Chile in 1960. It was a 9.5 on the moment-magnitude scale.**

- Today, the Richter scale is no longer in use. It has been replaced by the moment-magnitude scale, which is more precise, especially for larger earthquakes.

I AM HOME! I WILL REBUILD! I AM NEW ORLEANS!

MELTING OF THE POLAR ICE CAPS IN THE ARCTIC MEANS POLAR BEARS HAVE TO SWIM FARTHER TO FIND FOOD, WHICH HAS CAUSED MANY BEARS TO STARVE.

Carbon dioxide molecule

Cool It!

73 Totally Random Facts About CLIMATE CHANGE

"Climate change" is when typical conditions, including weather and temperature, change over a long period of time. • **In the past 100 years, Earth's global temperature has increased about 2° F (1° C).** • The ocean has risen 8 inches (20 cm) in the past 150 years. • **Many animal and plant species are near extinction due to loss of habitat, a contributor to climate change.** • The fuel sources that release carbon dioxide are known as greenhouse gases. • **The fuel sources that release the most greenhouse gases are coal, oil, and natural gas.** • Coal, oil, and natural gas release carbon dioxide, which traps heat from escaping Earth's atmosphere. This causes the global temperature to rise. • **Mosquitoes (unlike most other animals) are thriving despite the planet's increasing global temperature.** • The spread of mosquitoes has led to a spike in cases of deadly diseases such as malaria, yellow fever, and dengue fever in Africa. • **China produces 30 percent of the world's carbon dioxide emissions, more than any other country on Earth.** • The United States produces 15 percent of the world's carbon dioxide emissions, the second highest on Earth. • **Scientists believe that by 2100, the global temperature will rise about 3.6° F (about 2° C).** • In addition to carbon dioxide, methane is also a greenhouse gas. • **Over a 100-year period, methane has become about 30 times more destructive to the environment than carbon dioxide.** • The amount of methane in the air is 2.5 times higher than it was before the industrial revolution, a period of time when people were transitioning from handmade materials to machine-made materials. • **Livestock such as cows, pigs, and sheep release methane gas from their bodies. Their poop also releases methane. Because of this, raising livestock on a large scale contributes to global climate change.** • The rise in global temperature is causing the polar ice caps to melt. • **Since 1880, the global sea level has risen about 8 to 9 inches (20 to 23 cm) due to polar ice caps melting.** • The rising sea level means more areas around the world will have increased flooding. • **Changing temperatures are damaging certain animal habitats, forcing many**

A coal-fired power station

MALARIA
P.f
(15min)

animal species to migrate to new places. • The ocean's global temperature has increased about 0.6° F (0.3 C) in the past five to six decades. • **If all of Greenland's ice melted, the ocean would rise about 20 feet (6 m).** • Some of the fastest warming on Earth is happening on the Antarctic Peninsula. In February 2020, a temperature of almost 65° F (18° C) was recorded there! • **Due to global warming, the ice caps on mountains are vanishing.** • About 23 percent of the greenhouse gas emissions released in 2019 came from factories burning gas, coal, and oil to build and produce various products. • **The hottest years ever recorded have all happened since 2014.** • Currently, 2016 and 2020 are tied for having the hottest global surface temperatures on record. • **The nation of Tuvalu, located in the Pacific Ocean, is experiencing rising sea levels at a higher rate than other places. Two of its islands are already under threat of being submerged by the sea.** • Warming temperatures have caused the amount of ice loss on Antarctica to triple over the past decade. • **The ocean absorbs massive amounts of carbon dioxide, so the increase of this gas in the air is making seawater more acidic and harmful to sea life.** • Acid causes calcium carbonate to dissolve, and the shells of many marine animals contain calcium carbonate. The

THE GAS PASSED BY COWS, SHEEP, AND OTHER LIVESTOCK THROUGH BURPING AND POOPING MAKE UP 28 PERCENT OF THE METHANE GAS PRODUCED EVERY YEAR.

Hermit crab

A bleached coral reef

more acidic ocean water becomes, the harder it will be for animals to create hard shells to protect themselves. • **Warmer weather due to climate change has caused wildfires in many parts of the world, including areas of Australia and the American West.** • Studies show that an average 1.8° F (1° C) temperature increase in much of the western United States can increase the chances of large wildfires by 600 percent. • **Climate change doubled the number of wildfires that occurred in the western United States between 1984 and 2015.** • A drier climate has resulted in longer droughts and famines in various parts of Africa. • **Due to our changing climate, farmers in Africa haven't been able to grow enough food to meet demand.** • Since 2000, the number of people living in areas at risk of flooding due to rising sea levels has increased by almost 25 percent. • **Earth's ozone is a protective layer of the planet's atmosphere that blocks out harmful radiation.** • Some greenhouse gases can reduce Earth's ozone layer, making it thinner.

• **Higher sea levels and warmer ocean temperatures make hurricanes more powerful and more destructive.** • The rising global temperature is making hurricanes more likely to occur farther away from the equator. • **Coral reefs are dying because of the increased acidity of warming oceans.** • Warmer oceans cause microscopic algae to expel themselves from coral. Because algae give coral its bright color, their loss results in a totally white coral, an effect called "bleaching." • **The Amazon rain forest plays a vital part in absorbing carbon dioxide emissions and releasing oxygen.** • Deforestation of the Amazon rain forest results in less carbon dioxide being absorbed and more staying in the atmosphere. • **Carbon dioxide makes up about 76 percent of the greenhouse gases released into the atmosphere.** • Methane makes up about 16 percent of the greenhouse gases released into the atmosphere. • **Around a quarter of the greenhouse gas emissions created in 2019**

CARS, PLANES, AND OTHER VEHICLES ACCOUNTED FOR ABOUT 29 PERCENT OF GREENHOUSE GAS EMISSIONS IN 2019.

came from burning gas, coal, and oil to power electricity and heaters. • Climate change can cause an increase in snowfall in some parts of the world during the winter. This is because an increased amount of water is being evaporated into the atmosphere due to a warming climate. • **Scientists think that warmer Arctic air might be causing frigid polar winds to travel farther south into the eastern United States.** • If nothing is done to drastically cut down greenhouse gas emissions, Earth's sea level could rise 1 to 8 feet (0.3 to 2.4 m) by 2100. • **Extreme weather and water patterns caused by climate change can create stronger natural disasters that contaminate clean water supplies, making it harder for people to have access to**

BY 2050, THE ARCTIC WILL MOST LIKELY BE ALMOST COMPLETELY ICE FREE IF GREENHOUSE GASES ARE NOT REDUCED DRASTICALLY.

safe drinking water. • Rising sea levels allow more salt to enter freshwater, making it undrinkable. • **Preventing food waste can keep more carbon dioxide emissions from going into the air than restoring almost 440 million acres (178 million ha) of tropical rain forest.** • Due

to more intense rainfall, mountainous areas of Asia may be more prone to landslides, putting many people in danger. • **Carbon dioxide emissions from air travel grew about 75 percent from 1990 to 2012.** • Walking, biking, or taking a bus can help prevent up to 1.9 tons (1.7 metric tons) of carbon dioxide from entering Earth's atmosphere per year. • **A flight from London, England, to Montreal, Canada, produces about the same amount of carbon dioxide emissions as heating a house for one year.** • One commercial airplane flight releases the same amount of carbon dioxide into the air as a car does in an entire year. • **Rising carbon dioxide levels can reduce the nutritional value of crops because carbon dioxide can break down their proteins.** • One of the most environmentally friendly energy sources is solar energy, which generates energy from the sun. • **A carbon footprint is the estimated amount of greenhouse gases a person produces in their lifetime based on their lifestyle.** • LED bulbs use 90 percent less energy than normal lightbulbs, making them more environmentally friendly.

Reducing CO_2

- To reduce the amount of carbon dioxide produced by your computer, it's better to unplug it when not in use or charging to lower the amount of electricity you are using.

- **To reduce carbon dioxide emissions, wear warmer clothing inside during the winter instead of cranking up the heat.**

- Recycling and reusing materials help prevent climate change by reducing the number of items factories produce. In turn, this lowers carbon dioxide emissions.

- **Eating and buying locally produced food reduces the amount of emissions made by vehicles, because the food you're consuming doesn't need to travel very far.**

- Eating a plant-based diet can lower carbon dioxide emissions because plant foods don't produce large amounts of greenhouse gases the way animals do.

Solar panels in China

What a Gem

84 Totally Random Facts About BIRTHSTONE GEMS

A miner holding an uncut diamond

Ancient Egyptians wore amethyst gems into battle because they thought the stones helped retain their courage.

Tourmalines can become electrically charged when they are heated.

Opals can be black, but they are much rarer than white opals.

In ancient China, citrine stones were supposed to be given only to generous people.

Citrine is a second birthstone for the month of November and is named after the citron fruit because of its golden color.

Sailors used aquamarine stones as good luck charms.

Diamonds are one of the hardest natural materials on Earth.

Some white dwarf stars have cores made of diamonds.

The first known emerald mines were discovered in Egypt.

Historians have discovered that Cleopatra loved emerald stones and wore them as part of her accessories.

Pearls and amber are two gems that originate from a living organism.

Amber is made from hardening sap or resin from old pine trees.

Oysters make pearls as a defense against a foreign object that enters their shells, entrapping it in layers of hard, smooth material, turning into a pearl.

The red in rubies comes from an element called chromium. Chromium also contributes to an emerald's green color.

One zircon gem found in Australia was more than 4.4 billion years old, making it the world's oldest mineral.

Zircon can be clear, but also orange, blue, or green.

Peridot is formed by magma deep under Earth's surface.

Sapphires are so tough that only diamonds can scratch them.

Garnet grains can be used for filtering water.

The most prized color of rubies is referred to as "pigeon blood."

"Pigeon blood" ruby

Because tourmaline comes in so many colors, it is sometimes called the **RAINBOW GEMSTONE.**

By mixing garnet grains with pressurized water moving at high speeds, construction workers can cut through most types of metals.

Some models of Apple watches have sapphire crystals in their screens.

Turquoise was once believed to have originated from the country of Turkey and got its name from the French words *pierre tourques*, which mean "Turkish stone."

All the mined tanzanite in the world comes from a 3-mile (5-km) stretch of land in northern Tanzania.

Because tanzanite can only be found in a small strip of land, geologists believe that within the next 10 to 20 years, there will be no more tanzanite stones left to mine.

In Victorian England, sapphires were a popular gem for royal engagement jewelry.

The ancient Greeks believed that opals were formed by tears of joy from the god Zeus after he defeated powerful deities called the Titans.

The last empress of the Ch'ing dynasty in China was buried with her head on a tourmaline pillow.

Amethyst

Tourmaline comes in a variety of vibrant colors, including pinks, reds, oranges, greens, yellows, and blues.

The biggest aquamarine ever discovered weighed around 243 pounds (110 kg).

Aquamarine gets its name from the fact that it resembles the color of the sea—*aqua* means "water" and *marine* means "sea."

Leonardo da Vinci thought amethyst gems had the power to control evil thoughts and strengthen one's intellect.

Opals are formed when rainwater seeps through the ground, collecting silica deposits and entering cracks in stone. Once most of the water evaporates, the silica in the rock eventually turns into opals.

Sapphire

Opal

Emerald

The Hope Diamond, actual size

The Hope Diamond was donated to the Smithsonian Institution in 1958. The diamond is now on display at the Smithsonian's National Museum of Natural History in Washington, D.C.

The Hope Diamond has only left the National Museum of Natural History four times since it was donated: once to the Louvre in Paris, France; once to a museum in South Africa; and twice to the Harry Winston jewelry company in New York City.

Most amethysts are mined in the South American countries of Brazil and Uruguay.

Though diamonds are one of the rarest gems, a top-quality emerald can be worth more than a diamond.

It was once believed that a topaz made its wearer invisible to enemies.

In ancient Rome, emeralds were considered symbols of Venus, the goddess of love.

Ancient Romans believed that Neptune, the god of the sea, had a deep connection with aquamarine stones.

Alexandrite turns green in sunlight and red under lamp and candlelight.

During the time of the Roman Empire, pearls symbolized wealth, so the ruler Julius Caesar made it illegal for anyone other than the wealthy elite to wear them.

Pure zircon is colorless.

Opal is the national gemstone of Australia.

Only one percent of topaz gems appear red. The most commonly occurring colors are brown and yellow, but the gem has a wide range, including blue and pink.

Tibetans believe turquoise came from the heavens. It is Tibet's national gem.

Rubies are the most durable minerals after diamonds.

Peridot was once believed to help with anxiety and asthma.

Turquoise is one of the minerals used in King Tut's death mask.

Among the Maasai people, who discovered tanzanite, it's a tradition for new mothers to be given a tanzanite stone as a symbol of good luck and new beginnings.

Some people once believed that turquoise could change color to warn wearers to be careful or to protect themselves.

Some believe that the word *topaz* comes from the Sanskrit word *tapas*, meaning "fire."

A 17th-century Dutch pendant in the form of Neptune, made from a large pearl with enameled gold mounts set with rubies, diamonds, and smaller pearls

In ancient Greece, citrine was dedicated to Demeter, the Greek goddess of the harvest.

A pearl weighing 75 pounds (34 kg) found by a fisher in the Philippines is thought to be the largest in the world.

Opals have been discovered on Mars.

Between the 19th and 20th centuries, pearl divers in the ocean had a 50 percent mortality rate owing to shark attacks and drowning.

Alexandrite in different kinds of light

Tanzanite was only **DISCOVERED IN 1967,** much later than most other gems.

Tourmalines were only discovered to be their own gemstones in the 1800s. Before that, they were mistaken for everything from an emerald to a topaz.

All amethysts are purple. Their value is determined by the vibrancy of the color.

In 1971, aquamarine became the official gemstone of the state of Colorado, because so many have been discovered there.

Due to its extreme rarity, alexandrite is one of the most expensive gems in the world.

In Germany, aquamarines were once used in glasses to help people suffering from shortsightedness.

During the medieval ages, citrine stones were known as "merchant stones" because they were believed to help bring profits.

Peridot is one of the oldest gems to be mined. Ancient Egyptians mined these stones since at least 1500 BC.

Today's tradition of diamond engagement rings began in the 1930s as a marketing tool by a diamond company to boost its sales.

Because rubies are so rare and expensive, they're often referred to as the "king of gemstones."

During the Middle Ages, people believed that garnets protected them from having nightmares.

The earliest recorded diamond engagement ring was given in 1477 by Archduke Maximilian of Austria to Belgian duchess Mary of Burgundy.

Zircon sometimes has traces of uranium in it, making it slightly radioactive, but not nearly enough to be harmful.

During the Middle Ages, sapphires were thought to cure eye diseases.

Some people believe alexandrite inspires creativity.

Happy Birthday!

JANUARY: GARNET
Garnet is believed to keep people safe while traveling.

FEBRUARY: AMETHYST
Amethyst symbolizes courage.

MARCH: AQUAMARINE
Aquamarine was once believed to help with ailments of the liver, heart, and stomach.

APRIL: DIAMOND
Like amethysts, diamonds symbolize courage. They are also a symbol of love.

MAY: EMERALD
Emeralds are thought to represent rebirth and love.

JUNE: PEARL
For many years, pearls have been a symbol of purity.

JULY: RUBY
It was once thought that rubies protected people from evil. Today, they are also a symbol of love.

AUGUST: PERIDOT
Peridot symbolizes strength.

SEPTEMBER: SAPPHIRE
Sapphires symbolize wisdom. Throughout history, priests and kings have worn this gem.

OCTOBER: OPAL
Opals symbolize confidence and faithfulness. The word *opal* comes from the Latin word *opalus*, which means "precious jewel."

NOVEMBER: TOPAZ
Topaz symbolizes affection.

DECEMBER: TURQUOISE
Turquoise symbolizes success and good luck.

Fan the Flames

Statue of Prometheus at the Rockefeller Center, New York City

93 Totally Random Facts About FIRE

The first source of fire on Earth was lightning. Fire is a chemical reaction that releases light and heat. • **In Greek mythology, Hestia is the goddess of fire.** • According to Greek mythology, Prometheus, a giant Titan—a being said to have come before the gods—stole fire from the gods and brought it to the people of Earth. • **The U.S. Forest Service has a spokesbear called Smokey Bear, who educates people about how to spend time in the wilderness without causing wildfires.** • Ancient cultures, including Egyptians, Greeks, Romans, Inca, Maya, Aztec, and Zoroastrians, all worshipped fires as sacred. • **Fire requires fuel, oxygen, and heat to burn.** • A typical house fire will double in size every minute. • **According to Native American Cherokee legend, a water spider brought the first fire to people on her back.** • On July 18, AD 64, the Great Fire

PREVENT
SMOKEY
FOREST FIRES

of Rome began. It burned for six days and damaged most of the city. • **The Great Chicago Fire in 1871 was one of the greatest disasters in American history. It destroyed 17,450 buildings and 3.3 square miles (8.5 sq km) of the city.** • Though it's not known exactly how the Great Chicago Fire started, the weather was very dry and the city had many wooden structures, making the area vulnerable. • **The Great Fire of 1910, also known as the Big Blowup and the Big Burn, occurred in eastern Washington, Montana, and Idaho. After burning 3 million acres (1.2 million ha), it ended only because it rained.** • In the Native American Mohawk legend, a young boy named Three Arrows travels to a sacred mountain where gods give him the gift of fire to bring back to his people. • **In the Neolithic era, about 9,000 years ago, early humans used fire to clear fields and plant crops. This brought on the development of agriculture, as opposed to hunting and gathering for survival.** • For fuel to burn, it must be heated to a specific temperature. This is known as the ignition point. • **Every kind of fuel has its own unique ignition**

point. For example, the temperature at which wood burns is different than the temperature at which plastic burns. • Matches are made with a number of chemicals that have a particularly low ignition point, so just a few strokes of a matchstick against something rough can easily light a flame. • **According to Native American Apache folklore, a fox brought fire to people by stealing it from a village of fireflies and spreading its sparks across Earth.** • Fire has four stages. The first is ignition: Fuel and oxygen come together to create a chemical reaction. The second is growth: The heat of the first spark causes the fire to grow larger. The third is full development: The fire becomes fully grown as it consumes all available fuel. The final stage is decay: The fire eventually runs out of fuel and goes out. • **Fire is able to grow by spreading the heat it creates.** • Fire can spread when nearby areas get increasingly hot and catch fire; this is called conduction. • **Fire also spreads through convection—when a flame's gas drifts away to bring heat and fire to colder areas.** • Fire can spread when electromagnetic waves from a fire radiate heat; this is called radiation. • **On Earth, flames are teardrop-shaped, due to gravity.** • Because fire needs oxygen to

exist, a fire cannot happen naturally in space—because space has no oxygen. • **In the zero-gravity environment of the International Space Station, astronauts conducted an experiment to make fire. The flame had a spherical shape instead of a teardrop shape like it has on Earth.** • The term *flammable* is used to describe something that can catch fire when oxygen is present. • **Spontaneous combustion is when a fire starts without an outside heat source.** • Spontaneous combustion creates the fire that flies a liquid-fueled rocket. • **The more oxygen that is present, the hotter a fire will burn.** • In Australia, wildfires are called bushfires. • A pyroclimate is a hot, dry ecosystem where fire naturally happens and is needed for the environment to thrive. • **The two most common causes of forest fires are lightning and human activity, such as a downed electrical wire, a tossed cigarette, or a campfire left to burn unattended.** • There are more than a million firefighters in the United States.

Fighting the Dixie Fire, California, 2021

Lightning and lava cause 10 percent of forest fires. • **A pyrophyte is a plant that is either fire resistant or needs fire to reproduce. Plants such as manzanita, chamise, and scrub oak need their seeds to come into contact with fire to grow into plants.** • Some forest fires can be seen from outer space. • **Some animals need fires to survive. Karner blue butterfly caterpillars eat only wild lupine, a purple perennial flower that needs fire to grow.** • As many as 3 million square miles (7.8 million sq km) of Earth's surface are burned by fire every year. That's more than half the surface area of the United States! • **Deliberately setting a fire to clear overgrown areas and increase the amount of nutrients in the soil is called a controlled burn.** • The amount of U.S. land annually affected by forest fire is projected to double by the year 2050 due to warmer and drier conditions brought on by climate change. • **Black kite birds are known to fly toward fires to catch prey trying to escape the flames.** • There are about 30,000 fire departments in the United States. • **A sparkler can burn at 1800 °F (982 °C).** • In the United States, humans cause approximately 84 percent of wildfires. • **Smokejumpers are people who are trained to parachute out of planes and into areas affected by wildfires that a land vehicle cannot reach.** • Fire towers are tall structures made for watching wildfires. • **Lookouts are people who stay in remote fire towers and watch for forest fires during heavy lightning. They then report the locations of any fires they spot. Fewer people work as lookouts today due to advances in methods for detecting fires.** • Scientists and firefighters use satellites to track the direction and intensity of wildfires. • **A fire scientist studies fire behavior, weather conditions, and how fire affects its surroundings.** • Fuel specialists are people who plan controlled fires. • **Helitack crews are groups of firefighters who use helicopters to fight fires.** • A firestorm is a forest fire that radiates such intense heat that it creates its own wind system. • **A fire tornado is a spiral of fire. Heat rising from a fire creates an updraft, or empty space, that the fire fills.** • Fire tornadoes are also known

Black kite

A mirror is used to focus sunlight to **IGNITE THE OLYMPIC TORCH.**

as fire whirls and firenadoes, though they technically are not tornadoes because they don't occur from clouds to the ground. • **Fire tornadoes during volcanic eruptions are called lava whirls or volcanic fire whirls.** • The largest urban fire whirl ever recorded happened after an earthquake in Tokyo, Japan, in 1923. • **Smoke particles from a fire and water vapor in the air form pyrocumulus clouds.** • Pyrocumulonimbus clouds are large pyrocumulus clouds that result from firestorms. These can form lightning, in addition to rain and wind. • **A flashover fire happens when everything in an enclosed area suddenly catches fire at the same time.** • The color of a flame depends on how much oxygen it's getting. • **The color of a flame reflects how hot it is. A flame with a lower temperature will be red, orange, and yellow, whereas a flame with a higher temperature tends to be blue.** • Candle flames are blue at the bottom, where they are getting a lot of oxygen and are thus very hot, and yellow near the top, where less oxygen enters the flame. • **Fires burn faster at higher elevations than at lower elevations.** • Smoke from wildfires, even when naturally occurring, still causes air pollution. • **Global warming increases the frequency of forest fires by creating extreme heat and making areas drier.** • Some fuel sources, such as haystacks, compost heaps, and old newspapers, generate their own heat by rotting and can even burst into flames.

California wildfires seen from space

• Trees can burst into flames during a wildfire if the water within them turns to steam. • No one knows who invented the fire hydrant because the patent for it was destroyed in a fire in 1836. • **It's possible to start a fire using ice.** • Forest fires move faster uphill than downhill. • **A fire rainbow is a rare natural phenomenon when light appears like rainbow flames in wispy cirrus clouds.** • Fire stations used to be built with spiral staircases so the horses that pulled the fire engines wouldn't try to climb the stairs and get into the living quarters. • **A fire bomber is an airplane that drops fire retardant, a substance that puts out fires.** • Lava is a scorching 2282 °F (1250 °C), one of the hottest things on Earth's surface. • **Coal deposited in layers of rock in Australia has been burning for about 500,000 years. This area where the coal is deposited is known as a coal seam.** • The ancient Greeks started fire by using a mirror to concentrate, or focus, sunlight. • **The 1666 Great Fire of London destroyed 80 percent of the city center.** • The second deadliest blaze in U.S. history, the Peshtigo Fire in Wisconsin, broke out the same day as the Great Chicago Fire: October 8, 1871. • **Pistachios are so likely to spontaneously combust that they have special shipping codes to keep this from happening.** • Fire can make water. If you put a cold spoon above a flame, water will appear in the spoon. • **A candle flame burns at 1800 °F (982 °C).** • During a fire, smoke inhalation kills more people and animals than the flames. • **When combined with fire, 1 gallon (3.8 L) of gasoline can be as explosive as 30 sticks of dynamite.** • Fires spread quickly—a fire can become uncontrollable within 30 seconds. • **The chance of dying in a house fire is cut in half if the house has a working smoke alarm.** • The heat of a candle's flame melts the wax into a gas, which the fire then burns as fuel. • **The heat from a house fire can reach 1100 °F (593 °C) in less than four minutes.** • In a lab in Geneva, Switzerland, scientists created the hottest temperature ever recorded—more than 5 trillion kelvin—which is 300,000 times hotter than the center of the sun. • **A natural gas vent in Iraq known as the Eternal Fire has been burning for 4,000 years.** • The deadliest fire in the United States took place on the Mississippi River aboard the steamboat *Sultana* in 1865. • **There were 44,000 wildfires in the United States in 2021. Combined, these fires burned land equivalent to the area of the state of New Jersey.**

THAT'S SO RANDOM:

The First Fires!

THE EARLIEST KNOWN USE OF FIRE BY HUMAN ANCESTORS WAS ABOUT 1.6 MILLION YEARS AGO, according to evidence archaeologists discovered in Africa. Much later, between 300,000 and 400,000 years ago, Neanderthals, one of our closest extinct human relatives, began to learn to use fire regularly. **For early humans, fire changed the way of life. People could cook food, which added flavor and made it easier to eat.** Heat produced by fire kept people warm, which allowed them to live in colder places. **Fire also kept people safe by warding off wild animals.** Early humans used fire to see in the dark, allowing for travel at night. Fire also made it possible to harden points on wooden tools, making tools more useful.

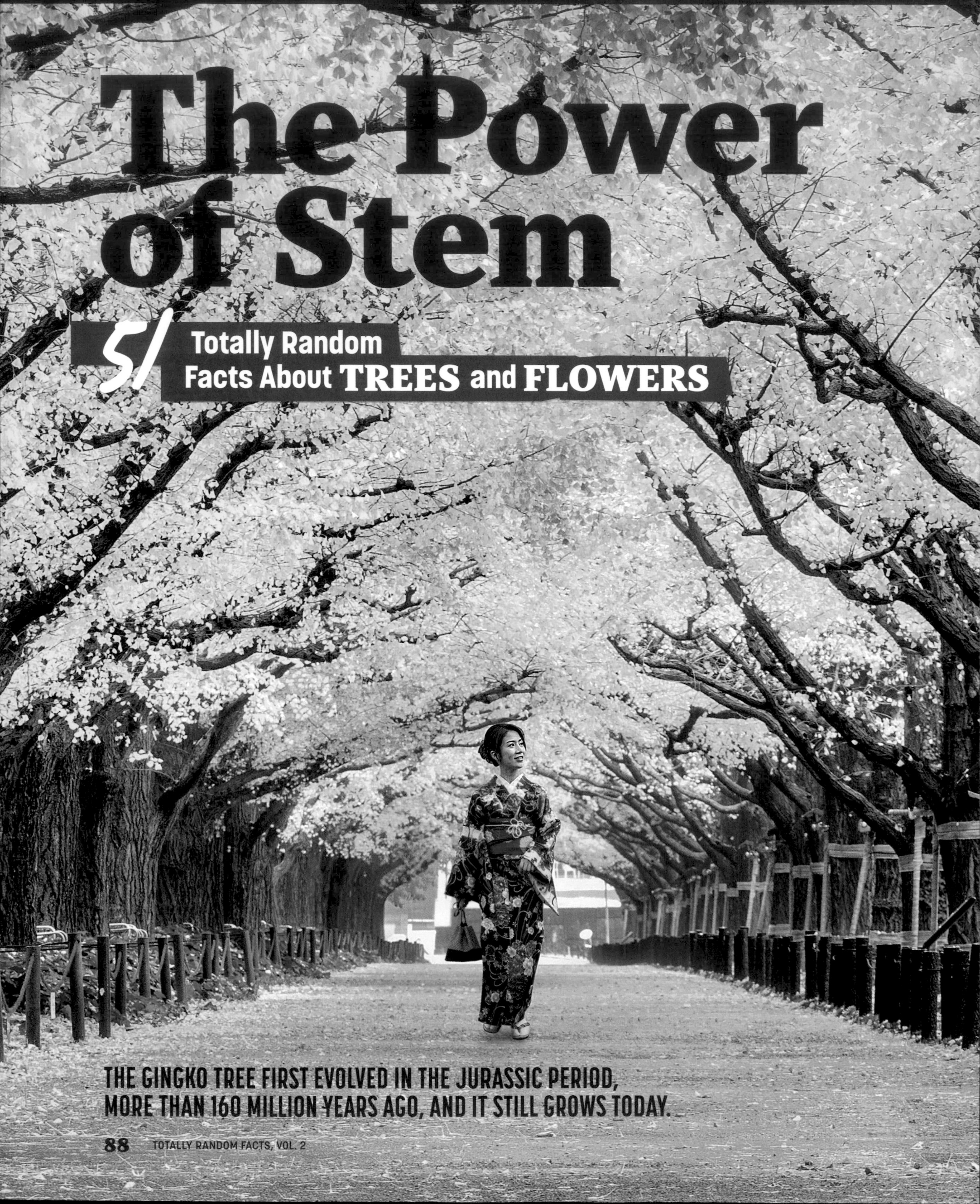

The Power of Stem

51 Totally Random Facts About TREES and FLOWERS

THE GINGKO TREE FIRST EVOLVED IN THE JURASSIC PERIOD,
MORE THAN 160 MILLION YEARS AGO, AND IT STILL GROWS TODAY.

Some of the structures created from the tree roots in Mawsynram, India, include platforms, ladders, and even bleachers for people to watch football games.

Trees planted around buildings can reduce the need for air conditioning by 30 percent.

Trees have a number of physical defenses to protect their leaves from animals that eat them. Some, like holly trees, have spiky leaves. Others can make their leaves taste bitter.

One of the most expensive flowers is an orchid that sold for more than $200,000 at auction.

Some bamboo species only flower once every 60 to 130 years.

There are more than 400,000 different flowering plants in the world.

The ghost flower, which usually has waxy white petals, contains no chlorophyll, the substance that makes plants green.

Ghost flower

Before trees existed on Earth, fungi grew 26 feet (8 m) tall.

Scientists were able to grow the seeds of a 32,000-year-old arctic flower after finding the seeds in the fossilized burrows of arctic squirrels.

Aboriginals, indigenous peoples of Australia, consider the boab tree to be sacred.

Moonflowers only bloom at night.

In India, the neem tree is thought to have healing properties and represents the maternal Hindu goddess Shitala.

In Europe, it was once thought a person could not tell a lie while under a linden tree.

Lilies are toxic for cats if ingested.

In 1997, environmental activist Julia Butterfly Hill climbed a tree in Northern California and stayed in it for two years to protest logging.

The manchineel tree is the deadliest of all trees, producing poisonous fruit and toxic sap.

"Prometheus," a now dead bristlecone pine tree in Nevada, was estimated to be almost 5,000 years old.

More than 500 flower species have gone extinct since the 1750s.

Some tulip bulbs can be used in cooking.

Fir trees can send water, carbon, and nutrients back and forth to each other through fungi in the soil.

When attacked by bugs, some species of trees and plants release chemicals into the air to attract the bug's predators.

Chrysanthemums have been used in traditional Chinese medicine for thousands of years.

The smallest flower in the world, the watermeal, is the size of a grain of rice.

Some of the bridges made from the roots of rubber fig trees have lasted more than 100 years.

Some flowers change color depending on the acidity of the soil.

Floriography is the language of flowers. Bouquets can be used to send coded messages.

Gingko leaves →

The agave plant only blooms once before dying.

The fastest-growing tree on Earth is the princess tree. In three weeks, it can grow almost 1 foot (30 cm).

Rangoon creeper flowers are thought to change color from white to pink to red depending on whether moths or butterflies are pollinating them.

Certain flowers only release pollen when a bee buzzes nearby.

Princess tree sapling

Scientists have found that spending time with trees can make people feel happier and healthier.

A dandelion flower needs a week to transform into a puffball of seeds.

Trees can warn each other that hungry herbivores are coming by releasing chemicals into the air.

There are more than 60,000 known species of trees.

Brazil is home to the highest number of different tree species.

The planet has 46 percent fewer trees now than when human civilization started.

Trees in urban areas can decrease the temperature by 9 °F (5 °C).

Chocolate cosmos flower

The chocolate cosmos flower actually smells like chocolate.

Trees have their own way of "migrating": Over time, seeds can disperse to different locations for new trees to grow.

The first trees on Earth, which grew about 500 million years ago, grew in wetland areas.

Tree leaves filter toxic gases from the air.

Some flower seeds can disperse up to 5 miles (8 km) in the wind.

THE PANDO CLONE IS A SINGLE ORGANISM MADE OF 47,000 ASPEN TREE TRUNKS COVERING 106 ACRES (43 HA). IT STARTED LIFE AS A SINGLE ASPEN TREE SEED.

Titan arum

The largest flower in the world, the titan arum, can grow to be 10 feet (3 m) tall and can weigh 23 pounds (10 kg). That's about as heavy as a small dog!

One of the rubber fig tree bridges in Mawsynram has two levels for people to cross!

Marigold flowers have medicinal properties such as helping to heal some minor skin conditions.

China uses the most paper in the world, followed by the United States and Japan.

THE LOTUS FLOWER WAS SACRED TO THE ANCIENT EGYPTIANS.

Getting to the Root of the Problem!

THE TOWN OF MAWSYNRAM IN MEGHALAYA, INDIA, IS THE RAINIEST PLACE ON THE PLANET. It receives 467 inches (1,186 cm) of rain per year—**13 times that of Seattle, Washington.** Because the environment is so damp, wood rots within a few years. This is a big problem when it comes to building bridges that last. **However, the people who live there have figured out a solution—using tree roots!** For centuries, the Khasi people have been planting rubber fig trees on either side of their rivers. It takes 15 years for the roots of these trees to grow long enough for people to start using them for river crossings. The roots are carefully woven into bamboo scaffolding built over the river to hold the roots as they continue grow. The roots take years to grow long enough to completely cross the rivers. Once that happens, the roots are tied to roots of the trees on the other side, creating suspension bridges sturdy enough to walk over. **As the roots grow over time, the bridges naturally become thicker and stronger,** even after the bamboo rots away. No wonder these structures are called living bridges!

The biggest living tree in the world is a giant sequoia named General Sherman. It's 275 feet (84 m) high and 36 feet (11 m) around.

The General Sherman Tree is also very old—it's been around for about 2,200 years!

GENERAL SHERMAN

The Grand Canyon is larger than the state of Rhode Island. • **A trip by car from the north rim to the south rim of the Grand Canyon is a 215-mile (346-km) drive!** • About 250 bird species live in the Grand Canyon. • **Of the many fossils in the Grand Canyon, none are dinosaur fossils.** • Aquatic fossils more than a billion years old have been discovered in the Grand Canyon. • **Eight species of fish are native to the Colorado River, which runs through an area of the Grand Canyon.** • Five of the eight native fish species found in the Colorado River of the Grand Canyon are found nowhere else in the world. • **Temperatures at the Grand Canyon can be drastically different depending on where you are in the canyon. The coldest temperature on record was –22 °F (–30 °C), whereas the warmest was 120 °F (49 °C).** • The Grand Canyon is 1 mile (1.6 km) deep, 277 miles (446 km) long, and 18 miles (30 km) wide. • **The Grand Canyon is one of the seven natural wonders of the world.** • The temperature in the Grand Canyon increases by 5.5 °F (3 °C) for every 1,000 feet (305 m) down into the canyon. • **Rock squirrels are native to Mexico and the southwestern United States and live in the Grand Canyon. But stay away, as they often bite tourists who try to feed them.** • The Grand Canyon is part of a pyroclimate,

THE GRAND CANYON CAN BE SEEN FROM SPACE.

meaning that fire is a necessary part of its ecosystem. • **President Theodore Roosevelt made the Grand Canyon a national monument in 1908, five years after his first visit.** • In 1919, President Woodrow Wilson signed the bill that would make the Grand Canyon a national park. • **The Grand Canyon has more than 1,000 caves.** • The slow-flowing Colorado River moves at about 4 miles an hour (6 kmh) and is up to 100 feet (30 m) deep. • **About 6 million people visit the Grand Canyon each year.** • Five Native American tribes have land within the Grand Canyon National Park. They are the Hopi, Navajo, Havasupai, Paiute, and Hualapai. • **The Grand Canyon is so large that it creates its own weather.** • Scientists believe that the Grand Canyon began as several small canyons that eventually merged to become one large canyon. • **The coldest point in the Grand Canyon, Bright Angel Ranger Station, and the hottest point, the Phantom Ranch, are only 8 miles (13 km) apart.** • Supai Village is located at the base of the Grand Canyon within the Havasupai Indian Reservation. There are 208 people that live there. • **Supai Village is the most**

Into the Deep

50 Totally Random Facts About the GRAND CANYON

remote community in the Lower 48 states. • Supai Village is also the only place where mail is still delivered by pack mule. • **Though the Grand Canyon is very deep, it's not the deepest canyon in the world. That record goes to the Yarlung Tsangpo Grand Canyon in Tibet.** • The lowermost rock layer of the Grand Canyon is 2 billion years old. • **The uppermost layer of rock in the Grand Canyon is 230 million years old.** • The name Grand Canyon was coined in 1869. Before this, it was known as the Big Canyon or the Great Canyon. • **The Grand Canyon is home to 22 species of bats, the most diverse population of bats anywhere in the United States.** • The rocks of the Grand Canyon are older than any species of dinosaur yet discovered. • **The Paiute Native American name for the Grand Canyon is Kaibab, which translates to "mountain lying down."** • The Skywalk is a lookout over the Grand Canyon that has a see-through bottom, allowing visitors to observe the 800 feet (244 m) between them and the ground below. • **The Grand Canyon was the 15th U.S. national park.** • Pink rattlesnakes are only found in the Grand Canyon. • **The layers of rock that make up**

20 South Entrance Road
Grand Canyon, AZ 86023
USA

the Grand Canyon include old lava flows. • The rock that makes up most of the Grand Canyon is red, but some layers are green, gray, pink, brown, or even violet. • **Ruins of Pueblo dwellings and other artifacts in the Grand Canyon suggest that people from the prehistoric era once lived there.** • The Grand Canyon is home to an underground hotel suite. It's 200 feet (61 m) down! • **In 1979, the Grand Canyon was established as a UNESCO World Heritage site—an area that has historical, cultural, or scientific significance.** • Though the Grand Canyon is very long, it is located in only one state: Arizona. • **Humans have lived in the area surrounding the Grand Canyon since the time of the last ice age.** • The oldest known rock in the Grand Canyon is called the Vishnu Basement. • **In 1902, the first car drove to the Grand Canyon. The car was steam-powered.** • The Havasupai people have lived in the Grand Canyon for more than 800 years. • **Roughly 1,750 types of plants have been discovered in Grand Canyon National Park.** • The Grand Canyon has an address. (It's 20 South Entrance Road, Grand Canyon, AZ 86023.) • **It was thought that the Colorado River began forming the Grand Canyon about 6 million years ago, but newer research shows that it could have started about 70 million years ago!**

The Skywalk

THE GRAND CANYON HAS MORE THAN 20 LAYERS OF EXPOSED ROCK.

A Major Empire

68 Totally Random Facts About ANCIENT ROME

Ancient Rome is thought to have been founded around 625 BC, though the actual date is not certain.

Nations conquered by Rome were often allowed to continue practicing their native religions, as long as they acknowledged the superiority of Roman gods.

Many Romans began worshipping gods of other religions, such as the Egyptian goddess Isis.

In ancient Rome, fathers were legally allowed to kill their entire family.

Julius Caesar was a Roman general and politician who helped build the Roman Republic.

Emperor Caligula

In 75 BC, Julius Caesar was kidnapped by pirates before eventually being released.

Emperor Caligula tried to leave for Egypt to be worshipped as a sun god.

Volcanic ash was a major ingredient in Roman concrete.

The Roman Empire spread across Italy, what is now England, Scotland, and Wales, and most other parts of Europe. It also went into parts of northern Africa and the Middle East.

In Rome's entire history, more than 40 percent of its emperors were assassinated, almost always by their own people.

To make sure that no one challenged his throne in 32 BC, Octavian (who would become known as Caesar Augustus) declared war on Egyptian queen Cleopatra and his political rival Mark Antony.

After 107 BC, Roman generals began to build armies that were loyal solely to themselves and not the state, leading to many civil wars and eventually the fall of the republic.

Map of the Roman Empire

The Roman army marched 25 miles (40 km) nearly every day.

Gladiators were viewed as celebrities; they even endorsed products and had clay action figures in their likeness.

Only 1 in 10 gladiator fights ended in death—usually by accident, as gladiators were trained specifically not to kill.

The Roman Colosseum could hold up to 80,000 spectators.

Julius Caesar was the great uncle of Augustus.

Ancient Romans had sewer systems, something very unusual for the time.

Multiple emperors participated in gladiator games for fun.

Roman emperor Caligula intended to make his horse, Incitatus, a consul (one of the highest positions in Rome's government).

AFTER ABOUT 450 YEARS AS A REPUBLIC, ROME BECAME AN EMPIRE WHEN OCTAVIAN ROSE TO BECOME THE FIRST EMPEROR, CAESAR AUGUSTUS.

In Roman mythology, twin brothers Romulus and Remus—said to be the sons of Mars raised by a female wolf—are believed to have founded Rome.

Julius Caesar took over Rome and the Senate, and established himself as a leader in 46 BC.

Caesar Augustus

A few months of the year are named after Roman numbers. September was the seventh month in the ancient Roman calendar, and in Latin *sept* translates to "seven."

In the same way, the first three letters of October, November, and December, translate to "eight," "nine," and "ten," respectively.

The Greeks influenced all parts of Roman culture, from architecture to literature, from the military to religion.

The gods of Greek mythology directly inspired most of the Roman gods.

Janus, the Roman god of transitions, had two heads.

The Roman calendar had only 10 months. Each month had 30 or 31 days.

To intimidate his opponents, Emperor Heraclius had his soldiers applaud him when he entered battle.

Ancient Roman legions (smaller groups within the army) had between 4,000 and 6,000 men.

In ancient Rome, only one hen could be served per meal.

The main language spoken in the Roman Empire was Latin.

It was illegal for chariot racers in ancient Rome to cast spells on their opponents.

Although not the biggest, the Roman Empire is the longest-lasting empire in history—more than 1,000 years!

The 18th Roman emperor, Commodus, who ruled from 177 to 192, tried to have Rome renamed as Commodiana, after himself.

Roman emperor Commodus renamed all the months after himself.

While in battle, Roman gladiators called andabata wore helmets that obstructed their vision.

Emperor Augustus created a postal system for the newly established empire.

One of the last Roman emperors, Romulus Augustulus, was nicknamed "little Augustus," in reference to his youth.

Romans were known to keep enslaved people who were prisoners of war, from other nations, or even Roman children sold into slavery.

More than a million people lived in the city of Rome during its peak in the Roman Empire.

In the year AD 238, Rome went through six emperors.

Rome was originally a small trading town where neighboring tribes gathered.

The Romans had giant constructs called aqueducts, or channels, that directed water from rivers and other water bodies to their cities.

Citizens of conquered lands were given the same rights of any Roman citizen, except for being able to vote.

Gladiator sweat was sold in pots to adoring fans.

Sometimes criminals were fed to the lions in Roman arenas.

Patricians, a group made up of noblemen and aristocrats, were the ruling class in Rome.

An escaped gladiatorial slave named Spartacus led a failed slave revolt from 73 to 71 BC.

Chariot racer Gaius Appuleius Diocles's winnings earned him equal to $15 billion in today's currency.

Emperor Hadrian, the 14th Roman emperor, had a 73-mile (117-km)-long wall built on what is now the border between Scotland and England. The wall was created to protect the area from invasion.

Aqueducts sent more than 370 gallons (1,400 L) of water per second into Rome.

A Roman slave collar. The inscription in Latin reads "I have escaped. Seize me. If you return me to my master Zoninus you will get a gold coin."

The Pont du Gard aquaduct in France

Chariot racing was the most adored sport in ancient Rome.

Emperor Commodus had himself sculpted as Hercules in statues that were created of him.

The Five Good Emperors era, which occurred between AD 96 and 180, got its name because of the peace that endured with the transition between each of these leaders. Before and after this, civil war had often broken out.

In the year AD 2, the Roman Empire had a population of around 65 million people, or around one-fourth of the entire human population at the time.

Mos maiorum was the moral code that all ancient Romans were expected to follow. It stated that one should do what one's ancestors would have done.

More than 500,000 people and 1,000,000 animals were killed in the Colosseum.

Julius Caesar and the Egyptian queen Cleopatra had a son named Caesarion.

Caesarion later became the king of Egypt.

The Colosseum in Rome

GLADIATOR BATTLES HAD REFEREES TO WATCH OVER AND POSSIBLY STOP FIGHTS BEFORE THEY GOT TOO DANGEROUS.

Bridges that ancient Romans built are still used to this day.

To show their power, Emperors Julius Caesar and Augustus added the months July and August, respectively, to the calendar—the months named after them.

The most common clothing in Rome was the tunic, which was a single rectangular piece of woven fabric pinned around the shoulders, similar to a Greek toga.

Roman families worshipped household spirits as well as the Roman gods.

The planets, except for Earth and Uranus, are named after the ancient Roman gods. Uranus is named for an ancient Greek god.

The Roman Empire collapsed in AD 476, partly because its large size made it impossible to manage and defend.

The Tower of London

Training for knighthood began between the ages of 7 and 10. ● **On average, it took 10 years to build a medieval castle.** ● Castles were large fortresses meant to protect politically important people of the time, such as kings, queens, and other members of nobility. ● **Most medieval castles were built in Europe.** ● The blade on a knight's sword was often double-edged, meaning each side was sharpened. One side represented loyalty and chivalry, whereas the other symbolized justice. ● **Knighting ceremonies varied, but one common practice was tapping each shoulder with the flat side of a sword.** ● The Tower of London's White Tower, one of the first castles in England, was built in 1066. ● **Knighting ceremonies were called dubbings.** ● During dubbings, soon-to-be knights were dressed in white, a symbol of purity; black, to represent the earth; and red, to represent blood. ● **When stone castles were originally built, they were smelly, cold, and dark.** ● Knights were called chevaliers in France and ritters in Germany. ● **Squires, the teenage trainees of knights, often followed them into battle as a way to prove** themselves. ● In medieval castles, the toilet was inside a large cupboard called a garderobe. ● **Every knight had a unique coat of arms, a symbolic picture with colors and graphics. These helped the knights identify one another while in armor.** ● Many medieval castles were built on hilltops to make it harder for invaders to reach them. ● **Castle towers are circular because the shape made them sturdier against prolonged attacks.** ● Castles often had very narrow windows called arrow slits where archers could safely fire at invading soldiers. ● *Chivalry* **is the term for the rules of behavior knights had to follow.** ● Boys training for knighthood would start as pages. Pages learned to read, write, and hunt. ● **When pages turned 12, they became squires. Squires would learn to fight, use weapons, and move in a suit of armor.** ● The Crusades were a series of religious wars in which European Christian knights and Muslims fought for control of Jerusalem and surrounding areas, which both groups considered to be holy lands. The wars occurred between 1095 and 1291. ● **During the Crusades, European knights from across Europe united to fight together, rather**

Conwy Castle, Wales, United Kingdom

Ye Olde Middle Ages

66 Totally Random Facts About MEDIEVAL KNIGHTS and CASTLES

than fighting for an individual country or lord. • Castles were often built with a large central room called the great hall, where most of the dining and gatherings occurred. • **Dungeons were prisons inside medieval castles, usually deep underground.** • Knights often fought under lords, individuals who were members of the aristocratic class and who owned land. • **Machicolations were holes built into the top of castle walls, from which soldiers inside would drop weapons such as rocks or shoot arrows.** • Sometimes soldiers poured hot sand or boiling water through the machicolations onto invaders. • **Boiling oil was also used to dissuade invaders, but only rarely because oil was very expensive.** By the 16th century, knights were no longer needed for combat, and the title of knight became an honor often given to nobility and people close to royal families. • **Today in the United Kingdom, the term *dame* is given to women who are knighted and the name *sir* is given to men who are knighted. A gender-neutral term has yet to be developed.** • To be a knight, it was necessary to be born into an aristocratic family, commit to a lifetime of training, have money to buy equipment and horses, and understand the rules of knighthood. • **Castles were originally made**

by the Normans, people who originated from Normandy and controlled England from 1066 to 1154. Castles first appeared around the ninth century in western Europe. **Knights became increasingly scarce with the development of war technologies such as powerful crossbows that made sword combat less effective.** • Before they were made of stone, castles were made out of wood. **England currently has 1,500 castles still standing.** • Dungeons were mostly used to force political prisoners to provide information that would benefit the king and queen of the castle.

Wales has **MORE CASTLES** than any other country in Europe.

• After the 16th century, advances in the use of cannons made castles much more vulnerable, because they weren't strong enough to withstand a cannon's blast. • **The largest castle in the world is Malbork Castle in Poland. It covers a sprawling 52 acres (21 ha) of land. That's about 40 American football fields.** • Many English kings owned multiple castles. • **Guest rooms in castles often had their own private chapels.** • The guest rooms were some of the safest parts of the castle because very few people were allowed into areas where visitors were staying. • **Some castles could hold more than 1,000 soldiers to defend the fortress.** • One place was worse for prisoners than the dungeon—the oubliette. This was a tiny vertical shaft so narrow that a prisoner couldn't sit down. • **Most servants lived within the castle walls.** • Some castle servants didn't have rooms where they could sleep. Instead, they slept wherever they

A knighting ceremony

could find space. • **Many castle cooks had to prepare meals for more than 200 people twice a day.** • During the siege of Kenilworth Castle in England in 1266, soldiers inside the castle went so long without food that they ate their leather belts. • **Dungeons weren't always underground. Sometimes they were in towers.** • To destroy castle walls, invaders sometimes dug deep underneath the wall and set explosives to collapse the structure. • **The floors of the great hall were often sprinkled with flowers and herbs to make the room smell better.** • The Bran Castle in Transylvania, part of Romania, was the inspiration for Count Dracula's castle. • **At the Český Krumlov, a castle in the Czech Republic, bears were kept in a protective ditch around the castle to keep out intruders.** • The Caerphilly Castle in Wales, United Kingdom, has a tower that leans more than the Tower of Pisa. • **Portcullises were large, heavy gates with spikes at**

Reenactment of a medieval jousting tournament

the bottom, often found at the entrance to medieval castles. • The highest-ranking castle servants were often the children of noble families from the area. • **Some of the moats in front of medieval castles were 30 feet (9 m) deep and 12 feet (3.6 m) wide.** • The castle on the island of Mont-Saint-Michel in France could only be reached by boat at high tide.

Castles from Around the World

• In 2015, Japan moved the 400-year-old Hirosaki Castle 230 feet (70 m) to fix its foundations.

• **The Amba Vilas Palace in Mysore, India, is home to a golden throne that former rulers of the area once used. It is brought out once a year during a religious festival. Otherwise, it is taken apart and the separate pieces are locked up in different areas of the palace.**

• Built in the late 1700s and located in the heart of Bangkok, the Grand Palace in Thailand is home to a special jade statue of the Buddha that only the Thai king and crown prince are allowed to touch.

• **The Smithsonian Castle in Washington, D.C., was completed in 1855. It is the oldest of the Smithsonian Institution's buildings, which include numerous museums.**

• Himeji-jo in Japan is a UNESCO World Heritage site. The castle is made up of 83 buildings, and what makes it even more unique is that it's made entirely of wood.

• **The Neuschwanstein Castle in Bavaria, Germany, inspired the castle at Disney World.**

Greta Thunberg

Change Makers

53 Totally Random Facts About PEOPLE WHO CHANGED THE WORLD

English botanist and photographer Anna Atkins was one of the first people to use photography for scientific purposes, including creating a photographic record of algae in the British Isles. • **Hugo Junkers was a German engineer and airplane designer. He is credited with pioneering the design of a metal airplane.** • Belva Lockwood, a lawyer and feminist who lived from 1830 to 1917, was the first woman to argue a case before the Supreme Court. • **The musical composer Johann Sebastian Bach, born in 1685, had five** brothers who all had the same first name as he did. • Nellie Bly was a fearless female journalist who set the record for traveling around the world in 72 days. • **Irish aviator Lilian Bland was the first woman to design, build, and fly her own airplane.** • Diana Vreeland was an

American fashion editor of *Harper's Bazaar* and *Vogue* magazines. She liked to iron her dollar bills and tissues before storing them in her purse. • **Madonna is the best-selling female rock artist of the 20th century.** • Rachel Carson was an early conservationist whose books, including *Silent Spring*, spoke out against the dangers of using pesticides. Many consider her the mother of the modern-day environmental movement. • **Rachel Carson published her first story at the age of 10!** • Civil rights activist Coretta Scott King, who was married to Dr. Martin Luther King Jr., graduated as the valedictorian (top student) of her high school class. She and her husband were inspired by Mahatma Gandhi's nonviolent form of protest and traveled through India on a pilgrimage. • **Genghis Khan, ruler of the Mongolian empire during the 13th century, created one of the first mail courier systems. Called "Yam," the network was a system of people on horses who would deliver communications from place to place.** • Historians aren't sure how Genghis Khan died or exactly where his body was buried. • **Claude Monet was a painter best known for his paintings of water lilies. He developed cataracts in his eyes, but only agreed to have surgery in one of them. Some think this resulted in him being able to see and paint a larger spectrum of color than most people see.** • Jesse Owens was famous for winning four gold medals in only one Olympic Games, matching a

IN 1954, DOROTHY DANDRIDGE WAS THE FIRST BLACK WOMAN TO BE NOMINATED FOR THE ACADEMY AWARD FOR BEST ACTRESS. SHE ALSO ACTED ALONGSIDE SIDNEY POITIER, THE FIRST BLACK MAN TO WIN AN OSCAR.

Jesse Owens Congressional Gold Medal

ATHLETE ~ HUMANITARIAN
ACT OF CONGRESS 1988
"DETERMINATION, DEDICATION, DISCIPLINE, ATTITUDE"

previous record set in 1900. Owens, who was Black, won gold at the 1936 Olympics, held in racist Nazi Germany. His wins crushed Hitler's cruel message of white supremacy. • **Alice Guy-Blaché was the first female film director. She was also the first woman to make a fictional movie instead of a documentary—many historians consider her to be the mother of the modern film.** • Edith Wharton was the first woman to win a Pulitzer Prize. She wrote more than 50 books in her lifetime! • **At the age of 20, Johann Sebastian Bach walked 280 miles (450 km) between two German cities to see a concert by a famous organist of the time. He would later become a famous composer.** •

AKBAR, INDIA'S EMPEROR FROM 1556 TO 1605, HAD DYSLEXIA AND NEVER LEARNED TO READ OR WRITE.

Joan of Arc was a French female warrior who lived in the 15th century. When the English army was invading France, she fought back because she heard voices in her head that she saw as signs from God. • **Nepali mountaineer Nirmal Purja became the first person to climb Earth's 14 highest peaks—all above 26,000 feet (8,000 m)—in less than seven months. The previous record had been about seven years.** • Eva Perón was a first lady of Argentina. She is credited with helping to pass a law that gave Argentinian women the right to vote. • **Olympic champion swimmer Michael Phelps has an unusually long "wingspan": 6 feet, 7 inches (2 m)—3 inches (7.6 cm) longer than his height. Most people have a wingspan the same length as their height.** • American painter Georgia O'Keeffe was widely considered to be the mother of American modernist art. O'Keeffe enjoyed painting New Mexico's deserts from the backseat of her car. • **Country singer, songwriter, and actress Dolly Parton holds the**

Guinness World Record for most decades with a top 20 hit on the U.S. Hot Country Songs Chart. • In 1995, Dolly Parton opened the Parton's Imagination Library, a nonprofit that provides books to children for free. In 2020, the library gifted its 150 millionth book! • **Medgar Evers was a civil rights activist and organizer who also served in the military, fighting for the U.S. during World War II. A white supremacist assassinated Evers for his activism in fighting for civil rights for Black people.** • At the age of 15, environmental activist Greta Thunberg decided to protest climate change by sitting outside the Swedish Parliament building every day. She has become an inspiration to young people all over the world to join the fight for a cleaner planet. • **Julia Child was a famous American chef who mastered the art of French cooking, but before her work as a chef, Julia wanted to become a spy.** • Scottish inventor and physicist Alexander Graham Bell is widely credited with inventing

MADAM C. J. WALKER WAS THE FIRST FEMALE SELF-MADE MILLIONAIRE. SHE CREATED A BLOCKBUSTER BUSINESS SELLING HAIR CARE PRODUCTS.

the telephone. His middle name was given by his father as a present on Bell's 11th birthday. • **Serena Williams is an American tennis champion, famous for winning more Grand Slam single competitions than any other person with 23 victories.** • John Ronald Reuel (J. R. R.) Tolkien was the English author of *The Hobbit* and *The Lord of the Rings* trilogy. He loved languages so much that he invented his own for fun. • **Ludwig van Beethoven was a German composer and musician born in 1770. As he grew older, he developed a condition that caused him to hear buzzing in his ear. Eventually, he went deaf but continued to compose music, including one of his most famous songs, "Ode to Joy."** • Comedian,

JRR TOLKIEN · THE LORD OF THE RINGS

talk show host, and actor Ellen DeGeneres became the first leading actor on television to discuss being gay. She also voiced Dory in the movies *Finding Nemo* and *Finding Dory*. • **Diana Nyad was the first person to swim from Cuba to Florida without a shark cage. She achieved this feat at the age of 64.** • Queen Elizabeth I of England and Ireland was actually third in line to the throne, but after the deaths of her brother and sister, she became queen and ruled for 44 years. • **Hedy Lamarr was a famous film actress and inventor who worked on a system to improve the aim of submarine torpedoes in WWII. Although her invention was never used for that purpose, it would eventually become Wi-Fi, GPS, and Bluetooth.** • Charles Dickens was an English writer, best known for his works *A Tale of Two Cities* and *Great Expectations*, in which he discusses the social divide between rich and poor. In a train accident once, he was in the only car not to fall from a bridge. • **Maria Mitchell, born in 1818, was both the first female astronomer in the United States and the first American scientist to discover a comet.** • Apple Inc. founder Steve Jobs was known for wearing the same outfit every day—a black turtleneck sweater and blue jeans. He owned about 100 of the same turtleneck. • **Beatrix Potter, author and illustrator of popular children's books, including**

DUTCH PAINTER VINCENT VAN GOGH ONLY SOLD ONE PAINTING DURING HIS LIFE. AFTER HIS DEATH, HOWEVER, HE BECAME FAMOUS. IN 2021, ONE OF HIS PAINTINGS SOLD FOR $35.8 MILLION.

The Tale of Peter Rabbit, used to write in code in her journals as a teenager. Her journals were discovered in 1952, but it took six years to crack the code! • Iva Toguri, later given the name Tokyo Rose, was a Japanese American radio broadcaster famous for her amusing Japanese radio program for American soldiers during WWII. She served six years in a U.S. prison, wrongly accused of treason, and was awarded a presidential pardon in 1977. • Musician and songwriter John Lennon is best known for being a member of the Beatles. He was also a cat lover—he had more than 11 cats over the course of his life! • Susan B. Anthony was a prominent figure in the women's suffrage movement for women's right to vote. In 1872, she was arrested and fined $100 for voting. • Rumi was a famous poet from the 13th century who wrote his work in four languages: Persian, Arabic, Turkish, and Greek. • Harriet Beecher Stowe was a writer known for her novels, including *Uncle Tom's Cabin*, which highlighted the cruelty of slavery. She was the neighbor of American writer Mark Twain. • During the era of silent movies, Mary Pickford was one of the earliest female Hollywood stars. When she cut her hair, it was such a shock to the public that it made the front page of *The New York Times*. • Charles Babbage was an English mathematician who was widely considered the father of computing. He is best known for engineering the world's first functioning automatic calculator. • In 1960, Ruby Bridges was one of the Black American children, and the youngest, to integrate schools in the South—she was escorted to school by federal marshals every day as angry white peers and their parents protested her enrollment. • On June 16, 1963, Valentina Tereshkova became the first woman to go to space. Though she was not a pilot or an astronaut, she was a parachutist, which gave her the experience to be accepted into the Russian space program.

Commander in Chief

71 Totally Random Facts About U.S. PRESIDENTS

George Washington was the only president elected who was not a member of a political party.

George Washington never lived in the White House. He became president in April 1789 and the White House wasn't completed until November 1800.

Richard Nixon was the first president to visit China.

The White House was at various times known as the President's Palace, the President's House, and the Executive Mansion.

George Washington on the way to his inauguration in 1789

Andrew Johnson was the only tailor to become president. He enjoyed wearing suits he sewed himself.

Rutherford B. Hayes was the first president to receive a phone call. He spoke with inventor Alexander Graham Bell.

Thomas Jefferson was the first president to be sworn into office in Washington, D.C.

The only president to be elected twice and serve two terms that were not back-to-back was Grover Cleveland.

The 41st president, George Herbert Walker Bush, once vomited on the Japanese prime minister.

Martin Van Buren was the first president born a U.S. citizen. The previous presidents were originally British subjects.

While in office, President Calvin Coolidge and his wife, Grace, had a pet raccoon named Rebecca.

Six presidents— Madison, Monroe, Polk, Buchanan, Garfield, and Carter—all had the first name James.

Dwight Eisenhower was the only president to have served in WWI and WWII.

Richard Nixon was the first president to visit all 50 states and the only president to resign from office.

John Tyler was the first president to get married while in office.

Andrew Johnson was the first president to be impeached, meaning he was accused of misconduct while in office.

Theodore Roosevelt officially named the presidential residence the **WHITE HOUSE** in 1901.

John Quincy Adams was known to swim in the Potomac River.

Jimmy Carter was the first president born in a hospital. He is also the longest-lived U.S. president.

Four U.S. presidents have earned a Nobel Peace Prize: Theodore Roosevelt, Woodrow Wilson, Jimmy Carter, and Barack Obama. Vice President Al Gore was also a recipient of the prize.

Lyndon B. Johnson had five dogs while in office. His two beagles were named Him and Her.

William Taft had a pet cow named Pauline Wayne. She often grazed on the White House grass.

Each person in Teddy Roosevelt's family had a pair of stilts.

James Garfield was able to write in Latin and Greek with different hands at the same time.

William Henry Harrison gave the longest inauguration speech to date, at nearly two hours. He also had the shortest presidency on record. It lasted only one month before he died of pneumonia.

There has never been a president who was an only child.

A ticket to the impeachment proceedings for president Andrew Johnson

Second president John Adams was the first vice president, serving under George Washington. Three presidents—Thomas Jefferson, John Adams, and James Monroe— died on July 4.

Franklin Delano Roosevelt was the first sitting president to fly in a plane.

George Washington gave the shortest inauguration speech. After being elected to a second term, his speech was only 135 words and lasted less than two minutes.

Statue of Franklin Delano Roosevelt, Washington, D.C.

19th-century dueling pistols

FROM DODGE CITY TO TOMBSTONE...

HIS GUNS WERE THE ONLY LAW!

RONALD REAGAN

LAW and ORDER

Color by Technicolor

DOROTHY MALONE   PRESTON FOSTER
ALEX NICOL   and introducing   RUTH HAMPTON

Andrew Jackson was said to have participated in more than 100 duels.

The youngest person to become president was Teddy Roosevelt. He was just 42 when he took office.

Harry S Truman's middle initial doesn't stand for anything, which is why no period follows the *S*.

George Herbert Walker Bush was the only president to have had four names.

James Monroe ran after the secretary of the Treasury with a pair of fire tongs until the secretary fled from the White House.

Calvin Coolidge was born on July 4—the only president born on Independence Day.

Herbert Hoover's first job was plucking bugs from potato plants. He earned one dollar for every 100 bugs.

The inauguration of James Buchanan was the first presidential inauguration to be photographed at the Capitol.

Teddy bears are named after Theodore Roosevelt, who was nicknamed "Teddy."

Abraham Lincoln was 6 feet, 4 inches (1.9 m) tall, making him the **TALLEST U.S. PRESIDENT.**

John F. Kennedy was the first president born in the 20th century, and the first Boy Scout to be president.

William McKinley was the first president to ride in a car.

Woodrow Wilson liked to paint his golf balls black so that he could find them when he played in the winter.

Before becoming president, Jimmy Carter had an accident on his peanut farm, which permanently bent one of his fingers.

Abraham Lincoln was the first president to have a beard.

William Henry Harrison had a pet goat while at the White House.

KENNEDY FOR PRESIDENT

Ronald Reagan was a Hollywood actor before he was president.

When George Washington was president, the presidential salary was $25,000 a year. Today, it's $400,000 a year.

Warren Harding was the first president to give a speech that was broadcast on the radio.

James Garfield was the first left-handed president.

James Garfield was really ambidextrous—both right- and left-handed.

Ulysses S. Grant was once given a $20 ticket for speeding his horse and buggy too quickly down a street in Washington, D.C.

Woodrow Wilson is the only president to have had a Ph.D.

Prior to his time as president, Harry Truman ran a men's clothing store.

Harry Truman's 1949 inauguration was the first presidential inauguration to be televised.

Gerald Ford spent some time as a model and once posed on the cover of *Cosmopolitan* magazine.

George W. Bush was head cheerleader of his high school cheerleading team.

George Washington was the only president elected unanimously—everyone who could vote voted for him.

Eight cities served as capital of the United States before Washington, D.C.: Philadelphia, York, and Lancaster, Pennsylvania; Baltimore and Annapolis, Maryland; New York City, New York; and Princeton and Trenton, New Jersey.

Barack Obama was the first African American and first person of color elected president of the United States.

After his presidency, William Howard Taft became chief justice of the Supreme Court.

Only twice in American history have a father and son both been president: John Adams (2nd) and John Quincy Adams (6th), and George H. W. Bush (41st) and George W. Bush (43rd).

In 1897, William McKinley's inauguration became the first to be recorded on film.

First Ladies and a Gentleman!

- First Lady Martha Washington appeared on a postage stamp.

- **Hillary Clinton is the only first lady to be elected to the Senate and also serve as secretary of state.**

- Of the first ladies, Rosalynn Carter was the first to have her own office in the East Wing of the White House.

- **First Lady Lou Hoover was fluent in Chinese. She was also the "first" first lady to make radio broadcasts across the country.**

- Before becoming the first African American first lady, Michelle Obama was a lawyer. She met her future husband after being assigned to be his adviser.

- **Douglas Emhoff, husband of Vice President Kamala Harris, became the first "second gentleman" when Harris, the first woman and first vice president of color, was elected in 2020.**

- First Lady Abigail Fillmore was an accomplished schoolteacher and first met future President Millard Fillmore when he was her student.

- **College professor Dr. Jill Biden is the only first lady to hold a doctorate degree and keep her full-time job while in office.**

- Eleanor Roosevelt was the longest-serving first lady at 12 years. She was also an accomplished diplomat and became a spokesperson for the United Nations.

144 Totally Random Facts About

Splendid Sports

Catching Waves, Making Moves, and Pushing the Goalpost

Gooooal!

49 Totally Random Facts About SOCCER

Soccer is the most popular sport in the world, with an estimated 4 billion followers.

Kit is the term used for a soccer player's equipment. Cleats are called "hooves."

The earliest game resembling soccer was invented by Chinese emperor Huang-Ti in 1697 BC. Players kicked a leather ball stuffed with cork and hair.

In soccer, a red card is a penalty given that removes a player from a game for the duration of that game.

The fastest a red card was given in history is three seconds after the start of the game.

The FIFA Women's World Cup championship was founded in 1991.

Before the FIFA Women's World Cup, some countries hosted their own championships for women's soccer. Italy did so in 1970 and Mexico in 1971. Both drew large crowds of spectators.

Soccer is played in almost every country, with approximately 250 million people playing worldwide.

In the United States, more than 11 million children and adults attend soccer camps each year.

Rules for soccer were established in England around 1863.

The U.S. Open Cup is the oldest ongoing American soccer championship.

The Brazilian soccer legend known as Pelé holds the Guinness World Record for the most career goals scored with 1,279.

Pelé is also the youngest player to win a World Cup, which he first won at age 17.

So far, only 23 players have scored 500 or more goals over the course of their careers in both club and international soccer.

Canadian professional soccer player Christine Sinclair has more goals in international play than any other woman.

The Los Angeles Galaxy has won the Major League Soccer Cup more times than any other team in the United States.

The soccer team with the most Olympic gold medals is the U.S. women's national soccer team, with four.

The first match of the British Ladies' Football Club in London, England, 1895

Pelé, voted the 20th century's best soccer player, also holds the most World Cup championships. He helped Brazil win three of their five World Cup championships.

Soccer teams vying to play at the World Cup play for two years leading up to the games to qualify.

Women's soccer became an Olympic sport in 1996. The U.S. team won the gold medal that year.

The World Cup is the most watched television event across the globe.

In Europe during the Middle Ages, inflated pig bladders were used as balls.

SOCCER IS KNOWN AS FOOTBALL in most other countries around the world.

A soccer field is officially called a pitch.

A pitch is 100 to 130 yards (90 to 120 m) long and between 50 and 100 yards (45 and 90 m) wide.

A professional soccer game is split into two 45-minute halves, making a game 90 minutes long.

With 16 goals to date, Germany's Miroslav Klose has the record for most World Cup goals.

Nearly 8 percent of American kids play soccer.

U.S. youth soccer has more than 3 million members between the ages of 5 and 19.

The Golden Ball is given to the best player of the FIFA World Cup tournament.

The Golden Boot is awarded to the top goal scorer of the FIFA World Cup tournament.

The Golden Glove is given to the best goalkeeper of the FIFA World Cup tournament.

The Golden Ball and Golden Boot were first given in 1982. The Golden Glove was first awarded in 1994.

The term *soccer* originated in England. It's a nickname for the word *association*.

Uruguay hosted the first ever World Cup tournament.

The United States set the record highest attendance at a World Cup.

Goals scored when a player butts the ball with their head are called headers.

Only six times has a country won the World Cup the year that it hosted the event.

The 1942 World Cup was canceled due to World War II.

The first live broadcast of a soccer match was in 1937.

On average, a soccer player runs about 7 miles (11 km) per match.

In 1974, Carlos Caszely of Chile was the first player to get a red card in a World Cup.

The largest soccer stadium in the world is in North Korea. It seats 114,000 people.

Goalkeepers are the only players on a soccer team who can touch the ball with their hands.

The first rubber soccer ball was invented in 1855.

Soccer balls used in games aired on TV are often black-and-white to be easily seen on the screen.

Lightning once struck and killed 11 members of the same soccer team.

The first international women's soccer competition took place between England and Scotland in 1881.

In 2007, FIFA first tested micro-chip technology to track the movement of a soccer ball relative to the goal to determine if a goal was actually scored.

Cristiano Ronaldo

The United States team celebrates winning the Women's World Cup for a record fourth time, 2019.

For the Win!

49 Totally Random Facts About ATHLETICS

The LA Dodgers baseball team was once Brooklyn, New York's baseball team. The team is named after the fabled ability of Brooklyn residents to "dodge" the city's streetcar system. • **Can of corn is the term for a fly ball that is easy to catch.** • In 1947, Jackie Robinson integrated professional baseball, becoming the first African American to play major league baseball. • **The record for longest single-season losing streak in basketball is tied between the Cleveland Cavaliers and the Philadelphia 76ers. Both teams had 26 losses in a row.** • Americans eat approximately 8 million pounds (3.6 million kg) of guacamole each Super Bowl Sunday. • **At every Major League Baseball game, "Take Me Out to the Ballgame" is played during the seventh inning.** • The average height of a National Basketball Association (NBA) player is 6 feet, 6 inches (198 cm). • **The average height of a Women's National Basketball Association (WNBA) player is about 6 feet (183 cm).** • NBA courts are made of maple wood, chosen for its strength and flexibility. • **With 27 wins, the Yankees have won the most World Series titles.** • In 2015, Mieko Nagaoka of Japan became the world's first centenarian (person in their 100s) to finish a 1,500-meter swimming race. She was 100 years old at the time. • **The longest game in NBA history took place on January 6, 1951, with six overtimes.** • The game with the most points in NBA history occurred on December 13, 1983. The score was 186 to 184. • **Harlem Globetrotter Ant Atkinson set the record for the longest successful basketball shot blindfolded at** 73 feet, 10 inches (22.5 m). • Eliud Kipchoge of Kenya ran the fastest marathon ever, completing the 26.2-mile (42-km) race in 2 hours, 1 minute, and 39 seconds. • **The NFL, or National Football League, began in 1920 as the American Professional Football Association.** • With her fifth winter Olympic medal win in 2022, bobsledder Elana Meyers Taylor became the most decorated Black Winter Olympian and the most decorated female bobsledder. • **Bobsledding was included in the very first Winter Olympics, held in Chamonix, France in 1924.** • The first NFL Super Bowl was played in January 15, 1967, between the Kansas City Chiefs and the Green Bay Packers. • **Instant replay, a segment of televised sports in which a notable or particularly exciting moment is replayed in slow motion, was introduced in the mid-1960s.** • The first string basketball nets came in the early 1900s. Before, peach baskets were used. • **On average, each NFL game has 67,254 in-person spectators.** • The Bears, the Browns, the Bills, the Giants, the Steelers, and the Packers are the only NFL teams that don't have cheerleaders. • **"Octopush" is a form**

ABOUT 70 BASEBALLS ARE USED IN AN AVERAGE BASEBALL GAME.

of underwater hockey. • The last NFL game to end with a score of 0-0 occurred in 1943. • **The oldest marathoner in the world is from Britain. At the age of 100, he ran a marathon in 8 hours, 25 minutes.** • Paul Hubbard, a deaf quarterback from Gallaudet University, invented the huddle so that he could more easily understand his teammates and prevent the opposing team from reading their

THE NORTH POLE MARATHON IS THE NORTHERNMOST MARATHON IN THE WORLD.

lips. • **The only team to play an entire season undefeated was the Miami Dolphins in 1972.** • On Super Bowl Sunday, Domino's Pizza delivers 11 million pizza slices. • **In the late 1800s, the term for running was *competitive walking*.** • Indian long-distance runner Budhia Singh is the world's youngest marathoner: He ran 48 marathons before the age of five. • **By the time someone has run 10 miles (16 km), their feet have touched the ground an average of 15,000 times.** • Boston's Fenway Park is the world's oldest baseball park. It opened in 1912. • **Chess boxing requires players to play four minutes of chess, then three minutes of boxing for 11 rounds.** • The Antarctic Ice Marathon is the world's southernmost marathon. • **Stefaan Engels, also known as the "Marathon Man," ran the distance of a marathon each day for a year, totaling 9,563 miles (15,390 km).** • The word *ski* came from the Norwegian word *skio*, which means "a piece of wood." • **Running is known to**

Zorbing

improve the immune system. • An Australian sport called crocodile bungee jumping is just that—bungee jumping over crocodile-inhabited waters. • **Yellow was chosen to make tennis balls easier to see on television. Originally, the balls were black or white.** • In the winter sport of curling, players wear a different type of shoe on each foot. One is the "slider" shoe, the other is a "gripper." • **The first baseball game played under electric lighting was in 1880 in Nantasket Bay, Massachusetts.** • The Cleveland Indians in 1929 were the first baseball team to wear numbers on the backs of their jerseys. • **Initially, the numbers on baseball players' jerseys were based on batting order.** • Badminton became an Olympic sport at the Games in Barcelona in 1992. • **When running, the force at which the foot touches the ground is between three and four times the runner's body weight.** • The sport of zorbing requires players to roll inside a large inflatable ball.

Catching a Wave

46 Totally Random Facts About *SURFING*

Surfari is the term used for surfers spending stretches of time exploring a coastline for surfing.

At Plymouth University in the United Kingdom, you can earn a degree in surf science and technology. This program prepares graduates for careers in the surf industry or related environmental companies with studies on surf culture, history, marketing, fitness, and environmental studies.

The invention of the wet suit allowed surfers to surf all year, even when the weather and water got colder.

Surfing is one of the world's most ancient sports. Five-thousand-year-old stone carvings of people surfing have been discovered in Peru.

Cymophobia is the fear of waves.

The term *surfing* in reference to browsing the web was first coined in 1992.

Three Hawaiian princes first introduced surfing to California in 1885.

Gary Saavedra of Panama holds the world record for longest continuous surf at 3 hours, 55 minutes.

The record for longest ride on a single wave occurred on the Amazon River and lasted for 37 minutes.

The term *channel surfing* in reference to browsing channels on a television was first coined in 1986.

Point break is the term for a wave crashing into land pointing out of the coastline.

A "barrel" is a wave that makes a tube shape in which a surfer travels through.

Kathy Kohner-Zuckerman is one of the world's first and most famous women surfers. She started surfing at the age of 15 in the 1950s.

The world record for the most surfboards on top of a car is 282.

The world record for the most people surfing on a single surfboard at once is 66.

In February 2020, Maya Gabeira of Brazil surfed a 73.5-foot (22.4-m) wave, making her the world record holder for the largest wave surfed by a woman. She broke her own previous record!

According to *Surfer* magazine, 66 percent of surfers think about sharks while they are surfing.

THE EISBACH RIVER IN DOWNTOWN MUNICH, GERMANY, IS ONE OF THE MOST POPULAR RIVER SURFING LOCATIONS IN THE WORLD.

Hawaiians surfing in the 19th century

Donald Dettloff is the world record holder for largest surfboard collection, with 647 surfboards to his name.

Linguists, people who study words, believe that the word *surf* originated from the coast of India.

Surfing was accepted as an Olympic sport in 2016 and debuted at the 2021 Summer Olympics in Tokyo, Japan.

There are four kinds of waves: rolling, dumping, surging, and standing. Surfers most often ride rolling and dumping waves.

Some surfers ride waves in Antarctica.

Tsurigasaki Beach near Tokyo, Japan, was the location of the first ever Olympic surfing competition.

Ancient surfboards were made of solid wood, making them very heavy.

Modern surfboards are made of fiberglass, a form of glass, and polyurethane, a form of plastic.

Hawaiian king Kamehameha was known to be a great surfer.

The part of surfing that requires the most technique and skill is standing up on the board just as the wave breaks.

A *Neptune cocktail* is the term for when surfers accidentally swallow ocean water when they wipe out.

Experienced surfers consider the shape of the shore and the depth of the water when surfing.

Skateboarding was invented as practice for surfing. Many surfers still practice their moves this way on land.

Hydrodynamics is a term that refers to the scientific study of the movement of water.

A strong wave is called a "swell." Swells are affected by wind patterns and storm systems.

Surfers are only able to surf waves that break, or "crash."

The annual Surf City Surf Dog competition, held in California, raises money to help animals.

Waves crash when the water under the surface can no longer support the height of the wave.

THE LARGEST WAVES IN THE WORLD ARE BELIEVED TO BE OFF THE COAST OF NAZARÉ, PORTUGAL. WAVES THERE CAN POTENTIALLY REACH 100 FEET (30 M) IN HEIGHT.

The largest wave ever surfed was 80 feet (24.4 m) tall in Nazaré, Portugal.

A river usually flows into the ocean, but when that flow reverses and ocean water flows into a river, it's called a tidal bore. Tidal bores create waves perfect for river surfing.

Shortboarding is a faster type of surfing in which the surfer is able to move at quicker speeds, but with more difficulty. Longboarding is a type of slower surfing on easier waves, making standing and balancing on the board easier.

The world's first surf competition occurred in Corona del Mar, California, in 1928.

The first international championship of surfing occurred in 1953 in Makaha, Hawaii, which saw the beginning of surfing as an international sport.

When surfing extreme waves, surfers sometimes need to be towed by boat or personal watercraft to get past the surf break.

The Hawaiian word for surfing is *he 'enalu*, meaning "wave sliding."

Surfers use wax on their boards to keep them from slipping off.

The famed tidal bore of China's Qiantang River, which only experienced surfers brave, is named the Silver Dragon.

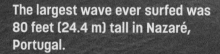

SPOT THE 13 RANDOM DIFFERENCES:

Turn to page 215 for the answers!

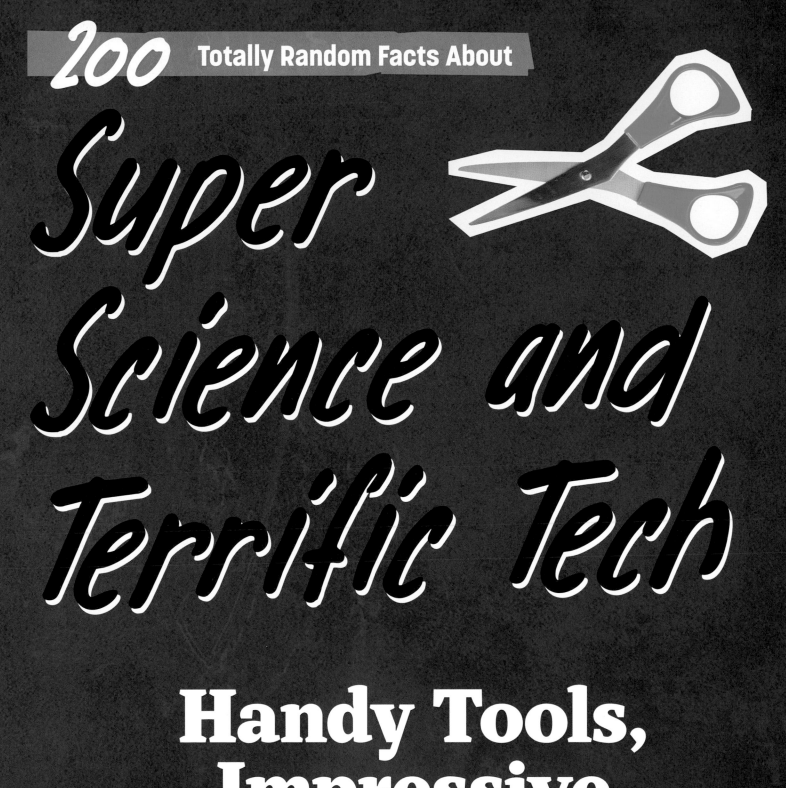

Super Science and Terrific Tech

Handy Tools, Impressive Inventions, and Things That Go

Human-Made

93 Totally Random Facts About TOOLS, INVENTIONS, and MACHINES

The short list of top inventions that changed the world includes the wheel, nail, compass, printing press, combustion engine (which powers things like cars and planes), telephone, and of course, the lightbulb.

When the fire engine was first invented in the late 1600s, it was originally called a "sucking worm."

Bullets were invented thousands of years before the gun. In the beginning, they were round, not pointed, and shot using slings.

The first forks were used in ancient Egypt, Greek, and Rome. Back then, they were two-tined and used just for cooking.

Computer scientist Alan Emtage invented the first ever search engine, called Archie, in 1990.

The U.S. Air Force created a supercomputer by combining 1,760 PlayStation 3 video game consoles.

Dr. Seuss tried to invent the Infantograph, which was supposed to predict what a couple's baby would look like, but it didn't work.

When the telephone was invented in 1876, people thought it ruined the craft of letter writing.

People were scared that the newly invented telephone would cause them to start hearing better with their left ear than their right ear (the left ear was most often used when making a call).

Air conditioners made it possible for warmer states such as Florida and Texas to be more easily inhabited year-round.

Umbrellas first appeared 4,000 YEARS AGO in ancient China.

The United States uses more energy to power its air conditioners than the continent of Africa uses for everything.

The world's oldest tool, a chipped stone, was discovered to be 3.3 million years old.

The first coin-operated vending machine was invented in ancient Egypt by a Greek engineer. It dispensed holy water.

Marvels

In the 1920s, American inventor **Earle Dickson created the Band-Aid because his wife was so accident-prone.**

An early type of scissors was used during the Bronze Age, around 1500 BC.

The Bronze Age was an era between 3300 to 1200 BC, when people first started to use metal instead of stone to make things such as tools.

Leonardo da Vinci created detailed concepts for various inventions, including predecessors to the tank, helicopter, diving suit, parachute, and plane.

The use of silk began thousands of years ago in China, where it was discovered that silk thread could be taken from the cocoon of a silkworm, then spun and woven.

The ancient Greeks played with hula hoops.

It's a myth that American politician Al Gore invented the internet.

The oldest known photograph was taken around 1826, and shows a window from the home of French photographer Joseph Niépce.

Hafting is the process of combining different elements or tools to make a better tool, such as a stone and a stick to make a spear.

Tools with blades connected to a handle are called hafted tools. They were invented around 500,000 years ago and led to the creation of more modern cutting tools.

Programing ENIAC (Electronic Numerical Integrator and Computer), 1945

The first computer was 1,800 square feet (167 sq m) and weighed 27 tons (24 metric tons), about the weight of **SEVEN LARGE ELEPHANTS.**

Chalk is made up of the shells of marine organisms.

Paper was invented in ancient China.

Matches were called "Lucifer matches" until 1830.

The microwave oven was invented by accident, when a scientist studying magnetrons (small tubes that generate radio waves called microwaves) noticed that a chocolate bar in his pocket had melted.

Archaeological evidence from South Africa shows that our human ancestors' earliest use of fire might have been about 1 million years ago.

An African American inventor named Garrett Morgan invented the three-light traffic signal in 1923.

Boomerangs were originally used thousands of years ago to scare prey into traps.

The first commercial microwave was 6 feet (1.8 m) tall and weighed 750 pounds (340 kg).

Screwdrivers have been used since the 15th century in France and Germany.

Some chain saws work underwater.

Archaeologists have found evidence that pottery wheels were used about 5,600 years ago— 300 years before wheels were used for chariots.

A chain saw's chain averages 60 miles an hour (97 kmh) while in use.

The ancient Sumerians of the eastern Mediterranean region used straws 5,000 years ago.

Early spoons were made of seashells attached to small sticks.

Stone knives have been used since the Stone Age, more than 2.5 million years ago.

During the Middle Ages, guests were expected to bring their own utensils to a meal.

China produces about 45 billion pairs of chopsticks every year.

Chopsticks first appeared in China about 5,000 years ago.

More people in the United States listen to the radio than watch TV.

In 1876, Alexander Graham Bell said the first words ever spoken into a telephone: "Mr. Watson—come here—I want to see you."

The first ever telephone directory was a one-page list of 50 people from New Haven, Connecticut.

Before people addressed the person on the other end of the phone with "hello," they greeted each other by saying "ahoy."

It took 10 hours for the first ever mobile phone to charge in 1983.

Before automatic switchboards were invented, people were hired to connect callers by hand on large switchboards.

When the inventor of the telephone, Alexander Graham Bell, died in 1922, all telephones stopped ringing for one minute to honor him.

Post-it notes were initially invented to be bookmarks that wouldn't tear the pages of books.

The Lightbulb—What a Bright Idea!

IN THE 1800S, SCIENTISTS STARTED EXPERIMENTING WITH INCANDESCENT LAMPS AS AN ALTERNATIVE TO CANDLELIGHT TO SEE AT NIGHT. After a fierce competition, Thomas Edison was the first to engineer a practical and inexpensive lightbulb in 1879. **His bulbs came with a complete system, including wiring and a generator to power them.** From that point on, people throughout the Western world started bringing electricity into their homes, **changing everything from how people worked, lived, and even slept.** These days, the LED bulb is considered the future of lighting. An international team of American and Japanese scientists in the early 1990s developed the blue LED bulb, which led to the development of the white LED bulb. **LED bulbs are less expensive, last longer than incandescent bulbs, and even require less energy to run, which is good for the environment.** No wonder our future is looking bright!

In 1910, telephones in New York had more than 6,000 female operators manning the switchboards.

Gunpowder was discovered by accident in ancient China, when early chemists were trying to make a potion.

A compass always point north because it's attracted to Earth's magnetic north pole.

Long before toothbrushes were invented, sticks with broken edges were used to brush teeth. They were called "chew sticks."

There are more **MOBILE PHONES** on Earth than people.

Tea bags were invented by accident in 1908, when a tea merchant in New York provided samples of tea in silk bags. Customers thought the bags themselves were meant to be dipped in the water, just like metal tea infusers.

Toothbrushes were first mass-produced in England in 1780. Toothbrushes weren't readily available in the United States until 1885.

In ancient China, compasses were originally used to tell the future.

The average pencil can write about 45,000 words.

The oldest known bow and arrow was made around 17,500 to 18,000 years ago in what is now modern-day Germany.

In 1802, before the invention of the lightbulb, British inventor Humphry Davy demonstrated how to create light when he passed electricity through a strip of platinum.

There are enough zippers made every year to circle the world 50 times.

Umbrella comes from the word *umbra*, meaning "shadow" or "shade" in Latin.

Umbrellas were originally used to protect people from sunlight, not rain.

In 1879, Thomas Edison invented the first commercially available lightbulb.

Gunpowder was originally used for FIREWORKS, not warfare.

Thomas Edison's lightbulbs could last 1,200 hours.

Safety glass was discovered when a scientist accidentally knocked over a glass flask and discovered that the residue of a chemical called cellulose nitrate that was once inside made the glass much more durable—instead of breaking into pieces, the flask cracked but didn't shatter.

More than 90 percent of the currency, or money, on Earth is digital.

The average pencil can be sharpened 17 times and still be usable.

When compasses started

being used for navigation, the compass was made up of a magnetic needle placed in a bowl of water where it could rotate freely.

Before being available to the average person, radios were used to communicate with ships at sea.

The computer mouse was invented in 1964, and was originally made of wood.

Pencils don't actually have any lead in them any longer. Pencil "lead" is now a mixture of graphite and clay.

Born in 1815, a British woman named Ada Lovelace was the first computer programmer.

In 1892, Sarah Boone, a woman who was born into slavery, became the inventor of an improved ironing board. At the time, garments were ironed on long wooden blocks. Boone created a sleek, curved design, which evolved into today's ironing boards.

Bowstrings were originally made from processed animal guts.

The smallest camera ever made is the size of one grain of sand.

In 1936, Russians invented a computer that ran using water.

The quill, which is a pen made from a feather, has been used since AD 700.

The space pen was a pen invented to work in space and underwater.

People tend to blink less when using a computer.

When cameras were first made in the 1820s, it took hours to take a single photo.

In 1761, Benjamin Franklin invented a musical instrument called the glass armonica, which used spinning glass and water to make sound.

Telescopes were invented in the Netherlands in 1608, after an eyeglass maker noticed that an image was magnified when he put two lenses in front of each other.

The biggest chain saw ever was 22 feet 11 inches (6.9 m) long and 6 feet (1.8 m) tall. It was named "Big Gus."

The average ballpoint pen has enough ink to draw a straight line 2 miles (3 km) long.

Walter Hunt invented the safety pin as a way to make money to pay off a $15.00 debt.

The stapler was first used by King Louis XV of France in the 18th century.

Hand axes have been used to break the bones of dead animals, dig for roots and insects, and cut wood.

In 2015, archaeologists in Kenya discovered stone tools that dated to more than 3 million years ago. They are the oldest tools used by early humans discovered so far.

PANDA POOP has been used to make tissue and toilet paper.

Let's Go!

107 Totally Random Facts About TRANSPORTATION

There were hot-air balloons in China as far back as AD 220 to 280. • **In 1930, two men drove their car in reverse all the way from New York to California—and back!** • A potter in the Middle East first invented the wheel about 5,600 years ago. • **In 1927, Charles Lindbergh became the first person to ever fly solo and nonstop across the Atlantic Ocean.** • The RMS *Titanic*, a luxury passenger ship that sank in 1912, remains 12,600 feet (3,840 m) under the ocean. • **A typical 747 airplane has more than 150 miles (241 km) of electrical wiring.** • The first submarine was built in 1620. • **The** farthest anyone has ever skateboarded is 7,555 miles (12,159 km), riding from Switzerland to Shanghai, China, in 2008. • There are hot-air balloons that look like Darth Vader, SpongeBob, Snoopy, and Shrek. • **In the United States, about 15.7 million trucks transport 70 percent of all freight around the country. If you lined up all those trucks end to end, they would reach the moon.** • The first ever boats were dugout canoes built in 8000 BC. • **The only living creatures capable of continuous flight are bats, birds, and insects.** • People who take public transportation reduce their chance of being in an accident by 90 percent

THE WORLD RECORD FOR THE LARGEST CARGO AIRPLANE TODAY GOES TO THE ANTONOV AN-225 CARGO JET, WHICH IS CAPABLE OF CARRYING 280 TONS (250 METRIC TONS)—THAT'S ABOUT 56 ELEPHANTS!

compared to driving a car. • **A German baron invented the bicycle in 1817.** • The U.S. military is working on special suits that would enable soldiers to fly. • **There are more than 45,000 helicopters in the world today.** • In the 1920s and 1930s, airships four times as long as today's jumbo jets took wealthy passengers for joy rides. • **Orville and Wilbur Wright designed and flew the first successful airplane in 1903.** • There are about 1 billion bicycles worldwide. • **The steel that makes up the Sydney Harbour Bridge in Australia can expand or contract up to 7 inches (18 cm) depending on the weather.** • In 1911, American aviator and writer Harriet Quimby became the first woman to receive a pilot's license. • **A type of iron-eating bacteria is eating away at the remains of the** *Titanic* **and will eventually eat the entire ship.** • Helicopters are also called whirlybirds, choppers, copters, and helos. • **According to statistics, airplane travel is safer than ground travel.** • The first trains were pulled along the tracks by horses. • **Leonardo da Vinci envisioned that people would fly 500 years before planes were invented.** • The Canadian National Railway has some of the world's longest trains at more than 2.5 miles (4 km) in length. • **The longest freight train ever was more than 4.5 miles (7.2 km)**

Richard Browning, founder of Gravity Industries, takes flight in his body-controlled jet-powered suit, Salisbury, UK.

long and traveled 171 miles (275 km) carrying iron ore through a part of Western Australia. • One of the most famous bridges in the world is the Golden Gate Bridge in San Francisco, California. The bridge is 8,981 feet (2,737 m) long and is held aloft by 80,000 miles (128,748 km) of cable wire. • **The first hot air balloon flight carrying a human lasted 20 minutes and took place in 1783.** • Some military planes can break the sound barrier, which is 768 miles an hour (1,236 kmh). • **Hot air balloons have been used to spy on enemies during wars.** • Train wheels only make contact with the rail in an area about the size of a silver dollar. • **In the United States, more cruise ships depart from**

Florida than from any other state. • Some submarines can spend months underwater. • **Leonardo da Vinci drew designs of a helicopter that he called the "Aerial Screw."** • Submarines were built and used during the American Civil War. • **The highest a hot-air balloon has ever flown is 68,900 feet (21,000 m).** • Helicopters are capable of vertical takeoffs and landings, and can hover, which allows them to reach difficult locations for emergencies. • **In 2020, U.S. households spent $9,826 on average on transportation.** • The railway system helped the North defeat the South during the American Civil War by transporting soldiers and weapons. • **When the *Titanic* set sail, it was going from Southampton, England, to New York City.** • The first passengers on a hot-air balloon flight were a duck, a rooster, and a sheep. • **Some trains can reach speeds of about 342 miles an hour (550 kmh).** • Because altitude causes dehydration, the average person loses 1.5 quarts (1.4 L) of water during a three-hour flight. • **In the 1990s, the U.S. military experimented with using skateboards for soldiers to get around.** • The longest train platform in the world is 4,938 feet (1,505 m) long and is located in the state of Karnataka, India. That's more

MOST CARS IN THE UNITED STATES HONK IN THE MUSICAL KEY OF F.

AT THE TIME OF ITS FIRST VOYAGE IN 1912, THE *TITANIC* WAS ONE OF THE LARGEST SHIPS IN THE WORLD AT MORE THAN 882 FEET (269 M) LONG AND 92 FEET (28 M) WIDE.

than the length of 14 American football fields. • **The Japanese SCMaglev train moves on a magnetic track. It holds the world record for the highest speed at 375 miles an hour (604 kmh).** • The world's largest cruise ship, Royal Caribbean's *Wonder of the Seas*, has a zip line, an ice-skating rink, a 92-foot (28-m) waterslide, and 24 swimming pools. It's about twice as long as two Washington Monuments placed end to end. • **Compared to traveling by car, traveling by public transportation is 10 times safer per mile.** • The world record for the largest passenger plane goes to the Airbus A380, which seats 532 people. • **About 50,000 people live full-time on houseboats in the United States.**

• The world's biggest helicopter was first flown in 1968 and could hold 196 people. • **The world's oldest bridge that is still in use was built in Turkey in 850 BC.** • In the United States, people took about 9.9 billion trips on public transportation in 2019. • **The longest tandem bike ever invented was 67 feet (20 m) long and could hold 35 riders.** • One of the busiest bridges in the world is the double-decker

Cruise ships in the Port of Miami, one of the busiest ports in the United States

INDEPENDENCE OF THE SEAS
NASSAU

George Washington Bridge, which connects New Jersey to New York City. • **Helicopters can help fight forest fires by dropping giant buckets of water on them.** • The Tour de France is the most famous bicycle race in the world. • **Over five centuries ago, the Inca civilization in South America used rope bridges in the Andes Mountains to cross canyons and gorges.** • Trains transport about 40 percent of the world's cargo. • **Water tanks on submarines fill and empty to submerge into and surface out of the water.** • The world record for the heaviest train is 95,000 tons (84,821 metric tons), which is about the same as 27,000 elephants. • **Planes can land themselves.** • Crews on a cruise ship speak in code to communicate with one another. For example, Bravo means "fire" and Alpha means "medical emergency." • **Americans board public transportation about 34 million times during the Monday to Friday workweek.** • In 1808, a duel in Paris took place in opposing hot-air balloons. • **The world record for longest paper airplane flight is 29.2 seconds.** • The first bicycle was called a "hobby horse" because it was made to replace the horse pulling a carriage. • **The longest hot-air balloon ride on record flew from Japan to Canada. It flew the 6,700-mile (10,783-km) trip at 245 miles an hour (394 kmh).** • Helicopters are often used to take photographs and videos from above. • **The Akashi Kaikyo Bridge in Kobe, Japan, is the longest suspension bridge in the world. It opened in 1998 and spans 6,529 feet (1,990 m).**

MODERN SKATEBOARDS WITH KICKTAILS (THE UPWARD BENDS ON EACH END) WERE INVENTED IN 1963.

• The U.S. president's plane, Air Force One, has a facility that can be used as an operating room. • **The first nuclear submarine, the USS *Nautilus*, was launched in 1954.** • Western Airlines, an airline service that began operating in the western United States in the 1920s, had its first passenger flight in 1926. The flight from Salt Lake City to Los Angeles cost $90 one way and took eight hours! • **In 1932, Amelia Earhart was the first woman to pilot a plane solo and nonstop across the Atlantic Ocean.** • Sled dogs have been used for transport for hundreds of years. • **You can build your own airplane from a kit that costs about $25,000.** • There were no restrictions of style, material, or color on the first car license plates in 1901: Some were made out of cardboard. • **There's a solar-powered airplane that can fly for 24 hours straight.** • Early submarines used steam, gas, and even muscle power. Today, nuclear-powered submarines are the fastest type and can stay

THE BICYCLE IS THE MOST ENERGY-EFFICIENT MODE OF TRANSPORTATION EVER INVENTED.

underwater the longest. • **Hot-air balloons cannot be used in the rain.** • **Helicopters use the same mechanisms as bees to lift off.** • On some cruise ships, the interior rooms have virtual views of the outside. • **There's a car that can run on wood chips.** • Some submarines can carry 100 people. • **The average commuter spends about 54 hours per year in traffic jams.** • Public transportation saves the United States 6 billion gallons (23 billion L) of gasoline every year. • **Cars, trucks, buses, and airplanes are some of the largest contributors to greenhouse gases, which contribute to global warming.** • Both horses and donkeys were tamed and used for transportation in 3000 BC. • **Donkeys are the oldest known pack animals—used to help transport heavy packs from one place to another.** • The world's smallest jet aircraft, the BD-5 Micro, only weighed 358 pounds (162 kg), and was in a James Bond movie. • *Bus* comes from the word *omnibus*, which means "for all."** • The first president to ride a train was Andrew Jackson in 1833. • **The very first form of transport was walking.** • Skateboarding became an Olympic sport in 2021.

Shanghai Transrapid Maglev magnetic levitation train station in Shanghai, China

The Big Yellow Bus

- The world's first school buses were horse-drawn carriages, which were first used in 1886.

- **There are 427,000 school buses in the United States.**

- School buses transport 26 million students daily in the United States.

- **A man in Indiana designed a jet-fueled school bus that zooms 367 miles an hour (590 kmh) and shoots 80-foot (24-m) flames from the back.**

- School buses are 70 times safer than any other vehicle.

- **School bus seats don't have seat belts because they were designed to be safe without them, sort of like an egg carton cushioning an egg.**

360 Totally Random Facts About

Into the Ocean

Coral Reefs, Cool Creatures, and More about the Deep Blue Sea

A scuba diver investigates the propeller of a sunken battleship.

THERE ARE AT LEAST A MILLION SHIPWRECKS STILL MOSTLY INTACT ON THE SEAFLOOR.

Rolling in the Deep

107 Totally Random Facts About the OCEAN

The average depth of the ocean is more than nine times as tall as the Empire State Building.

More is known about the surface of the moon than the bottom of the ocean.

More than 5 million microscopic organisms live in one teaspoon of saltwater.

The area between 656 feet (200 m) and 3,280 feet (1,000 m) below the surface of the open ocean is known as the twilight zone because sunlight begins to fade due to its depth.

Noise from large ships can damage invertebrates such as jellyfish and anemones.

The Mid-Atlantic Ridge is the longest mountain range on Earth, and it is under the Atlantic Ocean.

A tsunami is a series of gigantic waves caused by an event such as a volcanic eruption or earthquake.

A tsunami in the open ocean can move as fast as a jet plane.

Benthos is the name given to categorize living things that live on the ocean floor. These include sea grasses, coral reefs, and other marine ecosystems.

More than 99 percent of Earth's inhabitable space is in the open ocean.

The biggest wave was created by a tsunami that occurred in the Gulf of Alaska in 1958. It was 1,720 feet (524 m) above sea level.

The Dead Sea is almost 10 times saltier than the water in the ocean.

Earth gets about half of its oxygen from the ocean.

The ocean has absorbed more than 25 percent of the carbon dioxide created by humans in the last two centuries.

About 94 percent of all the water in oceans gets zero sunlight.

With nowhere to hide in the deep open ocean, some animals have evolved to be almost completely transparent.

Saltwater covers 71 percent of Earth's surface.

In the ocean, more than 95 percent of animals are invertebrates.

About 97 percent of all the water on Earth is saltwater.

Sound travels almost five times faster underwater than it does in air.

Anemone

THE OPEN OCEAN HAS FIVE LAYERS: THE EPIPELAGIC ZONE, THE MESOPELAGIC ZONE, THE BATHYPELAGIC ZONE, THE ABYSSOPELAGIC ZONE, AND THE HADOPELAGIC ZONE.

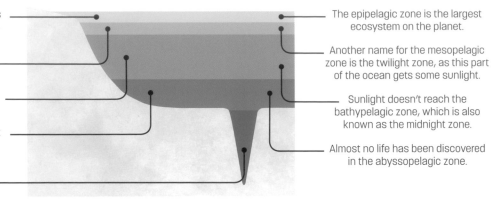

The epipelagic zone begins at the surface and goes to 650 feet (198 m) deep. Sunlight is prevalent here, so it's also called the sunlight zone.

The mesopelagic zone stretches from 650 feet (198 m) to 3,300 feet (1,006 m) deep.

The bathypelagic zone stretches from 3,300 feet (1,006 m) to 13,000 feet (3,962 m) deep.

The abyssopelagic zone stretches from 13,000 feet (3,962 m) deep to the seafloor. It's also called the abyss.

Hadopelagic zones are areas where massive trenches are present on the seafloor.

The epipelagic zone is the largest ecosystem on the planet.

Another name for the mesopelagic zone is the twilight zone, as this part of the ocean gets some sunlight.

Sunlight doesn't reach the bathypelagic zone, which is also known as the midnight zone.

Almost no life has been discovered in the abyssopelagic zone.

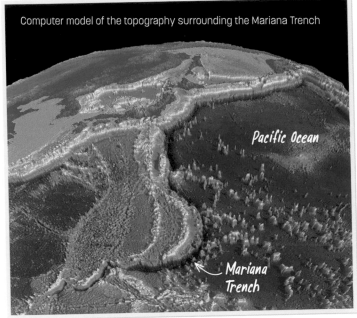

Computer model of the topography surrounding the Mariana Trench

Pacific Ocean

Mariana Trench

The Mariana Trench is almost 7 miles (11 km) deep. It is home to Challenger Deep.

Challenger Deep, the lowest point on Earth, is more than 36,200 feet (11,034 m) under the ocean's surface. That's deeper than Mount Everest is tall!

The pressure at the bottom of the ocean is about 500 times more than the air pressure at sea level.

Tsunamis can be caused by undersea volcanoes, landslides, and earthquakes.

Climate change has caused Earth's sea level to rise 4 to 10 inches (10 to 25 cm) in the last 100 years, and it is expected to continue rising.

Life originated in the ocean 3.4 to 3.8 billion years ago.

Of all life on Earth, 50 to 80 percent is estimated to live beneath the ocean's surface.

As of 2021, scientists have discovered at least 236,878 ocean-dwelling species.

It's estimated that there are 1 to 20 million ocean species undiscovered or incorrectly classified.

Seawater gets denser as it gets colder.

The largest current on Earth is the Antarctic Circumpolar Current. It is the only ocean current that completely circles the planet.

The Southern Ocean surrounds the South Pole. It is Earth's fourth largest ocean.

Around 75 percent of the world's volcanoes are underwater.

About 99 percent of all international communications are routed through underwater cables.

The open ocean refers to areas where sea life is far away from any shorelines.

Some of the smallest and largest animals to have ever lived exist in the ocean: These include the world's largest animal ever, the blue whale, and the teeny 1-inch (2.5-cm) pygmy seahorse.

Blue whale

An estuary is an area where a river and ocean meet, combining saltwater with freshwater.

The ocean is full of salt because the carbon dioxide in rainwater slowly dissolves rocks, which releases mineral salts into the water.

All of the world's oceans are actually connected in one massive body of saltwater.

The surface of the Pacific Ocean has less salt in it than the surface of the Atlantic Ocean.

A sea is a smaller section of an ocean and normally has landmasses on several sides.

People can float more easily in the Dead Sea because of how salty it is.

Earth's tides are created and controlled by the gravitational pull of the sun and moon.

The Arctic Ocean is the smallest of Earth's oceans. It's also the shallowest.

The ocean moves heat around the planet, preventing any part from becoming too hot or too cold.

Where freshwater and saltwater meet, the mix of water is known as brackish.

Intertidal zones are places where the ocean meets land.

A hurricane is formed from the combination of warm ocean water and powerful thunderstorms.

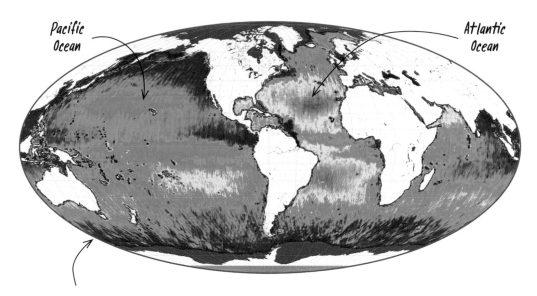

Pacific Ocean

Atlantic Ocean

Satellite imagery of global sea surface salinity (red is high salinity, blue is low salinity)

Gyres are systems of rotating ocean currents.

The global ocean conveyor belt is a constantly moving system of deep-ocean currents caused by changing temperatures and salt.

About 80 percent of all tsunamis take place in a region called the Ring of Fire in the Pacific Ocean.

Earth is the only planet in our solar system with oceans on its surface.

Some scientists think that there is an ocean beneath the icy outer layer of Jupiter's moon Europa.

The Southern Ocean is made up of the waters around Antarctica. It's also known as the Antarctic Ocean.

The Indian Ocean is home to an underwater plateau, an area of high, flat land. It is known as the Kerguelen Plateau.

The Kerguelen Plateau is larger than the state of California and might have once been covered wtih trees.

The tallest wave to hit land in history was at its peak taller than the Empire State Building.

Most of the Arctic Ocean is covered in sea ice.

THERE ARE ABOUT 25,000 ISLANDS IN THE PACIFIC OCEAN.

Icebergs off the coast of Greenland

In the ocean off Greenland, there's 5.4 million square miles (14,000,000 sq km) of sea ice—that's larger than the continental United States.

Some animals that live in the pitch-black parts of the ocean evolved bioluminescence. They glow in the dark to either attract mates or lure in prey.

Hydrothermal vents, which are located on the seafloor, are the result of tectonic plates moving around.

Hydrothermal vents pump out hot, toxic chemicals.

Mid-ocean ridges are the result of tectonic plates moving away from one another.

There are lakes and rivers deep underwater made from dissolving salt.

Each year, 10 to 50,000 icebergs are formed in the Arctic.

The biggest waterfall in the world, the Denmark Strait cataract, is underwater. Here, cold, dense water sinks under warmer water. Then, the water goes over a deep drop.

Ships on the ocean transport more than 90 percent of international trade.

The Denmark Strait cataract is 11,500 feet (3,505 m) deep.

Tsunami waves can reach higher than 100 feet (30 m).

An estimated 80 percent of the ocean remains unexplored and uncharted.

It takes about 1,000 years for water to make a complete trip around the ocean's conveyor belt.

ALMOST A THIRD OF THE WORLD'S OIL IS DRILLED FROM OIL FIELDS UNDER THE OCEANS.

Ahoy *Plastiki!*

AN ENVIRONMENTALIST NAMED DAVID DE ROTHSCHILD CAME UP WITH A CRAZY IDEA: What would happen if he made a boat entirely out of garbage and sailed it across the sea? In 2010, that's exactly what he did, skippering his self-made ship *Plastiki* from San Francisco, California, all the way to Sydney, Australia. This 8,000-mile (12,875-km) journey was quite an amazing feat considering **his boat was constructed from 12,500 plastic bottles attached by cashew-nut glue.** De Rothschild was out to prove the point that everyday items we throw away can be repurposed into something else spectacularly useful. Plus, there was a method to his madness: **De Rothschild wanted to call attention to the mountains of plastic trash floating around in our oceans.** In one area called the Great Pacific Garbage Patch, there's a collection of trash twice the size of Texas! **Here, unfortunately, plastic is more plentiful than kelp. Just think about how many boats that could make.**

The Pacific Ocean holds close to half of all water in the oceans.

Nutrient-rich sediment from dead plants and animals settles at the bottom of the ocean.

Saltwater freezes at about 28.4° F (–2° C).

Overfishing and global warming are some of the biggest threats to sea life.

Coral reefs make up 1 percent of the ocean but are home to nearly 25 percent of ocean species.

The Pacific Ocean is larger than all the landmasses on Earth put together.

The ocean is blue because water absorbs red light, leaving only the color blue visible to the human eye.

At least 15 percent of the ocean is covered by ice at some point during a year.

Hurricanes form over the ocean. Depending on where they occur, they have different names.

The biggest ocean waves are beneath the surface.

The ocean absorbs heat during the summer and releases it during the winter, regulating Earth's temperature.

In the Atlantic or eastern Pacific Oceans, tropical storms are called hurricanes. In the Indian and South Pacific Oceans, they are called cyclones. And in the western North Pacific, they are called typhoons.

The ocean has more than 22.4 million tons (20 million metric tons) of gold in it.

Because light can only get through about 650 feet (200 m) of water, and the ocean covers most of Earth, the majority of our planet is actually dark.

One of the loudest sounds ever recorded was from an icequake in the ocean. Scientists nicknamed the sound "The Bloop."

An icequake is a cracking iceberg breaking away from a glacier.

The Arctic Ocean is home to six species of seals.

The Pacific Ocean is wider than the moon.

More than 5.25 trillion pieces of plastic are floating in the ocean right now.

Around 40 percent of people live within 62 miles (100 km) of a coastline.

Scientists are able to predict when tsunamis will occur partly by studying the start time of a triggering earthquake.

Many scientists believe the ocean was formed billions of years ago by the releasing of water vapor and other gases from Earth's molten inner layers.

Water released from hydrothermal vents can blast water that's a scorching 750° F (400° C).

Gentle Giants

49 Totally Random Facts About WHALE SHARKS

A whale shark can grow to be 66 feet (20 m) long, which is longer than a full-size school bus. • **A whale shark's mouth can open up to 4 feet (1.2 m) wide.** • About 1,585 gallons (6,000 L) of water go through a whale shark's gills every hour. • **Shrimp, tiny fish, fish eggs, and plankton make up a whale shark's diet.** • Whale sharks can live up to 150 years old. • **Whale sharks aren't very fast swimmers. They glide through the water at 3 miles an hour (5 kmh).** • Whale sharks migrate thousands of miles every year to find new feeding grounds. • **Like catfish, whale sharks have small,**

WHALE SHARKS CANNOT BITE OR CHEW.

whisker-like sensors around their nostrils. • Each whale shark has a unique set of spot patterns on its backs. • **A whale shark will wait up to 14 hours to swoop in to eat fish eggs.** • A female whale shark can carry up to 300 babies at one time. • **Baby whale sharks reach maturity at 25 years old.** • Unlike most sharks, which have mouths located beneath their heads, a whale shark's mouth is at the front

of its head. • **A fully grown whale shark weighs about 40,000 pounds (18,143 kg).** • A whale shark's mouth has around 3,000 tiny teeth. • **A newborn whale shark is only 20 inches (51 cm) long.** • The whale shark is one of only three species of sharks that are filter feeders, sifting food from water they take in. • **To feed, a whale shark gulps gallons of water and then expels it through its gills to trap the plankton that it eats.** • Whale sharks are found in temperate and tropical waters worldwide, except for the Mediterranean Sea. • **Only 10 percent of whale sharks live to be adults.** • The whale shark gives birth to more babies than any other species of shark. This might be to increase the chance of their survival because many don't make it to adulthood. • **Many different species of fish swim close to whale sharks for protection from predators.** • Orcas and species of large predatory sharks are the main natural predators of young whale sharks that haven't reached adult size. • **Like other shark species, whale sharks are threatened by overfishing.** • Whale sharks make cough-like movements to clean out the filter pads in their mouths. • **A whale shark's mouth has between 300 and 350 rows of teeth.** • Whale sharks can dive more than 5,500 feet (1,700 m) below the surface. • **Young whale sharks in the wild have been observed playing with divers.** • Like other large filter feeders, whale sharks swim with their mouths wide open for plankton to float

THE WHALE SHARK IS NOT A WHALE AT ALL. IT'S A SHARK, AND THE WORLD'S LARGEST FISH.

Teeth ↗

• A whale shark has one nostril located on each end on its wide upper jaw. • **Using their strong sense of smell, whale sharks can determine how much plankton is in an area.** • Compared to other shark species, the whale shark has a proportionally smaller brain for its overall body size. • **Around 30 percent of the whale shark's brain is made up of the cerebellum (the part of the brain that controls motor coordination). This helps with migration and catching plankton.** • The ancestors of present-day whale sharks first appeared between 245 to 65 million years ago, during the Jurassic and Cretaceous periods. • **A whale shark's teeth are teeny, less than 0.2 inch (5 mm) long.** • Whale sharks were first discovered along the coast of South Africa in 1828. • **A whale shark's eye is only the size of a golf ball.** • Scientists are not sure of the purpose of the whale shark's spots. Some think it's a leftover trait from their bottom-feeding ancestors. Others think the spots protect whale sharks from ultraviolet radiation, could serve as camouflage, or might help the sharks recognize one another. • **The dorsal (back) fin of the whale shark can grow to be 4.9 feet (1.5 m) tall.** • A layer of mucus on the whale shark's body protects it from bacteria. Human touch can easily damage this mucus layer. • **Despite the massive size of the whale shark's mouth, its throat is only as wide as a quarter.**

in. Then they snap their mouths shut to trap their prey. • **Most of the time whale sharks live solitary lives, but they have been observed swimming in schools with hundreds of other whale sharks.** • Whale sharks evolved from small, bottom-feeding carpet sharks that swam along seafloors. • **A whale shark's skin is 4 inches (10 cm) thick and feels like strong rubber, making it very resilient to bites from predators.** • Whale sharks can often be found in shallow waters near the shore during seasonal plankton blooms (when plankton populations concentrate in certain areas to eat microscopic plants). • **Before whale shark pups are born, the mother produces a hard egg casing around each in her abdomen so that the pups are protected until fully developed.** • Unlike many other fish species, young whale sharks hatch inside the mother instead of in the water. • **Because whale sharks have small eyes compared to the size of their bodies, many scientists think these sharks might have poor eyesight and instead navigate primarily using their sense of smell.**

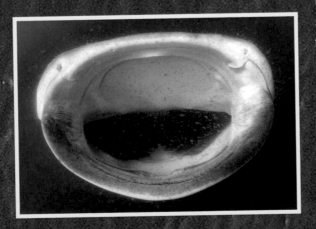

Rain Forest of the Sea

The Great Barrier Reef seen from space

AUSTRALIA 45c
Flatback Turtle

58 Totally Random Facts About the *GREAT BARRIER REEF*

The Great Barrier Reef is on the northeastern coast of Australia.

More than 900 islands make up the reef system.

The Great Barrier Reef is bigger than the Great Wall of China.

Visitors to the Great Barrier Reef bring in more than $6.4 billion in tourism revenue each year.

The Great Barrier Reef was dubbed one of the seven wonders of the natural world.

About 600 different species of coral make up the Great Barrier Reef.

The Great Barrier Reef is the only living thing that can be seen from space or such a far distance.

The reef is the largest living structure in the world.

The Great Barrier Reef includes about 3,000 reef systems and coral cays.

The average depths of the inner reef reach about 114 feet (35 m) below the surface.

There are about 150 mangrove islands in the Great Barrier Reef.

The deepest parts of the outer reef can reach around 6,561 feet (2,000 m) below the surface.

The Great Barrier Reef is larger than the country of Italy.

Sea turtles lay their eggs on the islands within the Great Barrier Reef.

More than 100 different species of jellyfish make their home in the reef.

Mangrove island

The Great Barrier Reef is home to about 215 different species of birds, including shorebirds and seabirds that nest in the area.

Corals spawn only once a year, usually during a full moon.

The world's smallest fish, the stout infantfish, and the world's largest fish, the whale shark, can both be found in the Great Barrier Reef.

The area that makes up the reef can hold up to 70 million football fields.

Some of the most venomous animals on Earth, including the box jellyfish and the blue-ringed octopus, live in the Great Barrier Reef.

The reef is at great risk of dying because of our warming climate and pollution.

The massive natural structure of the Great Barrier Reef is made of coral stuck together with algae.

The modern form of the reef is about 8,000 years old. Some of the coral in the reef is more than 500,000 years old.

About 30 different species of whales and dolphins live in the Great Barrier Reef.

Six out of seven species of sea turtle live in the Great Barrier Reef.

It is one of the most diverse ecosystems on the planet.

About 17 different species of sea snakes live in the Great Barrier Reef.

The temperature of the reef's surface water can reach 86 °F (30 °C)

Sea grasses found in reefs around the world provide safe hiding places for young animals such as crustaceans and fish.

Clown fish that live in tropical reefs rely on anemones to survive. The anemones provide food and protect them from predators.

More than 10,000 whales, including humpback and dwarf minke whales, migrate to the Great Barrier Reef each year from June to November to breed and give birth.

ABOUT 10 PERCENT of Earth's fish species live in the Great Barrier Reef.

Much of the sand in the Great Barrier Reef comes from parrot fish poop. These fish take in coral while scraping off algae to eat. They grind up the coral in their mouths and it comes out as sand.

The tallest points of the Great Barrier Reef are about 1,640 feet (500 m) high, which is taller than the Eiffel Tower.

Crustaceans in the Great Barrier Reef are on average less than 1 millimeter long.

About 50 percent of the coral in the Great Barrier Reef has been lost to climate change and pollution.

About 20,000 years ago the area that is now the Great Barrier Reef was aboveground and covered with forest.

"Stinger season" is a period of time from mid-October to May in when hordes of jellyfish migrate to the reef for the warm waters.

There are two types of coral in the ocean: soft and hard. Both are abundant in the Great Barrier Reef. They are identified partly by their texture and number of tentacles.

Soft coral attracts marine algae, which act as a major food source for herbivorous animals in the reef.

The most abundant hard coral in the Great Barrier Reef is the staghorn variety. This coral also becomes home to various marine animals.

More than 4,000 different species of mollusks live in the Great Barrier Reef.

Staghorn coral

Giant clam

The Great Barrier Reef is home to about 133 different species of sharks and rays.

Scientists believe that tourists only explore 10 percent of the Great Barrier Reef, leaving 90 percent of it untouched.

One of the biggest threats to the Great Barrier Reef is coral bleaching, which is when coral expels the algae in its body, putting the coral at risk of starvation and disease.

More than 2 million tourists visit the Great Barrier Reef every year.

The Great Barrier Reef became a protected marine park in 1975.

In 1981, the Great Barrier Reef was declared a World Heritage area because of its unique biodiversity and the important role it plays in the ecosystem.

The Great Barrier Reef as a whole is made up of different kinds of reefs, such as crescentic reefs, which are are crescent-shaped; planar reefs, which are flat; and ribbon reefs, which are winding like ribbons.

Outbreaks of the crown-of-thorn starfish, which eats coral, are another major threat to the Great Barrier Reef.

Dugongs, close relatives of manatees, **FEED ON SEA GRASS** that grows in the reef.

Large marine snails called giant tritons are predators of crown-of-thorns starfish. They have been bred and are being studied to see if they can stop the starfish from destroying more of the reef.

Corals only make up about 7 percent of the Great Barrier Reef. The reef has many other habitats in the reef, including sea sponge gardens and areas of sea grass.

Scientists think the Great Barrier Reef formed on top of another reef that dates back about 18,000 years.

Crescentic reefs are the most common type of reef in the Great Barrier Reef.

Within the Great Barrier Reef are the "ribbon reefs," 10 individual coral reefs that run 75 miles (120 km) long.

The Great Barrier Reef can be seen from the moon with the naked eye.

Crocodiles are occasionally found in the Great Barrier Reef.

Crown-of-thorns starfish

A Fin-tastic Fish

46 Totally Random Facts About SEAHORSES

Seahorses are actually fish. They are named for the shape of their heads.

The fin on a seahorse's back can beat 50 times per second.

Seahorses use their tails to anchor themselves to plants to eat and rest.

Some seahorses travel long distances by holding onto floating vegetation.

Seahorses don't have stomachs—their digestive tracts work so quickly that they don't need one!

A seahorse can inhale prey up to 1.1 inches (2.8 cm) away.

Seahorses eat up to 3,000 tiny crustaceans a day.

The pygmy seahorse is smaller than a postage stamp.

Seahorse mating rituals involve intertwining tails, dancing, and changing colors.

A seahorse can look in two different directions at once.

The body part that male seahorses carry their eggs in is called a brood pouch.

Some species of seahorses can give birth to about 2,000 babies at once.

Seahorses have small fins on the sides of their heads that they use for steering.

Male seahorses release their babies from their brood pouches a week after they hatch.

Unlike most other animal species, male seahorses give birth **INSTEAD OF FEMALES.**

Seahorses move up and down by adjusting the amount of air in their swim bladder.

Unlike many other seahorse species, the pot-bellied seahorse is a skilled swimmer and can travel hundreds of meters in one day.

Because of the seahorse's color-changing ability, scientists used to think there were about 200 species of seahorses.

Seahorses can only move a maximum speed of 5 feet (1.5 m) per hour.

The big-bellied seahorse is the largest species of seahorse—it's about the size of a banana.

Satomi's pygmy seahorse is the smallest seahorse species. It grows to be a little more than half an inch long (13 mm).

Seahorses strengthen their bonds with their mates by having daily greeting rituals.

The average seahorse can live to be around five years old.

The Bargibant's pygmy seahorse is covered in bright bumps to better **CAMOUFLAGE AMONG GORGONIAN CORAL.**

Most seahorses live in areas with a lot of marine plant life. Mangrove forests and sea grass beds offer shelter and food.

Seahorses are ambush predators.

When seahorses eat and are trying to attract a mate, they make noises that sound like lips smacking.

Just like with horses, a group of seahorses is called a herd.

Seahorses have a 90 percent success rate of catching their prey.

Over time, the jaws of seahorses have evolved to be fused shut with a small tubelike opening for the mouth.

Seahorses are toothless.

Baby seahorses eat on average 3,000 pieces of food every day.

Seahorse eggs hatch within 45 days.

Seahorse populations are at risk due to pollution of their habitats, being hunted for fake medicines, and the fishing industry.

A baby seahorse is often referred to as a "fry."

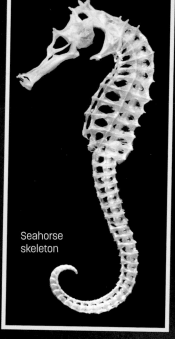

Seahorse skeleton

Though they are fish, seahorses don't have scales.

Seahorses have hard, bony plates along their bodies.

Unlike most fish, seahorses can also swim upward, downward, and backward.

Seahorses can change color to camouflage into their environments.

A seahorse courtship can last hours or even days.

Most seahorses mate with the same partner for life.

Seahorses can die of exhaustion if they try to swim during rough storms.

There are at least 47 different species of seahorses.

Seahorses were named after a Greek mythological creature called the hippocampus (*hippo* meaning "horse" and *kampos* meaning "sea monster"). It had the upper body of a horse and the lower body of a fish.

Some seahorses, like the long-snouted seahorse, live in cold waters.

The earliest seahorse fossils are around 13 million years old.

↖ *Ancient Greek pot showing a hippocampus*

ONE-THIRD OF AN OCTOPUS'S NEURONS ARE IN ITS BRAIN. THE OTHER TWO-THIRDS ARE IN THEIR ARMS.

Grab Masters

51 Totally Random Facts About OCTOPUSES

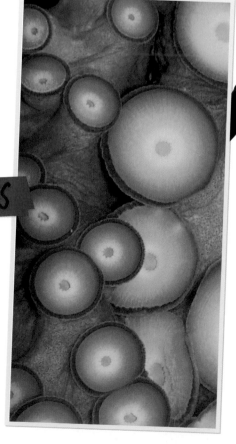

The male blanket octopus weighs 40,000 times less than the female.

Octopuses are invertebrates, animals with no backbone.

Scientists have found that octopuses are highly intelligent. They are considered to be the most intelligent of all invertebrates.

Octopuses live in every ocean in the world.

Humans and octopuses share a common ancestor, a wormlike animal that lived 600 million years ago.

Octopuses are able to smell and taste through their suction cups.

Using multiple arms, an octopus can lift 30 to 100 times its body weight.

If an octopus loses an arm, it will regrow.

Octopuses can travel as fast as 24.8 miles an hour (40 kmh).

The beak of an octopus is the only part of its body that isn't soft.

An octopus changes color not only for camouflage but also to communicate with others of their kind.

Octopuses are mostly solitary, meaning they live alone.

Octopuses are able to squirt water from a tube under their heads. The jet stream of water helps propel them forward when they need to move fast.

All octopuses have venom.

In captivity, octopuses have been observed solving mazes.

Fossils of octopus ancestors date back to 500 million years ago .

Octopuses are able to walk on the ocean floor.

The star-sucker pygmy octopus is the smallest known species of octopus. At full size, it's about 1 inch (2.5 cm) long.

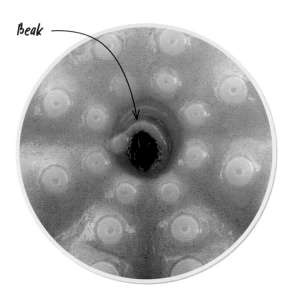

Beak

Star-sucker pygmy octopus, full size

Octopuses have three hearts.

The North Pacific giant octopus is the largest known species of octopus. It weighs 100 pounds (45 kg) and grows to 14 feet (4.3 m) long.

Octopuses are carnivores, meaning they eat meat.

SOME OCTOPUSES EAT SHARKS.

THE VENOM OF THE TINY 8-INCH (20-CM)-LONG BLUE-RINGED OCTOPUS CAN PARALYZE A HUMAN.

An octopus sheltering in an old clam shell

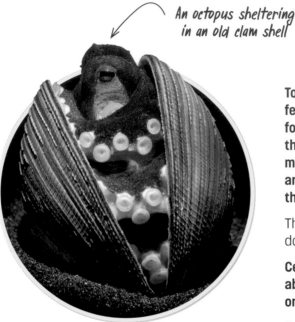

To show the researcher who fed her that she didn't like the food, an octopus in captivity at the University of Pennsylvania made direct contact for attention and then shoved the food down the drain.

There are more than 300 documented species of octopus.

Certain species of octopus are able to lay up to 500,000 eggs at one time.

Octopuses have rectangular-shaped pupils.

Octopuses see in black-and-white, which means they are color-blind. But scientists think they're able to detect color through their pupils, which helps them mimic their surroundings.

Octopuses don't have ears to hear, but scientists think they can sense some sound through a small organ called a statocyst.

In addition to changing colors, octopuses are able to change the texture of their skin.

When an octopus named Otto, who lived in a German aquarium, was bored, he squirted water into the light above his tank for multiple nights in a row. Each time, it short-circuited the lights in the whole building.

Otto the octopus also juggled hermit crabs and threw rocks at the glass in his tank.

Octopuses have blue blood.

The largest suction cups on the arms of the common octopus can hold 35 pounds (16 kg) each. This species has about 240 suction cups in each arm.

A mimic octopus mimicking a flatfish

Octopuses live in saltwater.

Dumbo octopus

Escape Artist!

SID THE OCTOPUS DESPERATELY WANTED TO FIND A MATE, BUT HE HAD ONE PROBLEM—he was housed in a tank all by himself at Portobello Aquarium in New Zealand. He had no choice but to make his escape. **On his first attempt, he disappeared through his tank's door into one of the aquarium's water drainage systems** and was found five days later. The aquarists returned him to his tank, but after several additional escape attempts, the aquarists decided that he'd be happiest in the wild. **Even as they were transporting him to the ocean, Sid tried to open the lid of the bucket holding him.** Oddly enough, he was released into the wild just before Valentine's Day—perfect for his quest to find a mate. The aquarists had some experience with runaway animals. Ten years earlier, an octopus named Harry—after the famous magician and escape artist Harry Houdini—**was found halfway up a staircase after sneaking out of his tank!**

A Dumbo octopus's webbed arms resemble an elephant's ears, which is how they got their common name—after Disney's Dumbo the elephant.

Scientists conducting research on octopuses have observed a giant Pacific octopus opening a childproof bottle of pills.

A California two-spot octopus in captivity unscrewed the valve at the top of her tank and released 200 gallons (757 L) of water, which flooded the building.

The Caribbean reef octopus has seven rows of teeth.

A female *Graneledone boreopacifica* octopus was observed taking care of her eggs for four and a half years. Most octopuses don't brood for this long.

During experiments, scientists have observed octopuses solving puzzles.

A giant Pacific octopus squirting ink at a diver

Dumbo octopuses live deeper in the ocean than any other known octopus species.

Scientists have recorded an octopus changing the color, pattern, and texture of their skin as many as 177 times in one hour.

Female octopuses die after their eggs hatch.

Octopuses are able to detect light through their skin.

When startled or frightened, octopuses can release black ink that hides them from a predator's sight so they can escape. The ink disorients and can also paralyze predators.

Most octopuses live between one and two years.

Octopuses have both long-term and short-term memory.

The blanket octopus isn't affected by jellyfish stings.

Scientists think that octopuses have distinct personalities.

To the Gills

49 Totally Random Facts About **MARINE FISH**

Catfish sometimes hunt pigeons. • **On a yearly basis, more fish are farmed than cows, pigs, sheep, and chickens combined.** • Haddock fish hum to attract mates. • **Some fish can change from male to female and vice versa.** • Human ears evolved from fish gills. • **An electric eel can produce enough electricity to stun a horse.** • It's impossible for a fish to close its eyes. • **The sailfish is the fastest marine animal, swimming at speeds up to 68 miles an hour (109 kmh).** • It's possible to determine the age of some fish by counting the rings on their scales. • **Some male fish protect their eggs by keeping them in their mouths.** • Some makeup is made using fish scales. • **The clown fish is immune to highly venomous animals called anemones.** • Moray eels have a second set of smaller jaws in their mouths to push struggling prey down their throats. • **Mudskippers mainly live in brackish waters. This fish can use its front fins to drag its way onto land, where it stays most of the time.** • The anglerfish has a pole-like structure on its head with a bioluminescent light at the end, which it uses to lure in prey similar to a fishing rod and lure. • **The flatfish has both of its eyes on only one side of its body.** • There are almost as many fish species as all other vertebrate species combined. • **As a defensive measure, schools of fish will team up to create massive balls, meant to both confuse predators and make the school look like one giant structure.** • Eels are a type of fish. • **The barreleye fish has a transparent head.** • The barreleye's eyes are tubular instead of round, and are

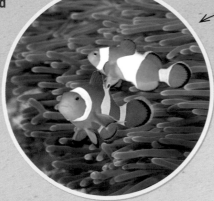

Clown fish

protected by its transparent head. • **Red-bellied piranhas bark.** • The flatfish camouflages itself by laying on the seafloor and staying still. • **A large and structured group of fish swimming together is called a school.** • Schools have no leader; instead, the fish self-organize into the group. • **Salmon can travel more than 6,000 miles (9,656 km) back to the spawning grounds where they were born.** • Carp, Japanese dace fish, and goldfish can see ultraviolet light. • **Fish have been on Earth for more than 500 million years.** • Most fish have darker tops

Fossil of one fish eating another fish

STINGRAYS HAVE NO BONES, BUT INSTEAD HAVE SKELETONS MADE OF CARTILAGE, WHICH IS THE SAME STUFF THAT MAKES UP A HUMAN'S EARS AND NOSE.

Beluga sturgeon

Freshwater Fish

- Nearly half of all fish species live in freshwater.
- **The world's smallest fish, the dwarf minnow, is only 0.3 to 0.5 inch (8 to 12 mm) long.**
- Some fish have natural antifreeze in their blood to adapt to freezing temperatures.
- **African lungfish have a pair of lungs and can breathe air. When lakes dry up during drought conditions, these fish can bury themselves underground and live for years until the lake refills.**
- There are more than 10,000 species of freshwater fish worldwide.
- **The beluga sturgeon is the largest freshwater fish in the world. It can grow up to 20 feet (6 m) long and and weigh more than 1 ton (900 kg).**

and get lighter on their sides, and then even lighter on their bellies to help blend in with the ocean water from above or below. This makes them less visible to predators. • **The cusk eel lives at depths up to 27,500 feet (8,382 m), deeper than any other species of fish.** • A flying fish can glide above water up to a distance of 650 feet (198 m). • **Lampreys and hagfish are species of fish without jaws. They live in both freshwater and saltwater.** • As a defense mechanism, the hagfish produces a thick slime that can clog a predator's gills. • **A puffer fish's venom is 1,200 times deadlier than the poison cyanide.** • A person is more likely to be killed by a toaster, dog, alligator, or lightning strike than by a shark. • **Though the shortfin mako is one of the fastest sharks in the world, it is slow to mature. It takes 7 to 9 years for males to fully mature and at**

least 18 years for females. • A shark's large liver contains oils that help it to stay afloat. • **Goblin sharks can push their jaws out of their mouth when trying to catch prey. These sharks are also pink.** • Most fish are cold-blooded, meaning their body temperature is the same as the water they're in. A few sharks, such as the great white, are warm-blooded. This means they can regulate their own body temperature, keeping it above the temperature of the water around them. • **A shark's skin feels like sandpaper.** • Spiny dogfish sharks have venom-containing spines on the front of their dorsal fins. • **Once the female yellowhead jawfish lays her eggs, the male holds the eggs in his mouth until they are ready to hatch.**

Goblin shark

The Amazing Human Body

From Teeth to Toes and Everything in Between

Material Substance

49 **Totally Random Facts About ANATOMY**

HUMANS HAVE ON AVERAGE ABOUT THE SAME AMOUNT OF HAIR AS CHIMPANZEES. OUR HAIR IS JUST SHORTER.

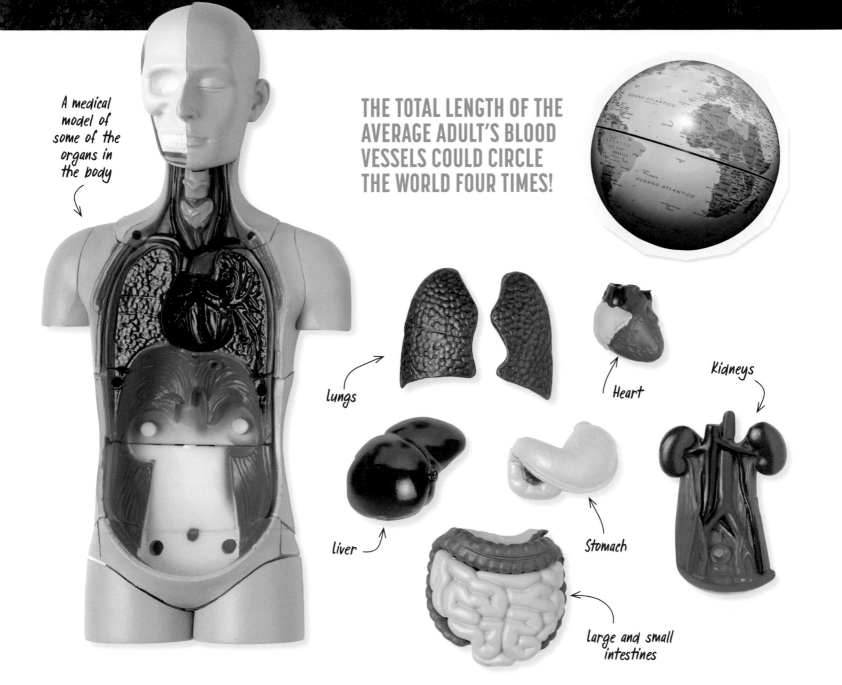

A medical model of some of the organs in the body

THE TOTAL LENGTH OF THE AVERAGE ADULT'S BLOOD VESSELS COULD CIRCLE THE WORLD FOUR TIMES!

lungs

Heart

Kidneys

liver

Stomach

large and small intestines

Bodies emit a small quantity of light that the human eye is unable to pick up.

Babies aren't able to produce tears until four weeks after they are born.

An organ is a combination of tissues that take a specific shape and serve a particular function.

The human body has 11 organ systems.

About 2.5 million sweat pores cover the human body.

Tiny hair-like structures in the nose called cilia help trap materials such as dust and dirt so they don't go into the lungs.

The liver is the only human organ that can regrow when damaged.

Blood isn't made up of just red and white blood cells. It also consists of a yellow liquid called blood plasma.

The femur bone in the thigh can hold up to 30 times the weight of the average person.

The smallest bone in the human body is the stirrup bone of the middle ear.

The heart is the only muscle in the body that does not experience fatigue.

Bone the size of a matchbox would be able to hold 18,000 pounds (8,165 kg).

Human ears are self-cleaning.

The pinkie finger is responsible for 33 percent of the grip strength of the human hand.

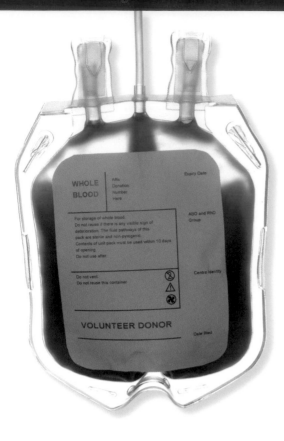

A substance called hemoglobin is what gives blood its red color. It also carries oxygen throughout the body.

Every taste bud has as many as 100 cells.

The shortest woman in the world stands 2 feet (61 cm) tall.

Blood plasma makes up more than half of your blood's content and helps carry nutrients throughout the body.

Human beings are about 0.5 inch (1 cm) taller in the morning than at night.

The speed at which nerves send and receive messages is 249 miles an hour (400 kmh).

Every minute, the human body loses 30,000 dead skin cells.

The average adult pees up to 60 liters per month. That's the equivalent of almost 16 gallons of milk.

Fingernails begin to develop in the womb at about three months.

Epithelial tissues cover the surface of our bodies and line internal parts such as organs.

A Turkish man stands 8 feet, 2.8 inches (251 cm) tall, earning him the title of the world's tallest man, according to Guinness World Records.

Rhinotillexomania **is the term for compulsive nose picking.**

Scientists believe that the evolutionary purpose of eyebrows is to stop sweat from getting into the eyes.

A Chinese woman who has lashes that are 4.88 inches (12 cm) long holds the record for longest eyelashes.

Muscle tissues are the only tissues in the body that are capable of contracting.

Connective tissues maintain the body's structure, partly by holding the organs in places.

The record for longest mustache goes to an Indian man who grew his more than 18.5 feet (5.6 m) long.

The human nose humidifies, or moistens, the air we breathe to prepare it to go into the throat and lungs.

By the age of 70, the average person has consumed 12,000 gallons (45,425 L) of water.

The Guinness World Record holder for the person with the longest fingernails went to an Indian man who grew the nails on his left hand 358.1 inches (910 cm) before he trimmed them.

Human beings are able to identify taste in just 0.0015 seconds.

A typical human cell

Ribosomes

Mitochondrion

Cell surface proteins

Nucleus

Centrosome

Rough endoplasmic reticulum

Smooth endoplasmic reticulum

lysosome

Golgi apparatus

Cytoskeletal fibers

THE AVERAGE PERSON COULD FILL A BALLOON WITH ONE DAY'S WORTH OF FARTS.

Bromidrophobia is the fear of body odors.

Humans are the only mammal that are predominantly two-legged, or bipedal.

The biggest muscle in the human body is the gluteus maximus.

The human body makes 25 million new cells every second.

The average person makes as many cells in the span of 15 seconds—more than 330 million—as the total population of the United States.

The human body contains 10 times more bacteria than cells.

The uvula is the hanging flesh at the back of the throat.

About 2 percent of people have a uvula with two points instead of a rounded end.

The human skin weighs anywhere from 8 to 11 pounds (3.6 to 5 kg).

If laid out flat, human skin would take up 18 to 22 square feet (1.7 to 2 sq m).

Anosmia is the term for a disease in which a person is unable to smell.

Eat It Up

77 Totally Random Facts About TEETH and the HUMAN DIGESTIVE SYSTEM

Nutrition is the process of how food is turned into energy to fuel the body.

Carbohydrates, proteins, and fats are the primary types of energy found in food.

On average, an adult eats up to 6 pounds (2.7 kg) of food per day.

The human digestive system is made up of nine organs.

Though teeth are part of the skeletal system, they are crucial to digestion: Teeth get the whole process started!

Adults have four canine teeth, which are the pointy teeth that are best for creating holes in food.

The human mouth has eight incisors, which are best for chewing small pieces of food.

Eight premolars and eight molars chew larger pieces of food.

The small intestine stretches between 22 and 23 feet (6.7–7 m) long.

The large intestine is a lot shorter than the small intestine at just 5 feet (1.5 m) long.

Farts are the release of gas from the digestive system. Gas accumulates when we swallow air while eating or drinking or by fermented bacteria from food, which gives gas its smell.

Most children have 20 teeth.

Most babies are born with a row of adult teeth behind a row of baby teeth. Both sets are "below" the gum line and are not yet visible.

In the ancient Maya civilization, holes were made in front teeth to place stones such as quartz or turquoise. Experts think this might have been done for religious reasons.

Before dentistry was an established job, barbers and blacksmiths were often left to do dental work such as tooth extraction.

Viking warrior

VIKING WARRIORS WOULD PAY FOR CHILDREN'S LOST TEETH SO THEY COULD BE WORN AS NECKLACES FOR GOOD LUCK.

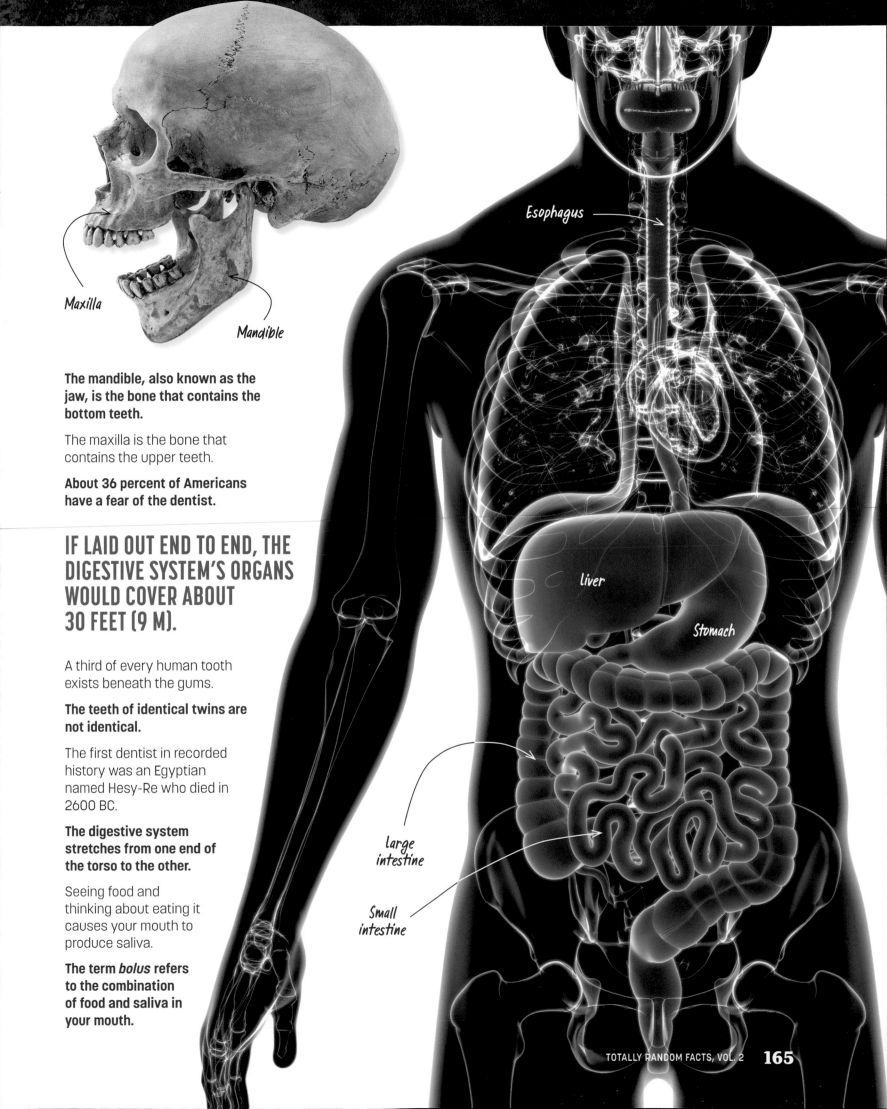

Maxilla

Mandible

The mandible, also known as the jaw, is the bone that contains the bottom teeth.

The maxilla is the bone that contains the upper teeth.

About 36 percent of Americans have a fear of the dentist.

IF LAID OUT END TO END, THE DIGESTIVE SYSTEM'S ORGANS WOULD COVER ABOUT 30 FEET (9 M).

A third of every human tooth exists beneath the gums.

The teeth of identical twins are not identical.

The first dentist in recorded history was an Egyptian named Hesy-Re who died in 2600 BC.

The digestive system stretches from one end of the torso to the other.

Seeing food and thinking about eating it causes your mouth to produce saliva.

The term *bolus* refers to the combination of food and saliva in your mouth.

Esophagus

liver

Stomach

large intestine

Small intestine

Cross-section of the small intestine

About 800 years ago in China, people attached animal hair to ivory or bamboo, creating some of the very first toothbrushes.

Before toothbrushes were invented, people would use twigs and leaves to brush their teeth.

A person spends five years of their life eating.

On average, it takes 30 to 40 hours for food to travel all the way through the digestive system.

Babies' teeth usually start emerging at about six months of age.

Most kids lose their baby teeth between the ages of 6 and 12.

The first known dental implant was a shell used to replace the tooth of a Maya woman in AD 600.

The bacteria that cause cavities can be spread from person to person by sharing utensils or food, and through saliva.

About 5 million teeth are lost each year due to sports injuries.

Peristalsis is the movement of muscles in the esophagus that moves the bolus from the mouth to the stomach.

Usually there are four wisdom teeth in the mouth, though for some, they never grow. Many people also have wisdom teeth removed if they don't grow correctly.

TEETH ARE AS UNIQUE AS FINGERPRINTS.

The stomach lining is regenerated in a five-day cycle because digestive acids in the stomach damage it.

Metal covers that adorn teeth for decoration are called "grills."

Bile is the term for a special substance produced in the liver that makes its way to the gallbladder, then reaches the small intestine where it helps to digest fats.

***Jejunum* is the word for the secondary region of the small intestine.**

Villi are tiny, string-like parts of the small intestine that take in nutrients.

In the Middle Ages, children would burn their baby teeth because of a myth that said if you failed to do so, you'd spend your afterlife looking for them.

Scientists think that the diet of early humans contained little sugar, and therefore they had fewer cavities.

Teeth are an essential part of nonverbal communication—which occurs without words or sounds created with your mouth. This includes body language such as smiling and making faces and hand gestures.

In ancient Egypt, people would use a mixture of crushed eggshells, ox hooves, and water to clean their teeth.

The modern toothbrush, made with nylon bristles and a shaped handle, was invented and became widely popular in the 1930s.

The electric toothbrush was invented in 1939.

THE HUMAN BODY MAKES BETWEEN 3 AND 8 OUNCES (85–227 G) OF POOP DAILY.

Scientists can learn our age, diet, and quality of health just by looking at our teeth.

A person imprisoned in West Virginia successfully escaped prison by braiding dental floss and scaling a prison wall.

Spray from a flushing toilet can reach a radius of 6 feet (1.8 m)—a good reason to keep your toothbrush far away from your toilet!

Though two minutes of brushing is required to fully clean your teeth, the average person only brushes for a total of 48 seconds—less than a minute—each day.

Plaque is the slimy substance that contains bacteria and sticks to teeth, causing tooth decay.

Plaque can contain 300 unique types of bacteria.

In Germany during the Middle Ages, a kiss from a donkey was thought to heal a toothache.

***Diastema* is the word that describes a gap between teeth.**

Former British prime minister Winston Churchill's dentures were auctioned off for $23,731.76.

Despite popular belief, President George Washington's dentures were not made of wood.

On average, a person spends 38.5 days of their life brushing their teeth.

The average person can chomp down with 200 pounds (91 kg) of force when biting.

Not all cultures tell the mythical story of the tooth fairy. In Spain, a mischievous mouse—El Ratoncito Perez—visits instead and leaves a coin behind.

Eating cheese increases the production of saliva.

Of every 2,000 babies, one is born with a tooth or more already grown in.

No two teeth are alike.

In 2019, doctors discovered that a seven-year-old boy had 526 extra teeth in his mouth.

In the Wild

- Though their mouths are no larger than the head of a pin, snails have upward of 25,000 teeth.

- **It's possible to estimate a dolphin's age by counting rings on its teeth.**

- Platypuses have no stomach.

- **Hippos have huge canine teeth! They grow up to 20 inches (51 cm) long—almost 2 feet!**

- Sharks are able to regrow their teeth whenever they lose them.

- **Pigs have 44 teeth.**

- The dragonfish, which lives deep in the ocean, has transparent teeth that are stronger than the teeth of a piranha.

- **Sharks can have more than 10,000 teeth over the course of their lives.**

- Naked mole rats have four long teeth on the outside of their lips to help them dig without getting dirt in their mouths.

- **Naked mole rats can also move each of their front teeth independently.**

Using Your Head

46 Totally Random Facts About THE BRAIN

Prefrontal cortex

Evidence of brain surgery dates as far back as 5,000 years ago, during the Stone Age.

It would take about 3,000 years to count each nerve cell in the brain.

Humans have the most developed brain of any species.

Of every organ in the human body, the brain requires the most time to develop.

Humans have the largest frontal lobe of any animal. It houses functions such as planning and organization.

Seeing stars, or seeing small points of light after you've hit your head, results from a blow to the brain's vision cells.

The cerebrum is the largest part of the brain. It controls muscle function, speech, thought, emotion, and communication.

The total surface area of the brain is between 230 and 470 square inches (1,500–3,000 sq cm).

Because a baby's brain can take in lots of new information in the early weeks of life, a baby babbles nearly every sound of every language.

Ancient Greek scientists and doctors were the first to believe that the brain was responsible for thought. Before that, they—like the ancient Egyptians— thought the heart was in charge of thinking.

THE TEXTURE OF THE HUMAN BRAIN IS SIMILAR TO TOFU.

If you flattened a human brain, it would take up about as much space as a backpack.

Ancient Egyptians didn't think the brain was needed in the afterlife. They believed the heart controlled emotions and thought.

The earliest known written record of the brain's anatomy dates to 1700 BC in ancient Egypt.

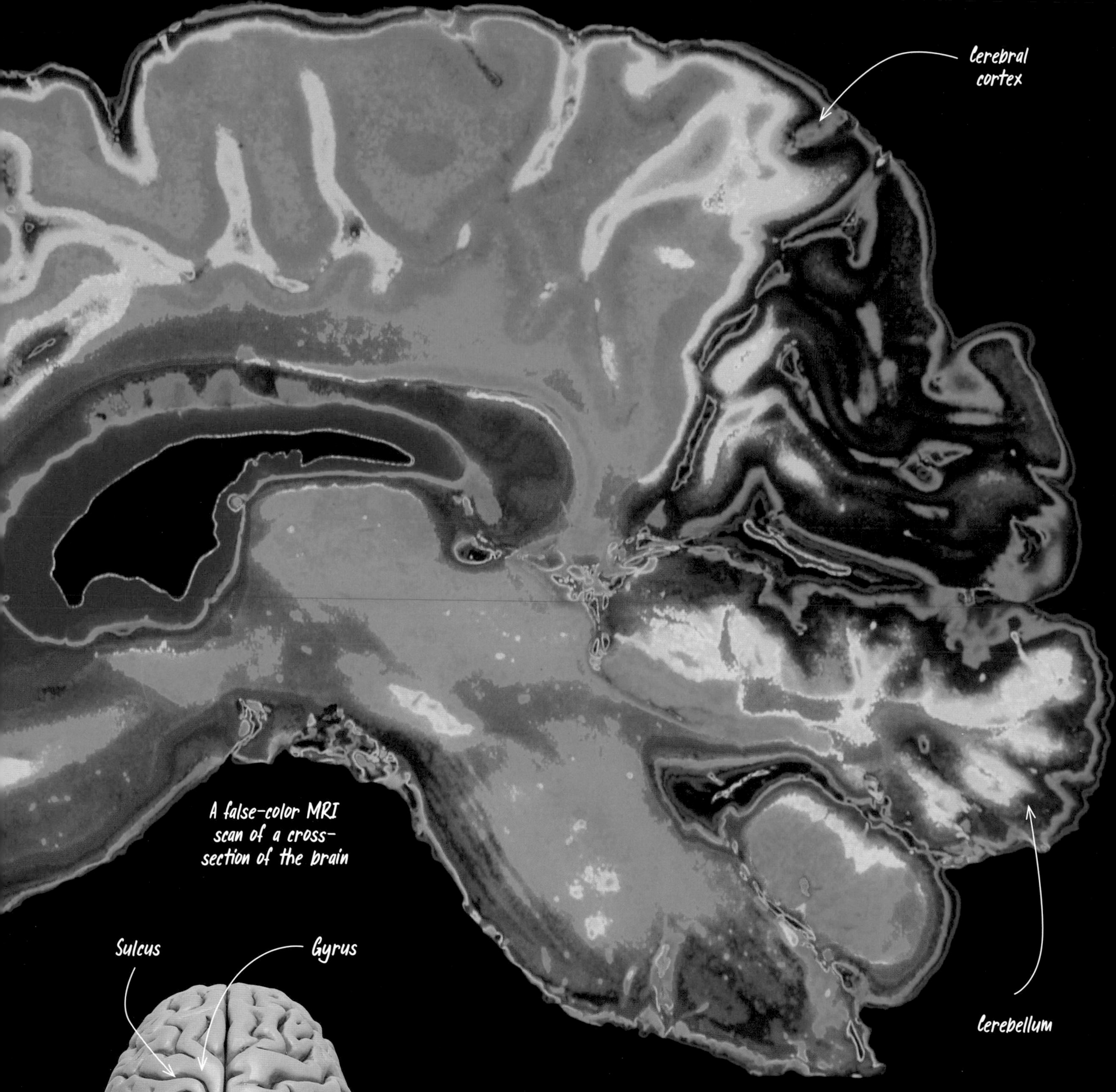

Cerebral cortex

A false-color MRI scan of a cross-section of the brain

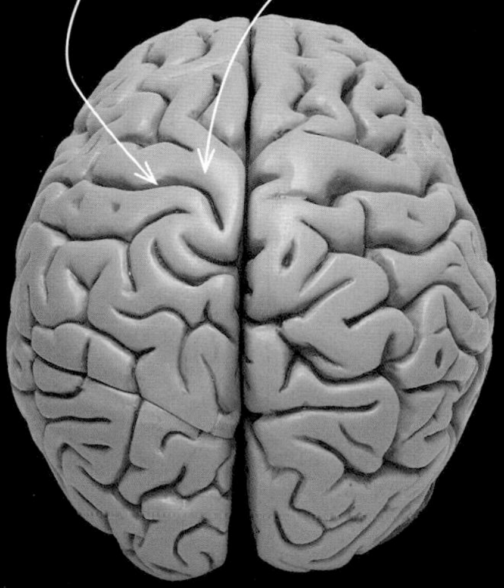

Cerebellum

Sulcus

Gyrus

The right side of the brain controls the left side of the body. The left side of the brain controls the right side of the body.

Sulcus is the scientific term for a brain fold.

A flat, non-folded area of the brain between the folds is known as a *gyrus*.

Wearing a helmet when riding a bike reduces the risk of a brain injury by 88 percent.

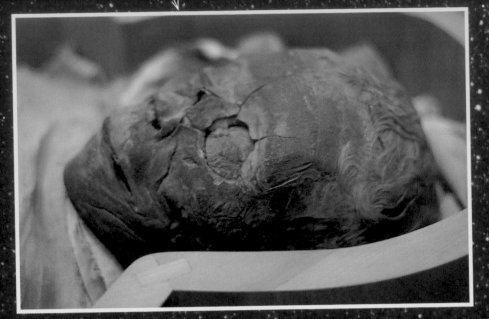

The brain can process an image that the eyes have only seen for 13 milliseconds.

Neurons are brain cells that receive sensory information taken in from the outside world.

Scientists know more about the universe than about the human brain.

A brain weighs about 2 percent of the total weight of the human body.

The left side of the brain is responsible for speech.

Your spinal cord stops growing at four years old.

The heaviest human brain on record was 5 pounds, 1.1 ounce (2.3 kg).

Background noise can alter how the brain perceives the taste of sweet or salty flavors.

Even when we sleep, the human brain is sending and receiving electrical signals.

The lightest human brain on record was 1 pound, 8 ounces (680 g).

"Sphenopalatine ganglioneuralgia" is the scientific name for brain freeze.

In addition to the tongue, there are taste-specific areas of neurons in the brain.

The fattiest organ in the body is the brain.

The human brain isn't fully formed until the age of 25.

When mummifying human remains, ancient Egyptians would remove parts of the brain through the nose.

Your brain's storage capacity is virtually unlimited.

Getting enough sleep is important for maintaining pathways in your brain.

Men tend to have larger brains than women, although increased size doesn't automatically imply increased intelligence.

The human brain is more complex than any other thing known in the universe.

It was a myth that Albert Einstein had a huge brain. His brain weighed 2.7 pounds (1.2 kg), which is about average.

THERE ARE ABOUT 400 BILLION STARS IN THE MILKY WAY GALAXY, BUT THAT'S NOTHING COMPARED TO THE NUMBER OF CONNECTIONS BETWEEN NERVE CELLS IN THE HUMAN BRAIN—100 TRILLION!

Awesome Animal Brains

- Squids' brains are doughnut-shaped.

- **There are 950,000 neurons in a honeybee's brain.**

- An elephant's brain weighs about 11 pounds (5 kg), about 8 pounds (4 kg) more than a human's brain.

- **The Clark's nutcracker is one smart bird! In winter, it can remember the locations of most of the more than 30,000 seeds it buried earlier in the year.**

- The smallest spiders have large brains relative to the size of their bodies, so their brains actually "spill" into their legs.

- **Scientists have discovered that narwhals send sensory information from their tusks to their brains.**

- Manta rays have a system of arteries and veins that surround their brains and help keep their brains warm.

Manta ray

Vision Quest

59 Totally Random Facts About EYES

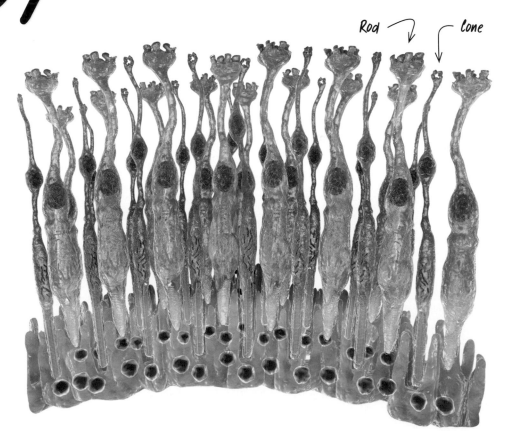

Rod ↘   Cone ↓

Night vision goggles are green because the human eye can differentiate more shades of green than any other color.

Only a small fraction of your eye is visible to the outside world.

Human eyes comprise millions of intricately connected working parts.

Eyes began to develop 550 million years ago in single-celled animals.

For people, eyes start to develop in the womb three weeks after a baby is conceived.

If laid end to end, humans shed 98 feet (30 m) of eyelashes over their lifetimes.

Each eyelash has a life span of 5 to 11 months.

The average adult has 100 to 150 upper eyelashes and 50 to 75 lower eyelashes.

Eyes are positioned in hollowed eye sockets to protect them.

Corneas are the only tissues in the body that don't have blood.

Your eyes include structures called rods and cones. Rods allow you to see shapes, while cones are responsible for detecting and deciphering colors.

Unlike other organs in the body, the eye cannot be transplanted because each eye has more than a million nerve fibers connecting to the brain.

About 80 percent of our memories are determined by what we see.

Eyes heal quickly from things like a minor scratch.

About 2 billion people in the world have some type of vision problem.

Up to 80 percent of vision problems worldwide are avoidable or curable.

About 2 percent of women have a rare genetic mutation that gives them an extra retinal cone, which means they can distinguish 100 million colors.

Human eyeballs are directly connected to the brain via the optic nerve.

People who are blind can still see in their dreams if they weren't born blind.

About 80 percent of what we learn is through our eyes.

Humans and dogs are the only species known to look at a person's eyes to seek visual cues.

Eyes are the body's second most complex organ after the brain.

Pupils dilate—get larger—by 45 percent when looking at something pleasant.

Human eyes don't reach full size until adulthood. They grow the most during the first two years of life.

Each eye contains 107 million light-sensitive cells.

Each of our eyes has a small blind spot. You don't notice the hole in your vision because your eyes work together to fill it in.

People generally read 25 percent slower from a computer screen compared to paper.

Every hour, your eyes can process about 36,000 bits of information.

Every second, your eye will focus on about 50 things.

Eyes use more brainpower than any other body part—up to 65 percent.

Your pupils can dilate up to 0.3 inch (8 mm), about the size of a blueberry.

A horizontal scan of the head, showing the eyes and brain

Heterochromia is the medical term for having **TWO DIFFERENT-COLORED EYES.**

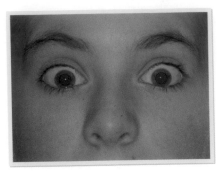

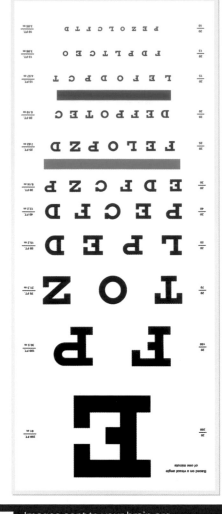

Eyes can look red in older color photographs because the camera's flash bounces off the back of the eye where there are lot of red blood vessels.

Your brain has to interpret the signals your eyes send for you to see.

The light-detecting cells in the retina can see about 500 different shades of gray.

Having two eyeballs gives us depth perception to determine how far away an object is from us.

The muscles in the eyes are 100 times stronger than they need to be to perform their function.

Everyone has one eye that is slightly stronger than the other.

In the right conditions and lighting, humans with average, healthy vision can see the light of a candle from 1.6 miles (2.6 km) away.

Your eyes can distinguish approximately a million different colors.

Ommetaphobia is an extreme fear of the eyes.

The human eye weighs about 0.25 ounce (7 g), which is a bit heavier than the weight of a pencil.

T Images sent to your brain are actually **BACKWARD AND UPSIDE DOWN.**

A blink lasts anywhere from 100 to 150 milliseconds.

It is possible to sneeze with your eyes open, but you have to work against the body's natural reflex that closes them.

The average person blinks 15 to 20 times per minute.

The shark cornea is nearly identical to the human cornea.

Your eye is the fastest contracting muscle in the body, contracting in less than a tenth of a second.

The optic nerve contains more than a million nerve cells.

If the human eye were a digital camera, it would have 576 megapixels.

Phosphene is the experience of seeing light without it actually entering the eye, like when you rub your eyes and see flashes of color.

A single eye has 107 million photosensitive cells.

We blink about every six seconds. That averages out to about 14,000 blinks per day.

Eyes blink less when reading and more when talking.

Babies and children only blink about two times per minute.

A person can blink up to five times in one second.

Your iris is about six times more unique than your fingerprint. A fingerprint has 40 unique characteristics, but an iris has 256.

We spend 10 percent of our waking hours with our eyes closed because of how often we blink.

The human eye blinks more than 11,500 times per day.

This street painting in the Netherlands is an optical illusion, making it seem like a fallen tree is over water.

163 Totally Random Facts About

Stellar Space

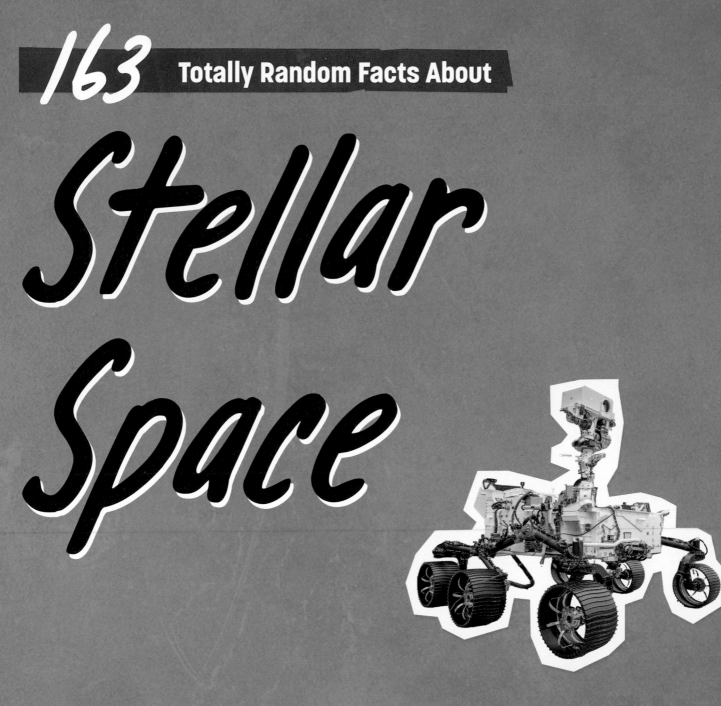

Shining Stars, Exoplanets, and Magnificent Mars

Stellar Performance

55 Totally Random Facts About STARS and CONSTELLATIONS

STARS ARE BORN
FROM NEBULAE,
WHICH ARE CLOUDS
MADE OF DUST AND GAS.

The Orion Nebula

At minimum, scientists estimate that there are more than 10 billion trillion stars.

A supergiant is a huge star—one hundreds of times larger than the sun.

The sun was born 4.6 billion years ago.

About 275 million stars are born each day.

Scientists think that the nebula dust that gave birth to the sun tasted like raspberries, based on its chemical content.

All stars visible from Earth exist within the Milky Way.

A CONSTELLATION IS A COLLECTION OF STARS THAT LOOKS AS IF IT IS A RECOGNIZABLE SHAPE.

The oldest stars in the Milky Way are about 13.6 billion years old.

Stars are made mostly of hydrogen and helium.

Most of the solar systems in our universe have two suns at the center instead of one.

Astronomer Annie Jump Cannon classified around 350,000 stars, more than any other person.

Hypatia of Alexandria, who lived between AD 355 and 415, is the earliest known female astronomer.

The smaller the star, the longer it lives.

There are 88 constellations.

Changes in season—from Earth's orbit—affect which constellations you can see in the night sky.

Astronomy is the science of space and the study of everything from stars to galaxies.

The largest constellation is Hydra, the Water Snake. It is made up of seven stars and takes up about 3 percent of the sky.

Astrology is the practice of observing the movements of stars and planets to draw conclusions about a person and their future.

Star patterns that are not constellations are called asterisms.

The sun's width is the size of 100 Earths laid end to end.

Stars have been discovered that are 10 times smaller than the sun, as well as some that are 100 times bigger.

Polaris, the North Star, is a part of the Little Dipper, a constellation shaped like a ladle.

After a star dies, it becomes a dwarf star, a neutron star, or a black hole.

A supernova is an extremely large explosion of a massive star.

Supernovae are by far the largest and most powerful explosions known to human beings.

The first supernova witnessed and recorded by people occurred in China in AD 185, more than 1,800 years ago.

Annie Jump Cannon

That's So Random: The Bear in the Sky!

URSA MAJOR, KNOWN AS THE GREAT BEAR, IS A CONSTELLATION IN THE NORTHERN NIGHT SKY. It has long been an object of fascination for humans, making an appearance in the Old Testament of the Bible and in Homer's *Iliad*, an epic poem written in 750 BC. **The ancient Greeks referred to this bear-shaped constellation as "the she-bear,"** and the ancient Romans called it simply "Ursa." Of the stars that make up Ursa Major, **the seven brightest combine to make up the Big Dipper,** a group of stars known to aid enslaved people in navigating to the northern United States and Canada in search of freedom. Ancient Hindu people believed that the seven stars of the Big Dipper represented the seven *rishis*— "sages" in Hinduism.

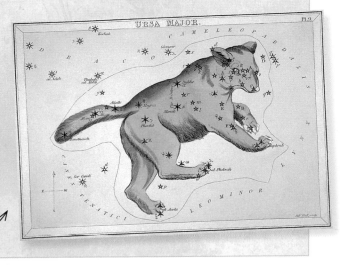

A 19th-century star chart of Ursa Major

An expanding shell of debris left behind after a supernova

A GALAXY IS A LARGE ACCUMULATION OF GAS, DUST, AND STARS HELD TOGETHER BY GRAVITY.

The Andromeda galaxy

Neutron stars form after a supergiant star dies and squashes to roughly the size of a small city, becoming very dense. Often, neutron stars become pulsars during this process: stars that release radiation in pulses, or bursts.

A black hole is an area of space that is very difficult to see because the gravitational pull is so strong that light is unable to escape.

When a star explodes, the materials that made it a star spread out into the universe to become other objects, such as planets, stars, or moons.

Neutron stars can be as small as about 16 miles (26 km) in diameter.

Because most natural elements in the universe are created inside of a star that eventually explodes, we are all made of stardust.

Most stars in the Milky Way are red dwarfs. They are the smallest type of star and the ones that live the longest. Because they are quite dim, they cannot be seen without a telescope.

When looking up at the night sky from a very dark area, you will be able to see between 2,000 and 2,500 stars at the same time.

A red dwarf star orbited by an exoplanet

The Andromeda galaxy is the most distant celestial body visible to the naked eye. It is 2.5 million light-years away. This means the light we see from Andromeda is 2.5 million years old!

The word *constellation* translates to "a set of stars."

The brightest star in our night sky is Sirius. It looks brighter than other stars because it is closer to our planet than many other stars.

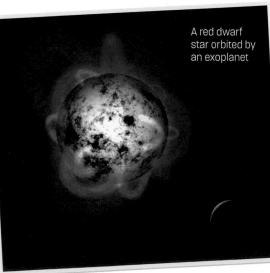

The sun's star classification is a G-type yellow dwarf star.

When studying the Murchison meteorite, which fell in Murchison, Australia, scientists discovered stardust that is 7 billion years old.

Today, it would take about 19,000 years for a human spacecraft to reach the next closest star, Proxima Centauri.

Stars get their huge amounts of energy from hydrogen atoms combining to form helium. This process is known as nuclear fusion.

After billions of years, stars use up all of their fuel and die. The sun will use up all of its energy in about 5 billion years.

THE STARS THAT MAKE UP THE BIG DIPPER ARE BETWEEN 80 AND 125 LIGHT-YEARS AWAY.

Types of Stars

- Stars are classified into seven categories: M, K, G, F, A, B, and O.

- M-type stars are red and the coldest type of star.

- K-type stars are between orange and red, and are colder than the sun.

- The sun is a G-type star. Stars in this class are yellow.

- F-type stars are between yellow and white. They have a brightness somewhat greater than the sun.

- A-type stars are white and have a brightness 10 times that of the sun.

- B-type stars are blue and white. They have a brightness between a hundred and a thousand times brighter than the sun.

- O-type stars have the highest temperature, are blue, and have a brightness a million times the sun's brightness.

- The International Astronomical Union is responsible for certifying the names of all celestial bodies, including stars and constellations.

- In a given constellation, the brightest star has the word *alpha* in its name, the second brightest has *beta*, and the third has *gamma*. For example, Alpha Centauri A is the brightest star in the constellation Centaurus.

- The scale by which the brightness of a star is measured was invented in 125 BC by Hipparchus, an ancient Greek astronomer.

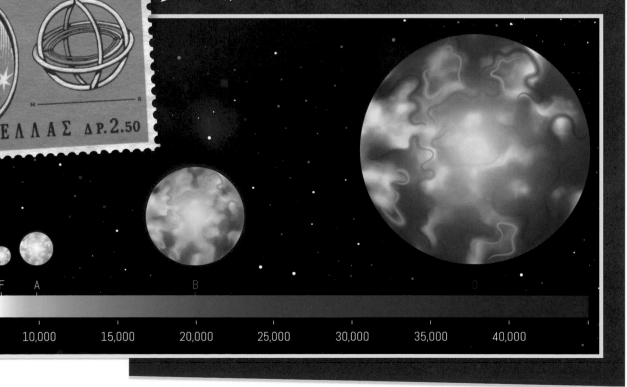

Hipparchus shown on a Greek stamp

Sapphires

An exoplanet is a planet that exists outside of our solar system—it can be a planet orbiting another star or one that exists on its own. • **Scientists are able to tell whether a planet is made of rock or gases by measuring its diameter and weight.** • Exoplanets were first discovered in the 1990s. • **Exoplanets are often discovered while scientists are looking for or studying other things.** • We don't yet have the ability to travel to an exoplanet—or any other planets! • **The first known exoplanet orbiting a sunlike star was 51 Pegasi b. It was also known as "hot Jupiter" because, like Jupiter, it's a gas giant. The planet exists 50 light-years from Earth.** • The smallest known exoplanet is between the size of Earth and Mars. It's called L 98-59b. **It is estimated that there are more than 6 billion Earthlike planets in the Milky Way galaxy.** • A possible new planet found by a telescope is called an exoplanet candidate.

Once it's confirmed to actually exist, it will be named an exoplanet. • **Scientists think that some exoplanets may rain glass, rubies, or sapphires.** • There are almost 5,000 known exoplanets, and that number is increasing all the time. • **Planet HD 209458 b, also known as Osiris, was the first exoplanet to be seen passing in front of its star.** • Astronomers believe that almost all sunlike stars have planets orbiting them, the way Earth orbits our sun. • **Exoplanets have their own atmospheres, like the planets in our solar system.** • Scientists think it's possible that there are more planets than stars in the universe. • **The exoplanet closest to Earth is Proxima Centauri b and is found in the constellation Centaurus.** • One of the ways scientists detect exoplanets is to measure their gravitational pull on stars. • *Exomoon* is the

Out of This World

36 **Totally Random Facts About EXOPLANETS**

An artist's impression of the exoplanet orbiting Proxima Centauri

term for a moon that orbits an exoplanet. • The first part of an exoplanet's name is taken from the telescope that discovered it. • **Another method of detecting exoplanets is to measure the difference in light from a star caused by an exoplanet passing between the star and Earth. When the planet passes between Earth and the star, the star's light dims slightly.** • Not all exoplanets are spherical—egg-shaped exoplanets have also been discovered! • **Some exoplanets orbit several stars at once.** • Several exoplanets have been discovered that are entirely coated in lava. • **Some exoplanets orbit dead stars—some of these planets may be 13 billion years old.** • Astronomers are looking for the existence of oxygen or a body of water as evidence that an exoplanet might sustain life. • **The super-Earth exoplanet 55 Cancri e**

Kepler space telescope

might have a core made of diamonds! • Water vapor has been detected on a super-Neptune exoplanet called TOI-674 b. • **Some exoplanets orbit their suns so closely that one year only lasts a few days.** • On 55 Cancri e, the length of a year is 17 hours and 41 minutes. • **CoRoT-7b was the first super-Earth exoplanet that was identified as being rocky.**

Types of Exoplanets

- There are four types of exoplanets: terrestrial, super-Earths, Neptune-like, and gas giants.

- **Terrestrial exoplanets are, at their biggest, the size of Earth and made of rock.**

- Super-Earth exoplanets are often made of rock, and they are larger than Earth yet lighter than Neptune.

- **Neptune-like exoplanets are larger than terrestrial exoplanets, roughly the size of Neptune or Uranus, and mostly made from gases.**

- Gas giants are very large exoplanets—often larger than Saturn or Jupiter—and have an extremely high temperature.

Scientists have discovered "puffy" exoplanets that **SHARE A DENSITY WITH STYROFOAM.**

Rockin' Red Planet

72 Totally Random Facts About MARS

Mar's moons,
Phobos and Deimos

North pole

Water ice clouds

Olympus
Mons

Northern
lowlands

Southern
Highlands

Valles Marineris

AROUND 4 BILLION YEARS AGO, MARS HAD RIVERS, LAKES, AND EVEN OCEANS.

The little water left on Mars is mostly frozen. Some liquid water might exist under the surface.

The Valles Marineris is the biggest canyon in the solar system.

At 2,500 miles (4,023 km) long, the Valles Marineris is nine times longer than the Grand Canyon.

At its deepest points, the Valles Marineris is 6 miles (10 km) deep—seven times deeper than the Grand Canyon.

Dust storms on Mars can have winds of 70 miles an hour (113 kmh).

In 1609, Galileo Galilei was the first person to ever see Mars through a telescope.

At only 3,700 miles (5,955 km) away from Mars, Phobos orbits closer to its planet than any other known moon.

Phobos orbits Mars three times a day.

Because Deimos is farther away than Phobos, it takes about 30 hours to make one orbit around Mars.

Mars is home to the largest mountain in the solar system, Olympus Mons.

Mars has four seasons. They are twice as long on the red planet than they are on Earth.

Mars appears red because of high amounts of a chemical called iron oxide in the planet's soil.

Robotic mining for water and fuel are crucial if the red planet is ever to be colonized.

In 1938, many people believed a Martian invasion was under way when a radio host was reading H. G. Wells's book *War of the Worlds* on air and listeners didn't realize it was just a story.

In 1976, the Viking landers were the first spacecrafts to land on Mars.

NASA hasn't sent rovers to any other planets other than Mars.

Mars has polar ice caps.

The atmosphere of Mars is 96 percent carbon dioxide.

Temperatures on Mars can drop to −284° F (−176° C).

Temperatures on Mars can reach up to 86° F (30° C).

Mars is 142 million miles (229 million km) from the sun.

Mars has two moons: Phobos and Deimos.

You can buy land on Mars through a website.

As of 2021, 323 rocks identified as from Mars have landed on Earth.

It would take seven months in a rocket ship to get to Mars.

The surface of Mars is a barren wasteland covered by rocks and sand.

After Mercury, Mars is the smallest planet in our solar system.

In a photo taken in 1998, a rock on Mars looks like a human face because of the sun's position and fog at the time.

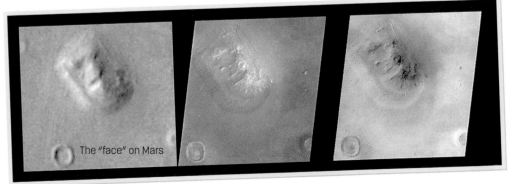

The "face" on Mars

Ingenuity

12.4 miles
20 km

Deimos and Phobos are named after the horses that pulled the god Mars's chariot.

The Hellas impact crater, the biggest crater on Mars, is 1,400 miles (2,250 km) in diameter. That's about the distance from Washington, D.C., to Austin, Texas.

The five NASA rovers that have been sent to Mars so far will remain there. They are Sojourner, Spirit, Opportunity, Curiosity, and Perseverance.

Scientists believe in the next 20 to 40 million years, the moon Phobos will be destroyed by gravitational forces.

When Phobos is destroyed, its broken pieces will likely become a ring around Mars.

Only about half of the 48 NASA missions to Mars have been successful.

A small helicopter called Ingenuity was carried to Mars on the Perseverance rover. Ingenuity made the first ever flight on another planet.

NASA's Perseverance rover team that is studying Mars includes more than 800 scientists and engineers from around the world.

The average temperature on Mars is –81° F (–63° C); however, the temperature at the north and south poles can plummet to –220° F (–140° C).

Olympus Mons is three times taller than Mount Everest and is a shield volcano.

It's possible that Olympus Mons is still active.

Mars orbits the sun at an average speed of 14.5 miles (23 km) per second.

"Marsquakes" are earthquakes on Mars.

Earth takes almost two trips around the sun in the time it takes Mars to take one.

When the sun and Mars are on opposite sides of Earth, Mars rises in the east at the same time the sun sets in the west. Mars sets in the west at the same time the sun rises in the east.

Mars is about twice as big as Earth's moon.

THERE IS BETTER MAPPING OF MARS THAN OF ALASKA.

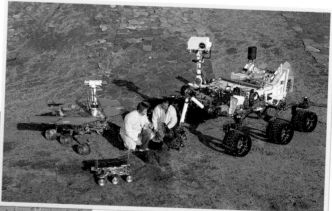

Two spacecraft engineers with Mars rovers: Sojourner, Mars Exploration Rover Project test rover, and Curiosity

Topographic map of Valles Marineris with its associated outflow channels and their surroundings, based on Mars Orbiter Laser Altimeter (MOLA) data

A dust storm photographed from the Mars Express orbiter

Mars Compared to Earth

- One hundred pounds (45 kg) on Earth is equal to 38 pounds (17 kg) on Mars.

- **Earth has about nine times more mass than Mars.**

- A Mars year is 687 days, almost double the days in an Earth year.

- **Earth's atmosphere is 61 times denser than that of Mars.**

- Mars has 62.5 percent less gravity than Earth.

- **Mars is about the same size as Earth's core.**

- A person could jump three times higher on Mars than they could on Earth.

- **You could fit about six Mars planets into one Earth.**

- Mars doesn't have a magnetic field like Earth does.

- **Seasons on Mars last about twice as long as they do on Earth.**

- A day on Mars lasts nearly 40 minutes longer than a day on Earth.

- **The sun looks a bit more than half the size on Mars than it does on Earth.**

- Mars has a similar amount of total land area to Earth. This is because most of our planet is covered with water, whereas the surface of Mars is all land.

SOME DUST STORMS ON MARS CAN COVER THE ENTIRE PLANET FOR MONTHS ON END.

The core of Mars may be similar to Earth's, but the structure remains a mystery.

Sounds on Mars are muffled and lower in volume than on Earth. If you heard them, it would sound like you're listening through a wall.

Whistles, bells, bird sounds, and other high-pitched sounds would be impossible to hear on Mars.

Some experts believe humans will begin colonizing Mars around the year 2050.

NASA's Ingenuity helicopter can take 3-D pictures of Mars.

Even if colonized, living on Mars will require space suits when outdoors. There is not enough oxygen in the atmosphere to breathe.

There is no evidence that life exists on Mars.

Sunset on Mars

Perseverance has five high-tech science cameras used for collecting scientific information. They take pictures of everything from sweeping landscapes to teeny rock granules.

Billions of years ago, Mars flowed with lava and water.

Rocks in some of the craters on Mars suggest that there were rivers on the planet at some point.

Photos of sedimentary rock give scientists clues about how erosion, wind, and water have changed Mars over time.

No humans have ever visited the red planet.

282 Totally Random Facts in a

Random
Roundup

Rolling Rides, Enticing Eats, and Other Totally Cool Topics

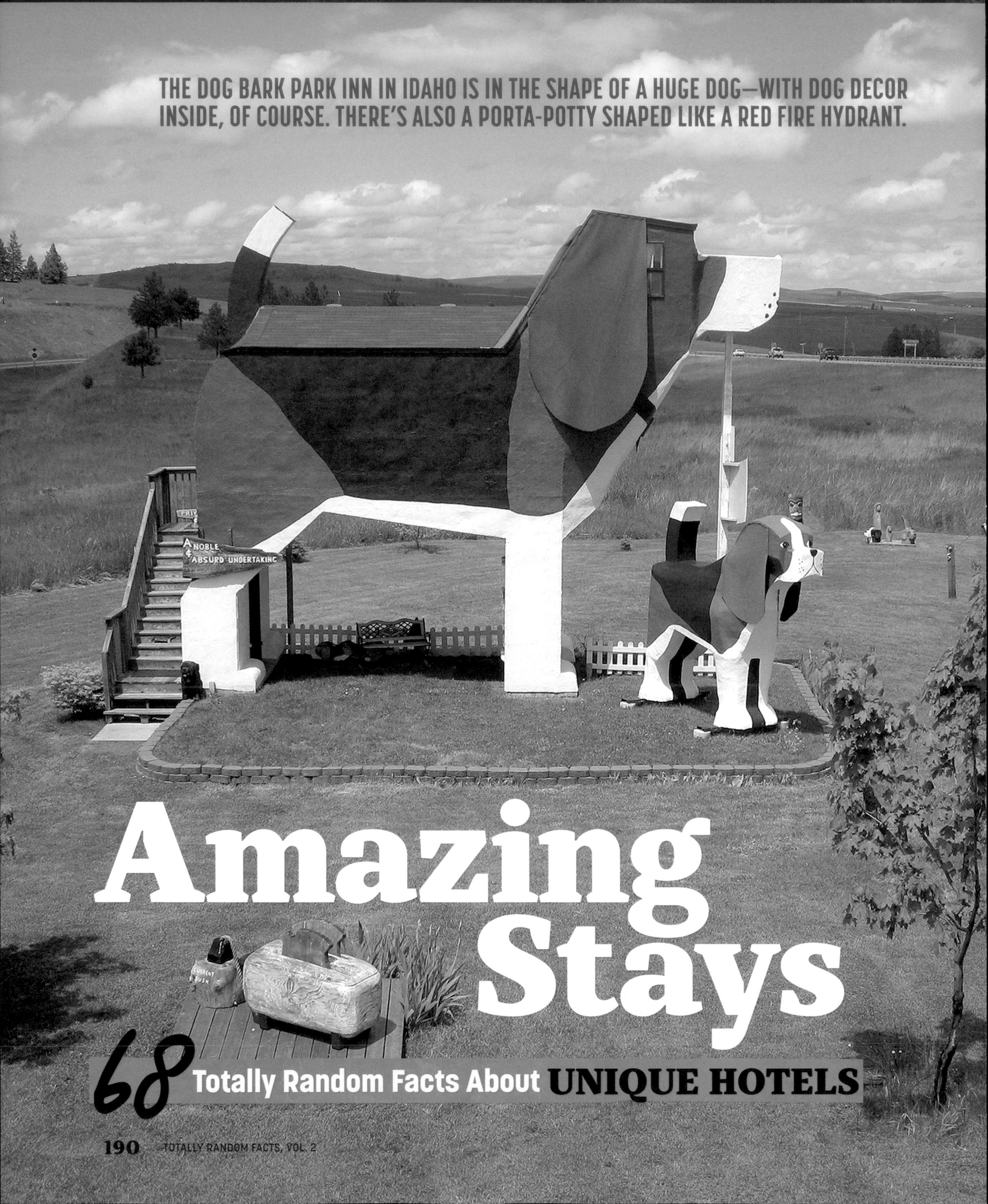

THE DOG BARK PARK INN IN IDAHO IS IN THE SHAPE OF A HUGE DOG—WITH DOG DECOR INSIDE, OF COURSE. THERE'S ALSO A PORTA-POTTY SHAPED LIKE A RED FIRE HYDRANT.

Amazing Stays

68 Totally Random Facts About UNIQUE HOTELS

At the Kakslauttanen Arctic Resort in Finland, you can see the northern lights—all from your very own igloo! And if that's too rustic for you, they also offer log cabins. • **The Montaña Mágica Lodge in Chile is built inside a volcano— complete with a waterfall and a wooden bridge.** • In New Mexico, Kokopelli's Cave is a 1,700-square-foot (158-sq m) hotel inside a cave. • **La Cabane en l'Air is a French hotel made of a series of more than 100 tree houses, connected by a rope bridge.** • At the Marriott Mena House hotel in Egypt, you can see the Great Pyramids from almost anywhere on the property. • **The Nickelodeon Hotel in Punta Cana, Dominican Republic, features the Pineapple Villa, inspired by the famous underwater home of SpongeBob SquarePants!** • Sweden's Sala Silver Mine is located in—you guessed it—an old silver mine found 508 feet (155 m) below ground. • **Costa Rica's Hotel Costa Verde is a refurbished 727 airplane, complete with a restaurant.** • Beijing, China, has the most hotels in the world, with more than 3,500. • **Attrap Reves is a hotel in France in which you can rent a bubble—a spherical hotel room with glass walls, that is!** • Save the Beach Hotel is a European hotel that is completely mobile and made out of trash that was found on beaches. • **The 4 Rivers Floating Lodge in southwestern Cambodia features floating rooms that sit on the Tatai River, surrounded by a lush jungle.** • The Balancing Barn hotel in Suffolk, England, is a hotel that is half-suspended in the air and half-built on a hill. It's literally balancing! • **Bolivia's Palacio del Sal hotel, even the furniture, is made entirely of salt.** • A fully functioning hotel in Belgium has an atomically correct

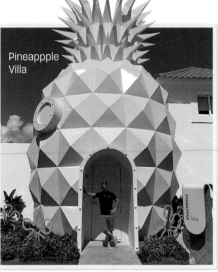

Pineappple Villa

sculpture of the human intestine. • **At the Kagga Kamma Nature Reserve in South Africa, guests can stay in special cave suites—rooms dug into the side of rock!** • The Crane Hotel Faralda is located in a refurbished construction crane in the Netherlands. • **No Man's Fort, a hotel in Portsmouth, England, was built in a military naval fort constructed between 1867 and 1880. It has a spa, a theater for live performances, and restaurants.** • SiloStay in Little River, New Zealand, is an environmentally conscious hotel built into long silos. Each silo even contains a full kitchen! • **The V8 Hotel in Stuttgart, Germany, is completely car themed. Each room has different auto decor and features such as a bed built into a vintage car.** • Das Park Hotel in Linz, Austria, offers rooms created from old sewage pipes. • **El Cosmico, a hotel in Marfa, Texas, offers a range of accommodations, from tents and teepees to vintage trailers.** • The Central Hotel & Café in Copenhagen, Denmark, is a hotel with only one room. • **The Sheraton Huzhou Hot Spring Resort in Huzhou, China, is commonly referred to as "the doughnut" because of its archlike shape.** • The Quinta Real Zacatecas in Zacatecas, Mexico, was built around a bullfighting ring built in the 1800s. • **The Arctic TreeHouse Hotel, located in northern Finland, is made up of tree houses in the Arctic. Here, you can enjoy views of the northern lights.** • The Burj Al Arab hotel in Dubai, United Arab Emirates, is in the shape of a ship's sail and sits on its own island in the Persian Gulf. • **The Hobbit Motel in**

THE WORLD'S FIRST HOTEL STAFFED BY ROBOTS IS THE HENN-NA HOTEL IN JAPAN. HERE, ROBOTS COMPLETE TASKS SUCH AS MANNING THE RECEPTION DESK AND SERVING COFFEE.

Treehotel

Icehotel

DO NOT DISTURB

Waitomo, New Zealand, is hobbit themed, with lodging modeled after Bilbo Baggins's on-screen home. • Treehotel in Sweden is a tree house hotel where each room has a different theme, from a UFO to a bird's nest! • **The most unique room at the Manta Resort on Pemba Island, Tanzania, is completely underwater. Guests are dropped off by boat and can watch marine life swim by from bed!** • Free Spirit Spheres in Vancouver Island, Canada, has sphere-shaped rooms tied to trees, so they can move with the breeze like gigantic wind chimes. • **The Boot Bed'n'Breakfast in Tasman, New Zealand, is shaped like a giant boot.** • Utter Inn, located in the middle of Lake Mälaren, Sweden, is a small red house on the water with a secret bedroom beneath the water's surface that has glass walls, allowing guests to see into the lake. • **Capsule Hotel in Sydney, Australia, is a hotel with rooms that are small pods—only large enough to contain a bed. Though small, they do have televisions!** • The Jaffa Hotel in Tel Aviv, Israel, used to be a monastery where priests lived. • **Fourteen themed hotels sit on the Las Vegas Strip, making Las Vegas, Nevada, the world record holder for the highest concentration of themed hotels.** • The rooms in Featherbed Railroad Bed and Breakfast Resort, located on Clear Lake in California, are in fact nine antique railroad cars. •

The Icehotel of Sweden offers both "regular" warm rooms and rooms made entirely out of ice. • Taj Lake Palace in Rajasthan, India, floats on a lake. • **Skylodge Adventure Suites in Sacred Valley, Peru, are small aluminum pods attached to the slope of a mountain.** • Cley Windmill in Norfolk, England, is a hotel in a repurposed windmill. • **The Hotel Everest View in Nepal is the world's highest hotel, located at an elevation of 13,000 feet (3,962 m).** • Alto Atacama hotel, in the Atacama Desert in Chile, is located in a place where until 2015 there was no rainfall in recorded history. • **Vatican City, the smallest country in the world by both land area and population, has only one hotel within its border.** • The first underground five-star resort in the world is China's InterContinental Shanghai Wonderland hotel. • **The First World Hotel in Malaysia is the world's largest hotel with 7,351 rooms.** • The world's oldest hotel is the Nishiyama Onsen Keiunkan of Japan, which has been in existence since AD 705. That's more than 1,300 years! • **The Fairmount holds the Guinness World Record for the "heaviest**

hotel re-located." Built in San Antonio, Texas, it moved five blocks via 36 dollies over six days. • The Fairmount's move cost $650,000. • **The world's largest hotel for insects was built in Warsaw, Poland, in 2021. The hotel is 3,156 cubic feet (89 cu m). That's the size of about 130 average-size refrigerators!** • One-thirteenth of all hotel rooms in the United States are in Las Vegas. • **The Marmara Antalya Hotel in Antalya, Turkey, was the world's first rotating hotel.** • Jules' Undersea Lodge of Key Largo, Florida, holds the Guinness World Record for first underwater hotel. • **To access the Jules' Undersea Lodge, hotel-goers must dive 30 feet (9 m) underwater.** • The world's most expensive hotel room is within the Hotel President Wilson of Geneva, Switzerland. It costs $83,200 per night. • **The Grand Hills Hotel and Spa in Lebanon holds the world record for largest hotel suite, with the room coming in at a total of 44,466 square feet (4,131 sq m). For comparison, the residence, ground floor, and state floor of the White House are a combined 55,000 square feet (5,110 sq m).** • A hotel chain known as the Peninsula Hotels in Hong Kong, China, owns the world's largest hotel fleet of Rolls-Royce luxury cars: 28. Each one is painted dark green. • **The Rotel is a hotel on wheels—in a bus, that is. It has locations across the world.** • The Bellagio Hotel of Las

Vegas holds the world record for the most fountains in a hotel. It's home to 1,000 fountains and a man-made lake. • **A hotel room in Hotel La Réserve, Paris, France, is themed after Magnum ice cream bars.** • The caveman room of the Madonna Inn Resort and Spa in San Luis Obispo, California, is made entirely of solid rock and includes a waterfall. • **Au Vieux Panier of Marseille, France, is periodically redesigned completely to reflect different themes, such as "Land of the Moon."** • The Sun Cruise Resort at Jeongdongjin Beach, South Korea, is a cruise ship that stays on land! It's located on a cliff overlooking the ocean. • **The Library Hotel in New York City has 10 floors, each themed after a category in the Dewey decimal system, a system used to organize library books.** • The Conrad Maldives hotel in the island nation of the Maldives has underwater suites built with all glass walls, so you can watch the marine life from your bed.

Hyatt Regency of San Francisco

THE HYATT REGENCY OF SAN FRANCISCO, CALIFORNIA, BOASTS THE WORLD'S LARGEST LOBBY AT 350 FEET (107 M) LONG AND 160 FEET (49 M) WIDE.

Dining at the Conrad Maldives

Delicious and

44 Totally Random Facts About FRUITS and VEGGIES

Fruits grow from the seeds of a plant's pollinated flower. Vegetables develop from any other part of a plant, such as the leaves or roots.

Crop is the term for a plant grown for the purpose of eating or selling.

People learned to grow crops about 11,500 years ago, when agriculture started to become a way of life.

The average pomegranate can have as many as 1,400 seeds.

Avocados first grew in the wild in southern Mexico about 12,000 years ago.

Before agriculture was practiced widely, early man found food by hunting wild animals and gathering wild-grown fruits, vegetables, and nuts.

Beets originally came from the Mediterranean region of Europe. This red root vegetable is not only edible, it can also be used as dye!

Corn was first grown by humans about 5,500 years ago in South America.

In colonial America, women hoping to marry would peel an apple and throw it over their shoulder. They believed that the peel would fall in the shape of the initial of the man they would marry.

Potatoes are the most commonly consumed fruit or vegetable in the United States.

Avocados were first farmed in 5000 BC. Archaeologists discovered this when they uncovered avocado seeds in the tomb of an Inca mummy.

AGRICULTURE IS THE SCIENCE AND PRACTICE OF GROWING CROPS AND RAISING ANIMALS FOR FOOD.

Nutritious

Baby carrots are not really young carrots. They are cut down to size from larger carrots.

Vegetables and fruits that are orange and yellow—such as sweet potatoes, pumpkins, and carrots—contain carotenoid pigments, which give them their color.

Red fruits and vegetables get their color from natural pigments called carotenoids, anthocyanins, and betacyanins.

In addition to red, anthocyanins produce many other colors in fruits and vegetables, including blue.

Peppers, pumpkins, cucumbers, pea pods, string beans, eggplants, okra, olives, avocados, corn, and zucchini are all actually fruit.

CARROTS CAN ALSO BE RED, PURPLE, AND YELLOW.

Native Americans not only ate cranberries, but they also used them to dye clothing and for medicine.

The "seeds" on the outside of strawberries are not actually seeds; they are fruits. Each one of these tiny fruits contains a seed.

In ancient Egypt, watermelons were buried with kings.

Bananas are actually berries because they grow from a flower, are soft in the middle, and have seeds.

Spinach is 91 percent water.

The red flesh around a pomegranate seed is called the aril.

Humans first started growing grapes around 6500 BC—that's about 8,000 years ago!

AVOCADOS ARE CONSIDERED BERRIES.

The first vegetable that was grown in space was a potato.

Artichokes are from the Mediterranean. The first recorded use of artichokes in food was in Italy in about 1400.

The pointy leaves of an artichoke plant can grow up to 3 feet (1 m). The part we eat comes from the center of the plant.

One apple tree can grow as many as 400 apples per year.

Ancient Egyptians harvesting grapes

BLUE PARROT
BRAND

CONTENTS
ONE HALF U.S.
STANDARD BBL.
OF CRANBERRIES

CAPE COD CRANBERRIES
COLLEY CRANBERRY CO.
DISTRIBUTING AGENTS
BOSTON, MASS.

A cranberry bed

Apples, peaches, cherries, quinces, apricots, and raspberries are all closely related to roses.

Tomatoes are technically fruits because they form from a flower and contain seeds. However, in the 1800s, the United States Supreme Court decided that they are also considered vegetables in the eyes of the law.

About 69 percent of food eaten across the world in a given country actually comes from another country.

Bananas were first grown agriculturally between 7,000 and 10,000 years ago in modern-day Papua New Guinea and Southeast Asia.

Ancient corn had the taste of an uncooked potato and had only between 5 and 10 kernels per cob.

Blueberries, cranberries, and Concord grapes are native to North America.

Humans first grew carrots about 5,000 years ago in an area that is now western Asia and the Middle East.

Black sapote

Buddha's hand

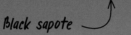

Fruits and Veggies You Probably Haven't Heard Of

- The African cucumber is also called a horned melon because the oval-shaped orange fruit is covered with spikes.

- **Native to Central and South America, the black sapote fruit has flesh the color and consistency of chocolate pudding.**

- Grown in India and China, a citrus fruit known as Buddha's hand gets its name from the many "fingers" that stick out from its center.

- **Durian fruit is the world's smelliest fruit—some people think it smells like rotten eggs, sweaty socks, and wet garbage. But in parts of the world, it's considered a gourmet food.**

- Fiddleheads are vegetables that are the coiled-up parts of the ostrich fern plant. They only grow in the spring, must be cooked before eaten, and taste grassy.

- **The most expensive fruit in the world is the Yubari melon, originally from Japan. It costs more than $11,000 for just one!**

- The largest fruit in the world grown on a tree is the jackfruit, which is native to parts of Asia. These huge fruits weigh more than 100 pounds (45 kg).

That's Creepy!

The Church of Bones

45 Totally Random Facts to MAKE YOUR SKIN TINGLE

Demodex folliculorum are a type of mite that eats dead skin cells on people. Without knowing it, many of us have small numbers of them on our bodies. • Emetophobia is the fear of throwing up. • *Rat king* is the term for when several rats' tails become entangled, and the rats are stuck together. • During England's Victorian era, people commonly took photographs with a loved one who had recently died as a way of honoring the dead and preserving their memory. • Anglerfish are able to open their mouths so wide that they can eat prey two times their size. • Imagine seeing a spider the size of a dinner plate. The world's largest tarantulas can get this big—up to 11 inches (28 cm)! • Although a tarantula mostly eats insects, it's able to eat small mammals. • Several species of tarantula are able to shoot hair containing a thin layer of venom from their bodies. • Tarantulas can swim. • Phasmophobia is the fear of ghosts. • The Asian vampire moth is known to drink animal blood. • The blood of spiders is clear. • Many people, aircraft, and ocean vessels have disappeared without a trace and without explanation in the Bermuda Triangle, a region between Florida, Puerto Rico, and Bermuda in the Atlantic Ocean. • The Church of Bones in the Czech Republic is in part made of human bones. • Historians widely consider a Celtic celebration called Samhain to be the original Halloween. It was believed that ghosts walked with the living during Samhain. • Vlad the Impaler was the nickname of Vlad III Dracula, who was born in Transylvania and became a prince of what is now Romania. He was known to be particularly bloodthirsty toward his enemies, which earned him the nickname. Many historians think the vampiric character Dracula was based on him. • In Latin, Dracula means "son of the dragon." • In the 18th and 19th centuries in New England, people would dig up suspected vampires and behead them to ensure that they didn't rise from the dead. • Safety coffins, invented in the late 19th century, were meant to allow someone to call for help if buried alive. • Though only about the size of a paper clip, the poisonous skin of a golden poison dart frog can be lethal with just a touch. • Some types of horned lizards can shoot blood from their eyes. • Statistically, it is more likely to die from a kick or stomp by a cow than from a shark. • Female black widows sometimes eat the males after mating. • Some lizards are able to drop their tails from their torsos. • *Cymothoa exigua* is a parasite that eats the tongues of fish and then uses its own body to replace the tongue. •

Tarantula

SOME ANCIENT MUMMIES STILL HAVE FINGERPRINTS.

Between July and September 1518, citizens of Strasbourg, France, spontaneously began dancing in the streets in an outbreak of mass hysteria called the Strasbourg dancing plague. • In the 18th and 19th centuries, dentures were made from human teeth. • Mourning jewelry, popular in the Victorian era, was meant to honor a loved one that had passed and was sometimes made with the hair of the deceased. • *Toxoplasma gondii* is a parasite that lives in cat feces and that rats and mice can contract, which causes them to be attracted to cats and their urine. • *Toxoplasma gondii* can also infect people, and for some, it can be dangerously harmful. • Jellyfish eat and poop from the same body part. • Teratoma are tumors that are able to grow organs, hair, teeth, and limbs. • Cuttlefish can change the color of their skin to create patterns that hypnotize their prey. • Rattlesnakes are able to both bite and release venom into their prey even after a rattlesnake is dead. • In the 16th century, English royalty used lead makeup as foundation, which caused skin discoloration, hair loss, and rotting

Mourning brooch containing the hair of a dead relative

teeth. • In the event that the sun exploded, the explosion wouldn't be visible on Earth for 8 minutes, 20 seconds. • Coulrophobia is the fear of clowns. • The human body sheds 77 pounds (35 kg) of skin over the course of a lifetime. • The average human creates 1.5 quarts (1.4 L) of mucus daily. • Boogers are actually dried mucus. • Some people interpreted the Aztec legend of the five suns as a prediction that the world would end by an earthquake in the year 2012. • Certain species of snakes are able to reuse the poison of poisonous animals they ingest. • The tiny venomous blue-ringed octopus is only 8 inches (20 cm) long but has venom 1,000 times more potent than cyanide. • If the huge supervolcano under Yellowstone National Park were to ever erupt, it would release ash for thousands of miles. • Cone snails are incredibly dangerous. They spear victims with a fatal toxin from their bodies.

THE GIANT SPIDER CRAB CAN GROW TO BE AS LARGE AS 10 FEET (3 M) WIDE.

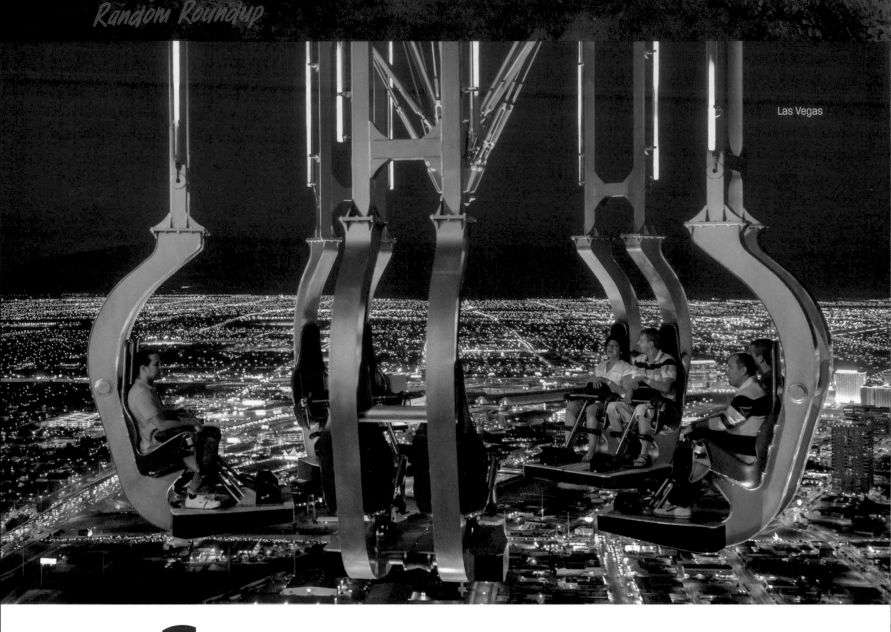

Las Vegas

Play Stations

5/ Totally Random Facts About THEME PARKS

The world's highest amusement park, in Las Vegas, Nevada, stands 1,149 feet (350 m) tall. It was built with help from helicopters.

Haw Par Villa, located in Singapore, is a theme park based on Chinese legends.

Ferrari World in Abu Dhabi is a Ferrari race car theme park and is mostly indoors.

Enchanted Forest is a fairy tale–themed park in Oregon that includes an attraction shaped like a giant witch's head. You can go inside through the door—her mouth!

Caribbean Bay water park in Gyeonggi-do, South Korea, has special rooms for park-goers to take naps before they head back to the park for more adventure.

The world's largest indoor theme park is in Abu Dhabi, United Arab Emirates (UAE). It features characters from Looney Tunes, among others.

The Children's Republic in Argentina is a theme park in which guests can spend time in a normal town—shrunk down to kid size. It has a theater, hotel, restaurant, and even a courthouse.

Suoi Tien Theme Park in Ho Chi Minh City, Vietnam, celebrates Buddhism. It is also home to 1,500 crocodiles.

The Aquaventure Waterpark in Dubai, UAE, has more than 100 waterslides!

Aquatica water park in Orlando, Florida, has a human-made beach that has no less than 1,360 tons (1,214 metric tons) of sand and upward of 60,000 types of plants.

Rolling With It!

TOWERING 130 FEET (40 M) HIGH AND FEATURING A PANIC-PROVOKING 87-DEGREE DROP, the Jersey Devil Coaster is **the world's most extreme roller coaster.** The ride was unveiled at Six Flags Great Adventure in New Jersey in 2021. **The orange ride features red, devil-decorated cars that hold up to 12 passengers.** The coaster, which has 3,000 feet (914 m) of track, **reaches speeds of 58 miles an hour (93 kph), and goes upside down three times during the two-minute experience.** You must be 4 feet tall (1.2 m) to ride!

The rides at the Watercube Waterpark in Beijing, China, were shipped to the city in parts and constructed on location.

Bollywood Parks, located in Dubai, UAE, is home to Bollywood SkyFlyer, the tallest swing ride in the world.

An amusement park in Las Vegas called Dig This Vegas lets you drive bulldozers and USE EXCAVATION EQUIPMENT.

Yas Waterworld, located in Abu Dhabi, UAE, includes the first hydromagnetic waterslide in the world.

WaterWorld Waterpark in Ayia Napa, Cyprus, is themed as ancient Greece, complete with shipwrecks and a Trojan horse.

The Chimelong Water Park of Guangzhou, China, is the world's most frequently visited water park, with 2,740,000 park-goers per year.

Chimelong Water Park

At Cedar Point, an amusement park in Ohio, all lost change is **DONATED TO CHARITY.**

The world's oldest amusement park, located in Denmark, is more than 400 years old.

One of the attractions at the Rush Mountain Adventure Park in South Dakota is an underground cave.

Some theme park workers have secret codes, used so that workers can communicate without alarming park-goers. "Code V" is the phrase workers at Disneyland use to inform one another that an amusement park-goer has vomited at the park.

The World Waterpark in Edmonton, Alberta, Canada, can handle 40,000 guests at one time.

Some roller coasters are recycled into new ones.

Doritos were invented at the now closed Casa de Fritos restaurant at Disneyland in the 1960s.

Juicy Water of London, England, holds the world record for largest residential water sprinkler at 21 feet, 1 inch (6.4 m) long, 5 feet, 10.87 inches (1.8 m) wide, and 5 feet, 1.8 inches (1.6 m) high.

The world's longest inflatable waterslide can be found in Vernon, New Jersey, and measures 1,975 feet (602 m) long.

Tropical Islands water park in Krausnick, Germany, is built inside the world's largest freestanding hall.

Tropical Islands

Crocosaurus Cove in Darwin, Australia, is a crocodile theme park in which guests can enter a glass box that is lowered 20 feet (6 m) into a pool filled with crocodiles!

PT. Ecomarine Indo Pelago in Bali, Indonesia, is the largest inflatable water park. It's designed to spell out the word Indonesia when seen from above.

Jens Scherer is the Guinness World Record holder for longest distance traveled on a waterslide over the course of 24 hours. He slid 94.54 miles (152.15 km).

Jens Scherer rode the ride 427 times in the 24-hour period.

An amusement park in Ohio boasting 18 coasters on 364 acres (943 ha) is known as the roller coaster capital of the world.

Mini-Europe, a theme park in Belgium, features tiny versions of popular attractions from around Europe, such as the Eiffel Tower and the Leaning Tower of Pisa.

Falcon's Flight in Riyadh, Saudi Arabia, is the world record holder for tallest, fastest, and longest roller coaster in the world.

Falcon's Flight will go faster than 155 miles an hour (249 kmh)!

The Mighty Mouse

- Disney World has the most guests of any theme park in the world—about 21 million per year.

- **Disneyland first opened its doors on July 17, 1955.**

- Parts of the outside of the building that houses the famous It's a Small World ride contain real gold.

- **Most of the plants inside Disneyland's Tomorrowland can be safely eaten.**

- Disneyland opened with 18 rides. Today, it has close to 100 attractions.

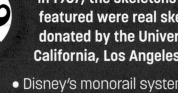

- **Approximately 200 feral cats live in Disneyland and roam the park at night to curb the population of unwanted rats.**

- A time capsule buried beneath Sleeping Beauty Castle is scheduled to be opened on July 17, 2035.

- **Thurl Ravenscroft, the voice actor who played Tony the Tiger and sang "You're a Mean One, Mr. Grinch," also voiced the portions of several Disneyland rides, such as the Haunted Mansion and It's a Small World.**

- Disneyland's admission in 1955 was $1.

- **While park-goers wait for their chance to enter the Star Wars-themed ride, a voice over a** loudspeaker asks for a "Mr. Egroeg Sacul,"—the name of George Lucas, with the letters arranged in reverse.

- Until the year 2000, workers at Disneyland were not allowed to have mustaches.

- **When the Pirates of the Caribbean ride first opened in 1967, the skeletons it featured were real skeletons donated by the University of California, Los Angeles.**

- Disney's monorail system was the first in the Western Hemisphere to run on a daily basis.

- **Walt Disney himself secretly kept a small apartment located on Disneyland's Main Street.**

- Disneyworld is just over 40 square miles (104 sq km). That's almost the size of San Francisco.

- **The Enchanted Storybook Castle at Shanghai Disneyland in China is the tallest of all Disney parks' castles.**

- The King Arthur Carrousel, located at Fantasyland in Disneyland has 68 horses, many of which are more than 90 years old.

Full Spectrum

46 Totally Random Facts About COLORS

A living thing that only sees in combinations of two colors (such as dogs) is called a dichromat. • **Color is the word we use to indicate the way we perceive different types of light.** • A living thing that sees in combinations of three different colors (such as humans) is called a trichromat. • **The human eye contains three types of cells known as cone cells.** • Humans have cone cells for the primary colors blue, green, and red. Most human beings see in combinations of these three primary colors. • **A small number of people are able to detect color between red and green. These people are called tetrachromats.** • Apes, chimpanzees, and African monkeys are able to see the same colors as humans. • **Babies can't see color when they are born. It takes about five months for babies to see all colors.** • All languages have more words to describe warm colors (orange, red, and pink, for instance) than cool colors such as blue, purple, and green. • **Plants get their green**

color from a chemical called chlorophyll, which helps plants absorb sunlight. • The visible spectrum of light—for example, the colors visible to the human eye—are the colors of the rainbow: red, orange, yellow, blue, green, indigo, and violet. • **Different colors have different wavelengths, which is how the eye is able to detect the differences.** • About 4.5 percent of people are unable to sense the complete visible spectrum of light. This is called color blindness. • **Colorimetry is the study of the measurement of color.** • During the reign of Cyrus the Great, king of Persia (modern-day Iran), it was illegal for anyone other than King Cyrus to wear the color purple. • **The color purple is also associated with royalty, because in the ancient world, the dye was produced from the mucus of a very rare sea snail, *Bolinus brandaris*. Because it was so hard to get, the dye was very expensive.** • Producing a single ounce of purple dye would take 250,000 snails. • **By the 1850s, people discovered how to create human-made purple dye that didn't require the snail; therefore, it became much less expensive.** • Color can affect the way food tastes. • **In the time of the Chinese Tang dynasty, only emperors wore *chihuang* (a red-yellow hue) because it symbolized the sun.** • A flame's color will change from red to blue as it becomes hotter. • **Scientists are able to determine the temperature of a star**

WORLDWIDE, BLUE IS THE MOST COMMON FAVORITE COLOR.

RESEARCHERS HAVE FOUND THAT YELLOW AND RED CAN MAKE YOU FEEL LIKE YOU'RE HUNGRY.

by its color. • The sun is 932° F (5500° C) and appears yellow. If the sun were cooler, it would be red, and if it were hotter, it would be blue. • **The Russian language distinguishes light blue and dark blue as separate colors, similar to the English language's distinction between dark and light red with the words *red* and *pink*.** • Red light does not penetrate the deep parts of the ocean. This means that red objects and substances in the deep ocean appear black. • **Sunlight contains every color of light in the visible spectrum—red, orange, yellow, blue, green, indigo, and violet.** • In the ancient Greek language, the word *kyaneos* was used to describe dark bluish colors. It was also used to describe purple. • **Red light has the longest wavelength, whereas violet has the shortest wavelength.** • Women are better than men at distinguishing between colors. • **The first known use of the word "orange" to describe color dates back to the early 16th century. The word "orange" derives from the Persian word, *narang*.** • White and black technically aren't colors. White is the combination of all wavelengths on the visible spectrum, whereas black is the absence of light. • **About 30 percent of people consider orange to be their least favorite color.** • People are more likely to remember something if they see it in color than in black-and-white. • **When placed in chicken coops, red lights help reduce stress for egg-laying hens.** • Chromophobia is the fear of one or multiple colors. • **Ancient Sumerians were likely the first group of people to have a word for the color dark blue.** • Egyptians were the first ancient peoples to develop a blue dye. • **The language of the Himba tribe of Namibia, Africa, does not have a word for the color blue. For them, blue is considered a type of green, not a separate color.**

What Colors Can Animals See?

- Dogs and rabbits can see blue and green, but not red.

- **Cats and squirrels can see blue and yellow, but not red.**

- Many spiders are able to see green and ultraviolet light, which is a color beyond purple.

- **Most insects are able to see blue, yellow, and ultraviolet light.**

- Rats are able to see blue, green, and ultraviolet light.

- **Because birds can see ultraviolet light, they are able to see colors in another bird's feathers that humans cannot see.**

Americans eat approximately 7 billion pounds (3 billion kg) of candy **EVERY YEAR.**

Sweet Treats

28 Totally Random Facts About CANDY

Bertie Bott's Every Flavour Beans, candy from the world of *Harry Potter*, include wax, pepper, avocado, marmalade, and caviar flavors.

Chocolate accounts for about half of the candy Americans consume yearly.

Five hundred and nine Peeps are made every eight seconds.

Cacao, the plant from which chocolate is made, is native to South America.

Until 1990 in the United Kingdom, Snickers chocolate bars were called Marathon bars. In 2020, they went back to that original name—Marathon!

The Guinness World Record for longest piece of licorice is 1,702 feet, 9 inches (519 m).

Two Swedish candy companies worked together on making the licorice and the record. The licorice took more than 13 hours to make.

More than 200 tons (178 metric tons) of Twizzlers are made each day.

Cacao trees can live as long as 200 years.

Germany consume more candy than per capita any other country in the world—29 pounds (13 kg) per person on average.

Dubble Bubble was the first brand of bubble gum in the United States. It debuted in 1928 and was even given to troops during World War II.

Candy corn is modeled after corn because, when it was invented, approximately half of Americans were farmers.

The *M*'s in M&Ms stand for the last names of the inventors of these candies: Forrest Mars and Bruce Murrie.

The German candy company HARIBO invented gummy bears in 1922. By the 1960s, they were given the name Gummibärchen, or "little gummy bears."

In Japan, you can find matcha green tea–flavored Kit Kat bars.

Jelly beans were invented during the Civil War.

Originally, jelly beans were sold in bags that held only one color.

Starburst candies were originally called Opal Fruit.

Sugar was first grown agriculturally in 8000 BC by the ancient people of present-day New Guinea.

The first chocolate made by a machine was in Barcelona, Spain, in the year 1780.

Ingesting 22 pounds (10 kg) of chocolate—the equivalent of 50 giant-size Hershey's bars—could be deadly to people.

HERSHEY'S HISTORY

- **Hershey's Kisses were first made in 1907.**

- **Hershey's Kisses were shaped like a square until 1921.**

- **The Hershey Company launched the Mr. Goodbar chocolate and peanut bar in 1925.**

- **In 1971, the Hershey's Tropical chocolate bar was sent to the moon with astronauts on the Apollo 15 mission.**

- **A 60-year-old Hershey's bar was once discovered frozen in Antarctica. Because it had been frozen, it was still edible.**

- **Seventy million Hershey's Kisses are made each day.**

Suoi Tien Theme Park, Ho Chi Minh City, Vietnam

Turn to page 215 for the answers!

Page numbers in *italic* refer to images.

A

animals. *See also* birds; cats; dogs; marine life; reptiles.
armadillos 6, 7, *7*
bilbies 46, *46*, 47
biofluorescence 67, *67*
bison 35, *35*
camouflage 14–15, *14–15*
chimpanzees 22, 160, *160*, 204
chipmunks 23, *23*
climate change and 76, *76*, 77, *77*
deer 3, 20, 22, *22*, 35
Diprotodon 48, *48*
echidnas 6, *6*, 7, 25
elephants 17, 22, 51, 171, *171*
emotional support animals 62–63, *63*
eyes 32, 36, 37, 47
gerbils 30, *30*, 31, 32, 33
guinea pigs 30, *30*, 31, 32, *32–33*, 33
hedgehogs 6, *6*, 7
hippos 19, *19*, 24, 167
horses 32, 62, 63, *63*, 87, 97, *97*, 101, *102–103*, 105, 131, 134, 135, *135*, 186, 203
kangaroos 22, *22*, 43, *43*, 44, *44–45*, 46, 47, *47*, 48, 49, *49*

koalas 22, 42, *42*, 43, *43*, 44, 45, 46, 47, *47*, 48
Kodiak bears 24, *24*
meerkats 21, *21*
monkeys 22, 24, *24*, 63, 204
naked mole rats 167, *167*
opossums 21, 43, 44, *44*, 48, 74
pandas 20, *20*, 21, 129, *129*
pigs 23, *23*, 62, 77, 114, 167
polar bears 76, *76*
porcupines 6, *6*, 7
possums 43, 44, *44*, 46, 47, 48
quolls 21, *21*, 48, *48*
rabbits 25, 30, *30–31*, 31, 32, *32*, 33, 74, 205
raccoons 24, 109, *109*
sloths 22, *22*
slow loris 19, *19*
snowshoe hares 14, *14*
squirrels 23, 67, *67*, 89, 92, 205
sugar gliders 45, *45*, 47, 48
Tasmanian devils 44, *44*, 45, 46
Thylacinus 48, *48*
tree kangaroos 46, *46*, 47
wildebeests 75, *75*
wolves 26, 28, *34*, *35*, 35–37, *36*, *37*, 97
wombats 22, 44, 47, *47*, 48
arachnids. *See also* insects
spiders *14*, 15, 16, 18, 21, 171, 198, 205
scorpions 16, *16*, 18, 67
tarantulas 198, *198*

B

birds. *See also* animals.
African gray parrots 65, *65*
Archaeopteryx 60, *61*
black kites 86, *86*
bluebirds 9, 10, *10*, 12
camouflage 14, 15, *15*
cardinals 8, *8–9*, 9, 10, 11, 12, 13
common cuckoos 10, 11, *11*
common potoos 15, *15*
crows 10, 11, *12*, 13
ducks 24, 25, *25*, 132
flamingos *12–13*, 21, *21*
hummingbirds 8, 9, 10, 11, 12, 13, *13*, 61
keas 65, *65*
macaws 64, *64*, 65
ostriches 22, *22*, 61
owls 13, *13*, 14, 21, *21*
parrots *63*, 64–65, *64*, *65*
pigeons 8, *8*, 10, 11, 12, 156
robins 8, 9, *9*, 10, *10*, 12
woodpeckers 8, 9, 10, 11, *11*
body
blood 16, 17, 18, 27, 56, 63, 100, 161, 162, *162*, 172, 174
bones 161, 165, *165*, 198, *198*, 203
brain 19, 29, 61, 168–171, *168–169*, 172, 173, *173*, 174
cells 162, *162–163*, 163, 168, 171, 173, 174, 198, 204
eyes 83, 105, 161, 162, 169, 172–175, *172*, *173*, *174*, 204–205

Guinea pigs have four toes on their front feet and three on their back feet. (See p. 33)

hair 53, 106, *106*, 107, 110, 160, *160*, 161, 199, *199*, 203
height 110, *110*, 162, *162*
intestines *161*, 164, 165, *165*, 166, *166*, 191
liver 83, 161, *161*, *165*, 166
muscles 161, 162, 163, *163*, 166, 168, 174
nose 161, 162, *162*, 170
teeth 127, 164, *164*, *165*, 166, *166*, 167, 199
buildings
  castles 100, *100–101*, 101, 102, 103, *103*, *188*, 203
  Church of Bones 198, *198*
  Great Chicago Fire 84, 85, *85*
  hotels 190, *190*, 191, *191*, 192, 192–193, *193*
  theme parks *188*, 200–203, *200*, *201*, *202*, *203*
  White House 108, 109, *109*, 110, 111, 193

C

cats. *See also* animals.
  Asian leopard cats 3, *3*
  cheetahs 2, 3, 4, *4*, 5, *5*, 56
  eyes 2, 25, 56, *56–57*, 57
  jaguars 2, *2*, 3, 4, *4*, 16
  kittens 3, 5, *5*, *56–57*, 57, 59
  Maine coon 56, *58*
  margay cats 3, *3*
  servals 3, 4, *4*, 5
  snow leopards 2, 3, *3*, 4, 5, *5*, 15
  tigers 3, 19, 20, 25, *25*, 59

D

dogs. *See also* animals.
  Border Collies 29, *29*
  Chihuahuas 29, *29*
  Great Danes 29, *29*
  Pekingese 26, *26*
  service dogs 62–63, *62*, *63*
  sled dogs *26–27*, 134

F

foods
  apples *55*, 194, *194*, 196, 197
  avocados 194, 195, *196*, 206
  black sapote 197, *197*
  Buddha's hand 197, *197*
  candy 126, 206–207, *206*, *207*
  carrots 32, 195, *195*, 197
  climate change and 78, 79, *79*

The White House was at various times known as the President's Palace, the President's House, and the Executive Mansion. (See p. 108)

  corn 194, *194*, 195, 197, 207
  cranberries 196, *196–197*, 197
  grapes 196, *196*, 197
  insects as 41, *41*, 55, *55*
  puffer fish 17, *17*
  sugar 54, 167, 207
  tea 128, *128*, 207
  utensils 124, *124*, 126, 166

G

geography
  earthquakes 59, 72, 75, 86, 139, 140, 143, 186, 199
  Grand Canyon 92–93, *92–93*
  islands 141, *141*
  Mars *184*, 185, *185*, 186, *186*, 187, *187*
  mountains 15, 47, 64, 77, 79, 105, 134, 139, 185, 186

H

history
  Abraham Lincoln 110, *110*
  Akbar 105, *105*
  Albert Einstein 170, *170*
  Andrew Johnson 109, *109*
  Augustus Caesar 96, *96–97*, 97, 98, 99
  Caligula 96, *96*, 97
  Colosseum 97, 99, *99*
  dentistry 164, 165, 166
  Dorothy Dandridge 105, *105*
  Elizabeth I 33, *33*, 106
  Ellen DeGeneres 106, *106*
  fire 84, 85, *85*, 86, 87, *87*, 124, 126
  Franklin Delano Roosevelt 109, *109*
  George Washington 108, *108*, 109, 110, 111, 167
  gladiators 96, 97, 98, 99, *99*
  Great Chicago Fire 84, 85, *85*, 87
  Harriet Quimby 131, *131*
  Hillary Clinton 111, *111*
  Jesse Owens 105, *105*
  John F. Kennedy 110, *110*
  Julius Caesar 82, 96, 97, 99
  knights 100, 101, *101*, 102, *102–103*
  Madam C. J. Walker 106, *106*
  Martha Washington 111, *111*
  Michelle Obama 111, *111*
  Napoleon 47, *47*
  Nellie Bly 104, *104*
  Ronald Reagan 110, *110*
  Steve Jobs 106, *106*
  Theodore Roosevelt 92, 109, 110
  Tower of London 100, *100*
  Vincent Van Gogh 107, *107*
  White House 108, 109, *109*, 110, 111
  World War I 8, *8*, 15, 28
  World War II 106, 115, 207

I

insects. *See also* arachnids.
  antennae 39, *39*, 54, 55
  ants 10, 18, 54, 55, *55*
  atlas moth 38, *38*
  bees 12, 18, 19, 55, 135, 171
  bioluminescence 66, *66*, 67
  butterflies 14, 39, 40, 41, 90

camouflage 14, 40, 41, *41*, 54–55, *54*

caterpillars 14, 19, 39, *39*, 40, 41, *41*, 86

death's head hawk moths 40, *40*

dragonflies 54, *54–55*, 55

fireflies 66, *66–67*, 67, 85

fleas 17, 55, *55*

Gray's leaf insects 54, *54*

hornet moths 40, *40*

hummingbird moths 40, *40–41*

mosquitoes 16, *16*, 17, 77

moths 38–41, *38*, *39*, *40–41*, 55, 90, 198

proboscis 39, 40, *40*

stick insects 14, *15*, 54, 55

M

marine life. *See also* animals.

anemones 15, 139, *139*, 147, 156

bioluminescence 66, *66*, 67, *67*, 142, 156

blue whales 19, 23, 61, 140, *140*

box jellyfish 18, *18*, 147

bull sharks 17, *17*

camouflage 14, 15, 17, 67, 145, 151, *151*, 153, 154, *154–155*, 155, 156, 199

clown fish 147, 156, *156*

coral 14, 67, 78, *78*, 139, 143, 146, *146–147*, 147, 148, *148*, 149, 151, *151*

dugongs 149, *149*

giant spider crab 199, *199*

Great Barrier Reef 146–149, *146–147*, *148*

hermit crabs *78*, 154

jellyfish 14, 16, 18, *18*, 67, *67*, 139, 146, 147, 148, 155, 199

Liopleurodon 61, *61*

manta rays 171, *171*, *193*

octopuses 14, 15, 16, 147, 152–155, *152*, *153*, *154–155*, 199

parrot fish 148, *148*

puffer fish 17, *17*, 157

seahorses 14, 21, 24, 140, 150–151, *150–151*

seals 24, *24*, 74, 143, *143*

sea snakes 53, *53*, 147

sea turtles 67, 146, *146*, 147

sharks 15, 17, *17*, 21, 24, 67, 82, *82*, 118, 144–145, *144*, *145*, 147, 149, 153, *153*, 157, *157*, 167, 174

squids 15, 66, 67, 171

starfish 149, *149*

stingrays 14, *156–157*, 157

sturgeon 157, *157*

whale sharks 144–145, *144*, *145*, 147

P

plants

apples *55*, 194, *194*, 196, 197

aspen trees 90, *90*

avocados 194, 195, *196*, 206

bamboo 89, 91, *91*, 166

black sapote 197, *197*

Buddha's hand 197, *197*

chlorophyll 89, 204, *204*

chocolate cosmos flower 90, *90*

corn 194, *194*, 195, 197, 207

cranberries 196, *196–197*, 197

eucalyptus 44, *44*, 45, 46, 47, 48

forest fires 84, *84–85*, 86, *86–87*, 134

ghost flowers 89, *89*

giant sequoia trees 91, *91*

gingko trees 88, *88*, 89

grapes 196, *196*, 197

living bridges 91, *91*

lotus flowers 91, *91*

mangrove trees 146, *146*, 151

pollination *40–41*, 41, 90, 194

princess trees 90, *90*

titan arum 91, *91*

R

reptiles. *See also* animals

boa constrictors 50, 52, *52*, 63, *63*

camouflage 14–15, *14–15*, 51, 53

crocodiles 149, *149*, 203, *203*

dinosaurs 60–61, *60*, *61*

geckos *14–15*, 15

king cobras 51, *51*, 52, 53, *53*

pythons 50, 51, 52

rattlesnakes *50*, 51, 52, 53, 93

sea snakes 53, *53*

sidewinders 50, 51, *51*

Stegosaurus 61, *61*

Suchomimus 60, *60*

Titanoboas 53, *53*

rocks and minerals

Alexandrite 82, *82*, 83

amethyst 80, 81, *81*, 82, 83, *83*

aquamarine 80, 81, 82, 83, *83*

birthstones 83, *83*

diamonds 80, *80*, 82, *82*, 83, *83*

emeralds 80, 81, *81*, 82, 83, *83*

garnet 80, 81, 83, *83*

gold *82*, 103, 105, *105*, 114, 143, *143*, 203

Grand Canyon *92–93*, 93

Mars 185, *185*, 187

opals 80, 81, *81*, 82, 83, *83*

pearls 80, *80*, 82, *82*, 83, *83*

peridot 80, 82, 83, *83*

rubies 80, *80*, 82, *82*, 83, *83*

sapphires 80, 81, *81*, 83, *83*, 182, *182*

tanzanite 81, 82, 83, *83*

topaz 82, 83, *83*

tourmalines 80, *80*, 81, 83

turquoise 81, 82, 83, *83*, 164

Suzhousaurus megatherioides was furry, and it waddled. Its name means "giant sloth-like reptile from Suzhou," because it looked a bit like the ancient giant ground sloth. (See p. 60)

S

space
  Andromeda galaxy 180, *180*
  astronomers 106, 179, *179*, 181, *181*, 183
  constellations 179, *179*, 180, 181, 182
  exoplanets *180*, 182–183, *182–183*
  Mars 82, 184–187, *184*, *185*, *186–187*
  Milky Way galaxy *170–171*, 179, 180, 182
  nebulae 178, *178*, 179
  red dwarf stars 180, *180*
  rovers 185, 186, *186*
  stars *170–171*, *178*, 179, 180, *180*, 181, *181*, 182, *182*, *187*, 204–205
  telescopes 129, *129*, 180, *180*, 182, 183, *183*, 185
sports
  baseball 8, *8*, 116, *116*, 117
  football 8, 89, 116
  jousting *102–103*
  Olympic Games *86*, 105, *105*, 114, 116, 117, 119, 135
  running 116, *116–117*, 117
  skateboarding 59, 119, 130, 132, 134, 135
  soccer 89, 114–115, *114–115*
  surfing 118–119, *118–119*
  zorbing 117, *117*

T

technology
  chain saws 126, 129, *129*
  computers 79, 124, 126, *126*, 129, *140*, 173
  greenhouse gases and *77*, 78–79, *78*, 135
  gunpowder 127, 128, *128*
  ironing boards *128–129*, 129
  lightbulbs 79, 124, 127, *127*, 128
  post-it notes 127, *127*
  pottery wheels 126, *126*, 130
  radios 107, 110, 111, 127, 129, *129*, 185
  robots 185, 191, *191*
  solar power 79, *79*, 134
  telephones *106*, 124, *125*, 127, *127*
  traffic signals 126, *126*
  umbrellas 124, *124*, 128
  utensils 124, *124*, 126, 166
  wheel 124, *124*, 130, 131

transportation
  airplanes 79, 87, *87*, 104, 130, *130–131*, 131, 134, 135, 191
  bicycles 131, 133, 134, *134–135*, 169
  cars 73, 78, *78*, 93, 124, 130, 132, 135, 193
  climate change and 78, *78*, 79
  dog sleds *26–27*, 134
  helicopters 86, 125, 131, 132, 133, 134, 135, 186, *186*, 187, 200
  hot air balloons 130, *130*, 131, 132, 134
  jet-powered suits 131, *131*
  public transportation 130–131, 133, 134, *134*, 135, *135*
  roller coasters 201, *201*, 202, 203
  Rotel hotel 193, *193*
  ships 129, 130, 131–132, *132–133*, 134, 135, 138, *138*, 139, 142, 193
  trains 106, 131, 132–133, *132*, 134, 135, *135*, 192

W

water
  aqueducts 98, *98*
  climate change and 77–78, 79, 140
  Mariana Trench 140, *140*
  ocean layers 140, *140*
  oil fields 142, *142*
  pollution 19, *19*, 143, *143*, 147, 148, 151
  salinity 140, 141, *141*
  sea ice 142, *142*
  shipwrecks 130, 131, 138, *138*, 202
  tsunamis 72, *73*, 74, 75, 139, 140, 141, 142, 143
  water parks 202, *202*
weather
  climate change 76–79
  dust storms 74, *74–75*, 185, 187, *187*
  El Niño 74, *74*, 75
  flooding 55, 72, 73, 74, *74*, 77, 78
  hurricanes 72, *72–73*, 74, 75, 78, 141, 143
  lightning 75, 84, 86, *93*, 115, 157
  Mars 185, 187, *187*
  tornadoes 72, 73, *73*, 74, 86

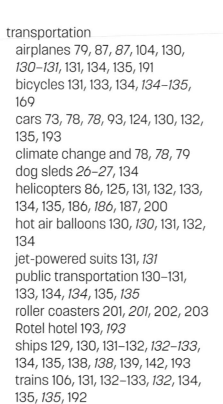

Surfers use wax on their boards to keep them from slipping off. (See p. 119)

Photo Credits

The publishers would like to thank the following for the use of their images. Although every effort has been made to credit images, the publishers will be pleased to correct any errors or omissions in future editions of the book.

t = top; b = bottom; l = left; r = right; c = center

123rf: pp. 63(tr), 161(tr), 208, 209, 215(br).

Alamy: pp. 5(tl,tr), 7(br), 8(bl), 11(tr), 15(tc), 19(cr), 28(tr), 36(b), 45(tl), 67(c), 74(tr,bl), 79(br), 82(bl), 85(br), 87(br), 89(bl), 91(tl,cr), 98(cr), 104(br), 105(tc,cr,bc), 106(br), 110(tcr), 115(tr,br), 117(bc), 129(tl,tr), 131(tr), 143(tr), 146(bl), 154(t), 157(cr), 185(tl), 186(cr), 191(c,bl), 192(tl), 193(br), 201(tcl), 203(tl), 206(cr).

Art Institute of Chicago: pp. 96(cl), 99(tr).

Pilley Bianchi: p. 29(br) (Pilley Bianchi, the copyright holder of this work, has published it under the Creative Commons Attribution-Share Alike 4.0 International License – https://creativecommons.org/licenses/by-sa/4.0/deed.en).

British Library, London: pp. 95, 101(br).

Photo courtesy of digthisvegas.com: p. 201(b).

Photo courtesy of Dog Bark Park Inn B&B: p. 190 (www.dogbarkpark.com/www.facebook.com/dogbarkparkinn).

Dreamstime: pp. i, ii(tl,bl), iv, v(tc,bl), vi(tc,bl), vii(tl,br), viii, 1, 2(tl,r), 3(tr,br), 4(t,bl,br), 5(b), 6(tr,cr,cl,bc), 7(tl,cr), 8(tr), 8–9, 9(tl,tr), 10(c,br), 11(tl,br), 12–13, 13(tl,cr), 14(c,bl), 14–15, 15(cl), 16(tr,cl,br), 16–17, 17(tr), 18(l,tr), 19(tr,bl), 20, 21(tr,cl), 22(tl,br), 23(c,br), 24(t,bl,r), 25(tr,br), 26(tl,br), 27(cl), 28(bl), 28–29, 29(tr), 30(tc,bl), 30–31, 31(tr), 32–33, 33(tl), 34, 35(tr,c), 36(tc,tr), 37(tr,cl,br), 38–39, 39(tr,bl,br), 40(tc,tr), 40–41, 41(tl,br), 42, 43(cr), 44(tr,cl,c,bl), 45(c), 46(bl), 47(tc,cl,bl,br), 48(bl), 49, 50(main photo,inset), 52, 53(tl,bl), 54(cl), 54–55, 55(tl,tcr,bcr), 56(tl,br), 56–57, 58(b), 59(tr,cr), 60(c,br), 61(c,br), 63(cr,cl,br), 64(l,cr), 65(tr,cr,bl), 66(c), 66–67, 68, 69, 70, 71, 72(tc,bl), 72–73, 73(tr,br), 75(cl,cr), 76(cr), 77(tr,cl,bc), 78(tl,tr,b), 79(cl,cr), 80(l,tcr), 81(tr,cl,cr), 82(tl,br), 83(tl,column of 12 birthstones), 84(tr,c), 84–85, 86(tr,cl), 86–87, 88, 89(tr,c), 90(tr,cl), 91(bl,br), 92–93, 93(tc,envelope,stamp,br), 94, 96–97(t,b), 97(tr), 98(tl,b), 99(cr,bl), 100(tc), 100–101, 102)cl), 102–103, 103(bc), 104(t), 106(tr,bl), 109(tr,cl,br), 110(bcl), 111(br), 112, 113, 114(l,bc), 115(bl), 116(tl,bc), 118(bl), 118–119, 119(cr), 120, 121, 122, 123, 124(tl,c,bl), 125(tr,b), 126(cr,bl), 127(tc,cr,b), 128(tc,bl), 128–129, 129(br), 130(tr), 130–131, 131(cl), 132(t,c,cl), 133(tl), 134(tr,c), 134–135, 135(cl), 136, 138, 139(br), 141(b), 142(tl,r,b), 143(cr,cl), 144(bl), 144–145, 145(bc), 146(cr), 146–147, 148(b), 149(tc,tr,bl,br), 150–151, 151(tr), 152(br), 153(tr), 154–155, 156(c,br), 156–157, 157(tr,bc), 158, 159, 160(l,br), 161(tl,body organs,br), 162(tl,tr), 163(tl,tr,br), 164(tr,bl), 165(tl,r), 166(tl,bl), 167(tr,cl,br), 168(c,bc), 160–169, 169(bl), 170(tr,cl), 170–171, 171(tr,bc), 173(tl,bl,br), 174(tc,tr,bl,b), 175, 176, 178, 179(tc), 180(br), 181(bcl,b), 183(bl), 187(bl), 188, 189, 191(tr), 192(tc,tr,bc), 192–193, 193(tc,cr), 194(tr,cl), 194–195, 195(t,c), 196(tr), 196–197, 197(tc,c), 198(tr,c,bc), 199(tr,b), 200(t), 202(tc,cl,b), 203(tr,c), 204(tl,cr,bc), 205(tl,bl,br), 206(t), 207(tl,c,bl,br), 210, 213, 215(bl,bc,br).

Courtesy of Enchanted Forest, Oregon: p. 200(br) (www.enchantedforest.com).

ESA (European Space Agency) © ESA/DLR/FU Berlin: pp: 186–187.

ESO (European Southern Observatory): pp. 182–183 (This file is licensed under the Creative Commons Attribution 4.0 International License – https://creativecommons.org/licenses/by/4.0/deed.en)/ Attribution: ESO/M. Kornmesser).

FunkMonk (Michael B.H.): p. 212 (FunkMonk (Michael B.H.), the copyright holder of this work, has published it under the GNU Free Documentation License –https://commons.wikimedia.org/wiki/Commons:GNU_Free_Documentation_License,_version_1.2). This file is also licensed under the Creative Commons Attribution 3.0 Unported License – https://creativecommons.org/licenses/by/3.0/deed.en).

Getty Images: pp. 32(bl), 35(b), 48(tl), 83(bc), 114(cr), 118(cr), 135(tr), 162(bl,bc), 185(cr), 196(cl,cr).

Dr Maria Guagnin: p. 27(br).

Photo courtesy of Guide Dogs of America/Tender Loving Canines (www.guidedogsofamerica.org): p. 62 (via Assistance Dogs International/www.assistancedogsinternational.org).

iStockphoto: pp. ii(r), 21(br), 25(tl), 26–27, 43(bl), 46(cr), 53(tr), 54(tl), 59(cl), 61(tr), 66(bl), 67(tl), 74–75, 76(main photo), 96(br), 110(cr), 132–133, 137, 147(tc), 148(tl), 152(t), 166(br), 172(tl), 191(cr).

Rob Lavinsky: p. 80(bc) (Rob Lavinsky, the copyright holder of this work, has published it under the Creative Commons Attribution-Share Alike 3.0 Unported License – https:// creativecommons.org/licenses/by-sa/3.0/deed.en)/ Attribution: Rob Lavinsky, iRocks.com – CC-BY-SA-3.0).

Library of Congress, Washington, D.C.: pp. 108, 110(tcl), 179(br)/Restored by Adam Cuerden, 211.

The Metropolitan Museum of Art, New York: pp. 82(tr), 110–111(t), 151(bcl).

NASA (National Aeronautics and Space Administration): pp. 86(bc), 92(tc), 141(tr), 146(tr), 177, 180(tl,tr,bc), 183(c,cr), 184(main photo, Phobos,Deimos), 185(br), 186(tc,bl), 187(c), 196(tl).

Nature Picture Library: pp. 3(tl), 12(cl), 21(tl), 22(br), 32(tl), 51(bc), 65(tl), 139(tr), 140–141, 150(bl), 153(b), 154(cl), 155(cr).

NOAA (National Oceanic and Atmospheric Administration/NOAA Office of Ocean Exploration and Research, Exploration of the Gulf of Mexico 2014): p. 155(tl).

NZ Marine Studies Centre: p. 155(t).

Science Photo Library: pp. 40(bc), 47(cr), 140(cl), 151(c), 172(bl).

Shutterstock Editorial: pp. 58(tl), 116–117.

Six Flags Great Adventure: p. 201(cr) (Six Flags Great Adventure, Wild Safari & Hurricane Harbor: 1 Six Flags Blvd, Jackson, New Jersey, USA 08527. www.sixflags.com/greatadventure; #MySixFlags; @sfgradventure on Twitter, Instagram & Snapchat; facebook.com/sixflagsgreatadventure).

Smithsonian Institution Archives: p. 179(cr).

Collection of the Smithsonian National Museum of African American History & Culture: p. 106(c) (Gift from Dawn Simon Spears and Alvin Spears, Sr.).

Smithsonian Tropical Research Institute (Close up of Whale Shark Teeth by D. Ross Robertson): p. 145(tl).

Roland Stadler: p. 63(tl) (via Foundation Swiss School for Guide Dogs for the Blind Allschwil/www.blindenhundeschule.ch and Assistance Dogs International/www.assistancedogsinternational.org).

US Army: p. 126(t).

Wellcome Collection: pp. 51(tr), 164(br), 199(tl)/ License: Attribution 4.0 International (CC BY 4.0) – https://creativecommons.org/licenses/by/4.0/.

Wikimedia Commons: pp. 10(tl), 33(br), 48(tr), 81(bl), 85(tl), 89(br), 90(b), 101(tr), 107, 109(cr), 111(tc), 119(tl), 129(bc), 153(cl), 170(cr), 174(tl).

Credits

Library of Congress Cataloging-in-Publication Data is available upon request.

ISBN 978-0-593-51646-1 (trade)
ISBN 978-0-593-51648-5 (ebook)

COVER PHOTO CREDITS:
Front Cover Photos: Shutterstock (all)
Back Cover Photos: Dreamstime (all)

MANUFACTURED IN ITALY
10 9 8 7 6 5 4 3 2 1
First Edition

Produced by Fun Factory Press, LLC, in association with Potomac Global Media, LLC.

The publisher would like to thank the following people for their contributions to this book:
Melina Gerosa Bellows, President, Fun Factory Press, and Series Creator and Author; Priyanka Lamichhane, Editor and Project Manager; Heather McElwain, Copy Editor; Chad Tomlinson, Art Director; Steve Hoffman, Factchecker; Jack Pecau, Editorial Intern; Potomac Global Media: Kevin Mulroy, Publisher; Barbara Brownell Grogan, Editor in Chief; Thomas Keenes, Designer; Susannah Jayes and Ellen Dupont, Picture Researchers; Heather McElwain, Proofreader; Tim Griffin, Indexer

SPOT THE 13 RANDOM DIFFERENCES:

p69 Awesome Animals

p121 Splendid Sports

p209 Random Roundup